cut here

The Complete Idiot's

Kid-Friendly Se

A great way to get your kids started online is to teach them to use kid-friendly search sites that help them find anything they want—and don't lead them to anything you don't want them to find. Here are some good ones. Turn to Chapter 14, "How to Search the Web Safely," for more information about safe searching.

Yahooligans!
www.yahooligans.com

America Online Kids-Only Search
www.aol.com/netfind/kids/

KidsNook
www.kidsnook.com

Ask Jeeves for Kids
www.ajkids.com/

Online Safety Sites

Many sites offer information on how to keep your kids safe. Here are some good places to go to find more information:

SafeKids.Com
www.safekids.com

CyberAngels
www.cyberangels.org

National Center for Missing and Exploited Children
www.missingkids.com

NetParenting.Com
www.netparenting.com

Yahooligan's Guide to Staying Street Smart on the Web
www.yahooligans.com/docs/safety/

SafeTeens.Com
www.safeteens.com

KidShield
www.kidshield.com

The FBI's Parents Guide to Internet Safety
www.fbi.gov/library/pguide/pguide.htm

SmartParent.Com
www.smartparent.com

The New York Public Library's Safety Net for the Internet
www.nypl.org/branch/safety.html

Acronyms

Acronym	Short for	Acronym	Short for
AKA	Also known as	FYI	For your information
BRB	Be right back	IMHO	In my humble opinion
BTW	By the way	LOL	Laughing out loud
FAQ	Frequently asked question	ROFL	Rolling on the floor laughing
FWIW	For what it's worth	TTFN	Tata for now

que®

Safe, Fun Places for Kids to Visit

The Internet is a big place, with lots of great things for kids to do. Here are just a few of the safe places that kids can go online:

Sites for Younger Kids

Seussville
www.randomhouse.com/seussville

The Cartoon Network
www.cartoonnetwork.com

PBS Kids
www.pbs.org/kids

The Color Site
www.thecolorsite.com

Disney.Com
disney.go.com

Sites for Older Kids and Teens

GusTown
www.gustown.com

Headbone.Com
www.headbone.com

World Kids Network
www.worldkids.net

FunBrain.Com
www.funbrain.com

KidsLoveAMystery.Com
www.kidsloveamystery.com

Cyberteens
www.cyberteens.com

Teen-Net
www.teen-net.com

Sites for Parents

Why should kids have all the fun? The following list shows some of the best sites for parents:

FamilyPC Magazine
www.familypc.com

Family and Home Guide
www.family-home.com.sg/

parent soup
www.parentsoup.com

Family.Com
www.family.com

Parents.Com
www.parents.com
familyeducation.com
www.familyeducation.com

Box Planet
www.spiltmilk.net

ParentTime
www.parenttime.com

ParenthoodWeb.Com
www.parenthood.com

ParentsPlace.Com
www.parentsplace.com

ParentsTalk
www.parents-talk.com

Parenting Q&A
www.parenting-qa.com
ParentZone.Com
www.parentzone.com

Interactive Parent
www.interactiveparent.com

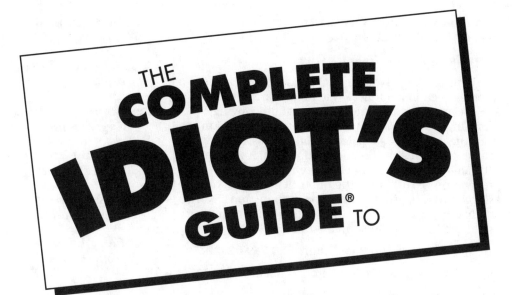

THE **COMPLETE** **IDIOT'S** **GUIDE®** TO

Protecting Your Child Online

Preston Gralla and Sherry Kinkoph

A Division of Macmillan USA
201 W. 103rd Street, Indianapolis, IN 46290

**The Complete Idiot's Guide to
Protecting Your Child Online**

Copyright © June 2000 by Que

International Standard Book Number: 0-7897-2422-7

Library of Congress Catalog Card Number: 00-101715

Printed in the United States of America

First Printing: June, 2000

01   00   4   3   2   1

Trademarks

All terms mentioned in this book that are known to be or suspected of being trademarks or service marks have been appropriately capitalized. Que cannot attest to the accuracy of this information. Use of a term in this book should not be regarded as affecting the validity of any trademark or service mark.

Warning and Disclaimer

Associate Publisher
Greg Wiegand

Acquisitions Editor
Stephanie J. McComb

Development Editor
Gregory Harris

Managing Editor
Thomas F. Hayes

Project Editor
Karen S. Shields

Copy Editor
Molly Schaller

Indexer
Sharon Shock

Proofreader
Harvey Stanbrough

Technical Editor
Mark Hall

Illustrator
Judd Winick

Team Coordinator
Sherry Gregory

Media Developer
Craig Atkins

Interior Designer
Nathan Clement

Cover Designer
Michael Freeland

Copywriter
Eric Borgert

Production
Jeannette McKay

Contents at a Glance

Contents

About the Authors

Preston Gralla is executive editor for ZDNet and the author of 16 books, including *The Complete Idiot's Guide to Protecting Yourself Online*, the best-selling *How the Internet Works*, and several Internet books for children. As a recognized Internet expert, he appears regularly on TV and radio shows and networks, including the *CBS Early Show*, CNN, MSNBC, CNBC, and many others. Preston has written about the Internet for many newspapers and magazines, including *USA Today*, the *Los Angeles Times*, *FamilyLife*, *FamilyPC*, and *PC Magazine*. He lives in Cambridge, Massachusetts, with his wife and two children.

Sherry Kinkoph has authored more than 40 books over the past seven years on a variety of topics, including computer books for kids. *How to Use Microsoft Office 2000*, *The Complete Idiot's Guide to Excel 2000*, and *Sams Teach Yourself Quicken 99 in 10 Minutes* are a few of Sherry's recent publications. A native of the Midwest, Sherry currently resides in Fishers, Indiana, and continues in her quest to help users of all levels and ages master the ever-changing computer technologies.

Dedication

To Jacob and Joshua, my favorite Web surfers.—Sherry Kinkoph

To my kids Gabe and Mia, who teach me new things about the Internet (and life!) every day.—Preston Gralla

Acknowledgments

Thanks to the folks at Macmillan USA: acquisitions editor Stephanie McComb, development editor Gregory Harris, project editor Karen Shields, copy editor Molly Schaller, indexer Sharon Shock, and proofreader Harvey Stanbrough.

Special thanks to the folks at NetNanny for their enthusiastic assistance—thanks, Dusty and Nika!

Tell Us What You Think!

As the reader of this book, *you* are our most important critic and commentator. We value your opinion and want to know what we're doing right, what we could do better, what areas you'd like to see us publish in, and any other words of wisdom you're willing to pass our way.

As a Associate Publisher for Que, I welcome your comments. You can fax, email, or write me directly to let me know what you did or didn't like about this book—as well as what we can do to make our books stronger.

Please note that I cannot help you with technical problems related to the topic of this book, and that due to the high volume of mail I receive, I might not be able to reply to every message.

When you write, please be sure to include this book's title and author as well as your name and phone or fax number. I will carefully review your comments and share them with the author and editors who worked on the book.

Fax: 317-581-4666

Email: consumer@mcp.com

Mail: Greg Wiegand
          Associate Publisher
          Que
          201 West 103rd Street
          Indianapolis, IN 46290 USA

Introduction

Let's face it: when you're a parent, it's a scary world out there these days. Nothing seems safe for you or your kids anymore. It's not safe to leave the house—somebody might mug you or hijack your kids in your car. It's not safe for them to stay in the house—it's full of sharp objects and deadly chemicals disguised as cleaning supplies. Now it's not even safe for them to use your computer—someone might steal their identity or harass them electronically. What's the world coming to?

Cyberstalking, online pedophiles, hacking, computer viruses—sounds like pretty spooky stuff, doesn't it? These topics have been in the news frequently this past year. Whether you and your family are brand new to this phenomenon called cyberspace or you've been online for some time now, you might be wondering what you've gotten your-selves into. Is the Internet safe, and more importantly, is it safe for your kids?

Before you give up and cancel your Internet account, stop and get the real scoop on Internet dangers. This book can help you make heads and tails out of the information superhighway as it relates to your child. If you're like many parents today, keeping up with the ever-changing computer technologies is an ongoing battle. Kids typically know more about computers than their parents do. You need an edge, and this book is it—slice through the misinformation and hype, and get the information you need to make the Internet safe for your family.

Why Do You Need This Book?

The Complete Idiot's Guide to Protecting Your Child Online straightens out all the hoopla associated with the Internet. Why an Idiot's Guide? Of course you're not an idiot, but learning about all this new-fangled computer technology can make you feel like one. And unless you have a degree in Geekology, spending all your time learning every-thing you need to know about the Internet just isn't up there on your list of things to do today. You've got work to complete, you've got a family to raise, and you've got a life.

This Idiot's Guide tells you all about potential online dangers and how you and your family can deal with them. Learn how to use filtering software, how to set family guidelines for Internet usage, and how to safely search the Internet. If you're con-cerned about making your computer cybersafe, this book can assist you and give you valuable tips on what to do if you and your kids encounter anything dangerous online.

How Do You Use This Book?

There are no rules with this book. You don't have to read it from cover to cover unless that's what you really want to do (although we hope you will never put it down). Each chapter presents a topic in easy-to-understand language complete with examples and suggestions. Just pick and choose the topics that interest you. We've broken the book into four parts:

➤ Part 1, "Kids and the Internet," provides a brief look at how kids use the Internet today, what's really going on out there in cyberspace, some history into how this whole thing got started, and even a chapter for the Internet-impaired. (Here's your chance to get computer hip.)

➤ Part 2, "The Real Dirt on Online Dangers," covers the major online dangers that can affect your child. Learn all about online chatting, email issues, marketing techniques, newsgroups, online games, and other potentially ugly stuff on the Internet.

➤ Part 3, "Preparing Your Computer," explains how to make your computer a safe place for kids when they use the Internet. Find out about parental controls and filtering software you can employ.

➤ Part 4, "Preparing Your Kids," gives you valuable tips for setting up guidelines in your household for Internet usage. Here's where you also find help when you encounter online dangers and an exhaustive look at kid friendly sites your children (and you) will enjoy.

In addition to these parts, you'll find a glossary in the back that covers all those geeky technical terms that are commonly associated with the Internet.

Scattered throughout each chapter are useful tips to help you along the way.

Techno Talk

Look to these boxes to learn about geeky terms and concepts.

Check This Out

These tip boxes contain hints, short-cuts, and other useful information.

Caution

Check these tip boxes for warnings or other important information you need to know.

That's about all there is to using this book. You're now ready to jump in and learn all about protecting your child online. Safe surfing!

Part 1
Kids and the Internet

It's a brave new world. If you don't believe it, look at your kids the next time they use the computer. Odds are, they're chatting with seven friends simultaneously, sending and receiving instant messages with four others, listening to MP3 music files they've downloaded from the Internet, and watching an online video of the 'N Sync "boy group"—and they're doing all this while researching an essay on the "dark lady" of Shakespeare's sonnets for school.

Welcome to the 21st century, Mom and Dad. Things aren't the way they were when you grew up. I think we're not in Kansas anymore.

In this first part of the book, you learn about all the good things your kids can do on the Internet, find out what kinds of dangers they face by going online, and learn how the Internet started and how we got to where we are today.

And, of course, you learn what to do if your kids know more about computers than you do. (Which, no doubt, they do.)

So come on along. Let's get started with the basic information you need to make sure your kids are safe and secure whenever they go online.

Chapter 1

What Do Kids Do on the Internet?

In This Chapter

➤ How the Internet has become part of kids' lives

➤ The ways the Internet helps kids with school and research

➤ How kids use the Internet to keep in touch with friends and family

➤ The ways kids use the Internet for their hobbies and sports

➤ Other reasons why kids use the Internet

The television news and newspapers are full of scary stories about cyberstalkers, online pornography, and other dangers the Internet poses to children. Because of that, it's easy to think of the Internet as an evil place where children should never tread.

But the truth is, the Internet has many great things to offer kids. And those are things that never make the 10 o'clock news. The Internet makes the world a better place for kids. In this chapter (before you learn about all the dangers and how to protect your kids against them in the rest of the book), we tell you all the *good* things about the Internet. So read on to find out all the ways that kids use the Internet for good.

Holy Mackerel! They Do All That? What Kids Do Online

It's 8:00 p.m. on a typical night in the Gralla household. Ten-year-old Gabe is on a kids' Internet search site looking for information about the Underground Railroad for a school project that's due tomorrow. (As usual, he leaves the writing until the last minute! What kid doesn't?) In between searches, he checks his email, happily reads a message from his grandmother in Florida, and sends her a note, telling her about his week in school. Later on, after his schoolwork is done (or at least, so his parents hope!), he loads up his favorite online strategy game and plays with dozens of other kids all over the world. Or maybe he heads to one of the chess sites—in which kids find chess partners to play online—and play a few lightning games. And before the evening is done, he checks the Web site his soccer coach set up to see when the next practice is. He might even go to his favorite sports site to check the latest scores online as well. Go Celtics!

Fifteen-year-old Mia is on the computer in her room, checking the online version of the *Encyclopedia Britannica*, in search of articles to help her write her essay detailing the differences between Romanesque and Gothic architecture. While taking a break, she notices that her seventeen-year-old cousin, Erica (who lives across the country in California), has just jumped online, so they send instant messages to each other about how Erica's college application process is going. After a few minutes, Erica logs off, and Mia chats with her high school friends about their essays. Later, after all her homework is done (once again, so her parents hope!), she checks the Web site of the American Ballet Theater ballet camp she'll be attending this coming summer. Afterward, she heads to another Web site and downloads some new furniture, rooms, and clothing for her favorite game, the real-life simulation *The Sims*.

Check This Out

The *Encyclopedia Britannica* Is Free Online

From your now-distant youth, you might remember the world's best encyclopedia, the *Encyclopedia Britannica*, a weighty series of tomes that to your young mind seemed to hold the accumulated wisdom and knowledge of the world. Your parents probably had to mortgage your house to buy the set, but it was worth it, considering how it helped your education. Well, now you're a parent, and here's one way, at least, that your life is easier than your parents'—the *Britannica* is now completely free online. Anyone can go to www.britannica.com and use the entire encyclopedia free.

Welcome to the world of kids, circa early twenty-first century. Just about every aspect of their lives is bound, one way or another, to the Internet. From school to friends, family, hobbies, entertainment, communication, and beyond, the Internet is thoroughly intertwined with their daily lives.

Headlines are made weekly, it seems, about the dangers the Internet poses to kids. This entire book, in fact, is devoted to showing you how to make sure your kids stay safe when they head online. But the truth is—despite the well-publicized dangers—the Internet is one of the best things that has ever happened to childhood. It broadens kids' worlds, enables them to talk with their extended family across the country, gives them instant access to all the information gathered in the world, and generally enriches their lives.

In the rest of this chapter, I show you all the ways kids typically use the Internet—and show you how it makes their lives fuller and richer. There's time throughout the rest of the book to talk about dangers and to teach you how to protect your kids. But let's start here at the beginning: the reasons kids go online and how they make use of the Internet. As you go through the rest of the book, remember—kids go online for important reasons, so don't try to block everything they do on the Internet.

Making the Grade: Using the Internet for Schoolwork

The way your kids are taught subjects such as math and writing are probably different than the way you were taught. But that's not the biggest difference between your kids' education and yours. The biggest difference is the Internet.

The Internet makes it much easier for your kids to do research and get help with their schoolwork—in fact, using the Internet is like giving kids the world's largest library at their fingertips. And they'll never have to pay overdue fines!

And the Internet also makes sure your kids have the best, most up-to-date information. Even if your local library or school system has a less-than-stellar set of reference books, your kids can get the best and latest reference tools free.

Through online research, the entire world is accessible to them. Although there are countless ways for kids to use the Internet for homework, here are some of the primary ways:

➤ Kids can use online encyclopedias and other reference sources that used to be available only at libraries or for a great cost. The amount of information available to them is mind-boggling. The *Encyclopedia Britannica* is pictured in Figure 1.1.

➤ Kids can get direct help from teachers and experts in the subject matter they're researching. In areas such as Homework Help on America Online (keyword, "Homework Help"), teachers and other experts answer kids' homework questions and point them toward places where they can get more information. It's like having a personal tutor whenever they want.

Figure 1.1

Free, free, free! Excellent reference sources, such as the Encyclopedia Britannica, help kids with research and their homework.

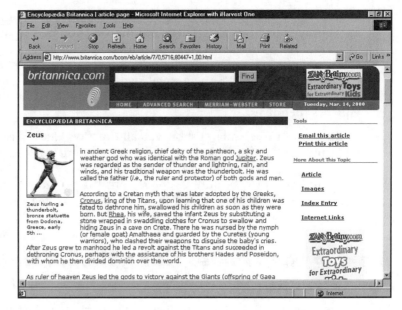

➤ Kids can get help from other kids with their schoolwork. Often, kids are the best sources of help. The Internet enables kids to get help from kids all over the world, not just in their classes.

➤ Kids can use kid-friendly search sites, such as Yahooligans! at www.yahooligans.com, to get research and information from Web sites across the Internet.

➤ Kids can get direct help from their teachers. Increasingly, teachers, not just kids, are online. Some of them make their email addresses available to their students, so kids can send email asking for help or further information. Many teachers even post homework assignments and information about the class and subject matter on their Web sites.

Some Classes Require That Projects Be Created on the Internet

The Internet has become so much a part of school that in some classes, projects are required to be completed online. For example, Preston's daughter, Mia, has to complete one of her high school history projects by building a Web site about a topic. Internet access has become a necessity, as well as a luxury, at many schools.

➤ Kids use the Internet for their schoolwork in countless other ways as well. The ways they use it are bound only by their imagination.

➤ Kids can get the text of classic books free online. Among the sites that let you read free classic books is www.worldwideschool.com/library/catalogs/bysubject-top.html.

Keeping in Touch with Friends and Family with Chat, Messaging, and Email

Kids live to talk. They're the world's greatest communicators. Through friends and talking with others they learn about themselves, about the world, about others…in short, to a great extent, the way they shape their personalities, try out personas, and just plain have fun is to talk, talk, and talk some more.

In past generations, that meant tying up the telephone. Today, it means chatting and emailing on the Internet. (Although anyone with a teenager knows it still means the telephone as well. It's not uncommon for a teenager to be talking on the phone with friends at the same time she's online chatting and sending instant messages to other friends—often the same ones she's talking with on the telephone!)

There are a number of ways kids talk to others online. Here are the top ones:

➤ **Chat**   Kids love to yak with other kids—about anything, everything, and nothing. They can do it on chat areas, especially on America Online (see Figure 1.2). People usually don't use their voice in chat areas; instead, they type words on the keyboard. Chat areas are also available on Web sites. And on the Internet, chat areas are called IRC channels. In general, an IRC channel isn't as good a place for kids to chat as America Online, because IRC channels are unregulated.

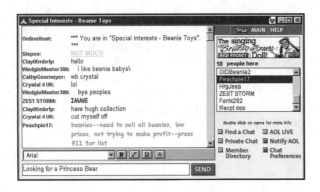

Figure 1.2

Yakking away…here's a chat area on America Online. In this one, kids talk about Beanie Babies.

➤ **Instant Messaging** In a chat area, everyone can see the messages that every-one sends—it's like a giant living room in which everyone talks at once. In instant messaging, kids can hold one-on-one conversations with another person via instant message software. They can also hold many one-on-one conversa-tions at the same time. The most popular way to do this is with America Online. But even if kids don't have America Online, they can use a piece of software that runs on the Internet called AOL Instant Messenger that allows anyone to send instant messages to people on America Online or to other AOL Instant Messenger users.

➤ **Message boards and newsgroups**—Message boards are public bulletin boards on which kids can leave messages. They read what's on the board, leave a mes-sage, and then leave. This way, people don't have to be on the boards at the same time to leave and read messages. America Online has popular message boards, as do some Web sites. But the biggest discussion areas in the world are what are called Internet newsgroups. Newsgroups have nothing to do with the news. A newsgroup is just another word for an Internet message board. Kids need special software to read newsgroups, although they can also use newsgroup-reader soft-ware built into America Online. Both Netscape Navigator and Internet Explorer include newsgroup-reading software, as does the Microsoft Outlook email program. Pictured in Figure 1.3 is the newsgroup software built into Outlook.

➤ **Email** It's not uncommon for kids to send and read a dozen or more email messages a day. They're constantly sending and receiving email from friends and acquaintances. Some kids also use email to get in touch with their teachers. Pictures and files can be attached to email. They're called, not surprisingly, *attachments*. (How about that! Some Internet terminology actually makes sense!)

What Does IRC Stand For?

IRC stands for Internet Relay Chat. IRC has been used on the Internet for years, since even before there was a World Wide Web. To use IRC, you need special software. For more information about IRC, turn to Chapter 5, "Chat, Chat, and More Chat."

➤ **Personal Web sites** Kids might know a whole lot more about the Internet than you do. Many know how to build Web sites. It's actually not that hard to do, because many sites, such as www.geocities.com, include easy-to-use tools that enable anyone to build their own Web pages. Kids use these Web pages as a way to communicate with each other and the world. For example, both Gabe and Mia have built several of their own Web pages, most notably about the Pokémon phenomenon.

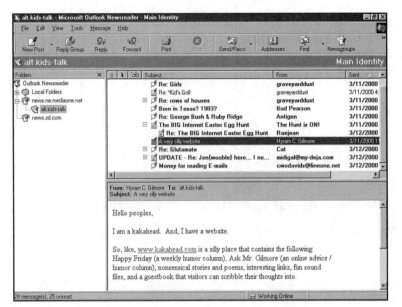

Figure 1.3

All the news that's fit to read—here's how kids read newsgroups using the Outlook newsgroup reader.

Check This Out

Your Kids Can Make Friends All Over the World

In the olden days when you were a wee one, kids sometimes had pen pals from other countries. These days, kids regularly send and receive email and have chats with kids all over the world. It's just one more way the Internet brings kids all over the world closer to one another.

Ain't We Got Fun! How Kids Use the Internet for Hobbies and Sports

If your kids have hobbies, whether it be ballet, reptile-collecting, or Pokémon cards, they can make hobbies more fun using the Internet. The same thing holds true for sports. Kids can use the Internet for hobbies and sports in many ways. Here are some popular ones:

13

➤ **Kids can participate in discussion areas about their hobby or sport.**
Discussion areas, as I outlined earlier in the chapter, are among the most popular destinations for kids. And there are thousands of discussion areas devoted to
hobbies and sports.

A Real-Life Story About Rabbits and the Internet

Several years ago, Mia wanted to get a pet rabbit as a new addition to the Gralla
household. At a farm, she almost got a cute little dwarf rabbit, but her dad, Preston
(that's me!), thought it would be a good idea to do some research to see if that
was the best breed for kids to have. So Mia went home, hopped onto the Internet, and found several message boards devoted to rabbits. Soon she was corresponding via email with a rabbit breeder who steered her away from the dwarf
breed because they tend to be foul-tempered and not suitable for kids, and
instead recommended a *mini-lop*—a small, lop-eared rabbit with a gentle disposi-
tion. After some final research on a Web site devoted to rabbits, the decision was
made—a mini-lop it would be! Based on Mia's Internet research, the Grallas
bought a grey-haired mini-lop that Mia named Polichinelle—and it's a happy,
affectionate member of the household. Score one for the Internet! Without it,
none of this would have happened.

➤ **Kids can visit Web sites devoted to their hobbies or sports.**   Thousands
of Web sites are devoted to hobbies and sports, and kids love visiting them.

➤ **Kids can build their own Web sites about their hobbies or favorite
sports.**   With all the Web-building sites on the Internet—such as www.geocities.
com, www.angelfire.com, and others—it's easy for kids to build Web sites about
their favorite hobbies and sports. Around the Gralla household, Pokémon fever
never lets up. Figure 1.4 shows a Web site that Mia built about her favorite, Mew.

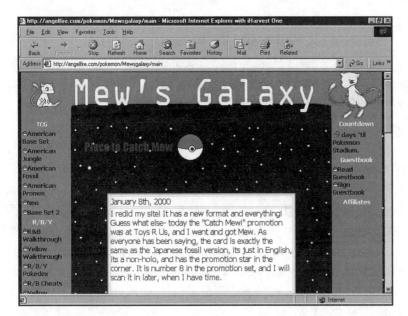

Figure 1.4

All Pokémon, all the time—kids love to build sites about their hobbies. Here's a site built by Mia Gralla and devoted to Mew of Pokémon fame.

But Wait, There's More! Other Ways Kids Use the Internet

Even all of that doesn't begin to encompass all the things kids do online. Here's a short list of other things kids do online. And you can be guaranteed that there's a whole lot more they do:

➤ **For entertainment**   Kids can download high-quality music files, known as MP3 files, and listen to music from the Internet. They can also watch videos, listen to Internet-only radio stations, and visit entertainment sites such as www.mtv.com.

➤ **To download files**   The Internet is full of tens of thousands of programs and files that can be downloaded free. Some kids live to download.

➤ **To play online games**   What fun is playing a game against a computer? None, as far as many kids are concerned (including Gabe Gralla). What kids *really* want to do is play games against others online. From board games like chess to strategy games like *StarCraft* to blast-'em-ups like *Quake*, thousands of kids every day are pitted against one another. And often, they chat with each other while they play.

➤ **To surf the Web**   Kids are like adults in this way—sometimes they just want to surf the Web from site to site, seeing what they can find along the way.

15

The Least You Need To Know

Although you want to protect your kids when they're online, keep in mind that the Internet is a great boon to kids and childhood. So make sure that when your kids go online, you keep the following in mind:

➤ The Internet has become an integral part of every aspect of kids' lives, so make sure that while you protect your kids, you give them full access to the Internet.

➤ The Internet is a great place for kids to do research for schoolwork and to get help from teachers.

➤ Kids use the Internet as an important way to keep in touch with friends and family by chatting, sending instant messages, and visiting message boards.

➤ The Internet is a great place for kids to talk to others about their hobbies and sports, and even to create Web pages about their hobbies.

➤ Kids also use the Internet to download files, get music, play online games, and surf the Web.

Chapter 2

A Walk Down the Bad Side of Cybertown

In This Chapter

➤ Find out what evil lurks on the Internet

➤ See eye-opening statistics for online crime

➤ Put everything into perspective

Here's a great analogy of the Internet for you: The Internet is like a town. Okay, a really big, globally-encompassing town. (Bear with me here.) Although there are certainly many good things about a town—such as the library, post office, parks, YMCA, and shops—there's always a seedy section somewhere with a reputation for murder and mayhem, an area of questionable atmosphere and influence. This area of town often has flashing neon lights that say "XXX," unsavory citizens hanging out on street corners and in dark, shadowy alleys, and so forth. You get the picture, right?

Although the good things about the Internet far outweigh the bad, the bad stuff generates much more press. To help you better understand what goes on, let's take a walk down the bad side of cybertown. Don't worry, it's daylight and you should be safe, plus you're not even logged on, are you?

The Stories

No doubt you've heard numerous stories in the news about the underbelly of the Internet. With the Internet gaining popularity on a daily basis, the bad side of cybertown will continue to make headlines in newspapers and on the nightly news. Here's a peek at just a few stories that made the headlines:

California   A 50-year old security guard in Los Angeles sought revenge against an ex-girlfriend using the Internet as his tool. Posing as his ex, he entered chat rooms and online bulletin boards and solicited rough sex and rape, giving out her real name, address, and phone number. Guess what happened? Six guys showed up at her house. Thankfully, she wasn't harmed; but her ex is now serving six years in prison.

Maryland   The FBI, investigating the abduction of a 10-year old boy, discovered widespread distribution of online child pornography which led to seizures of pornographic material in 20 U.S. cities across the country. Sadly, the boy is still missing.

California   A male student (an honors student, by the way) at the University of San Diego stalked five female classmates over the course of a year, sending them sexually explicit email that implied he was following them everywhere they went. He was caught and sentenced to six years in prison. He claims he committed the crimes because the women were laughing at him and inviting others to ridicule him as well. Oddly enough, the victims had never met the guy.

Arizona   Several attorneys general in 13 states, including Arizona, went after online tobacco merchants selling *bidis* (flavored cigarettes imported from India) to minors. The sites were not verifying the ages of purchasers. The Arizona attorney general may pursue suing the vendors if the practice doesn't stop.

Washington D. C.   The FTC is investigating several popular kids' Web sites that allegedly use deceptive marketing practices to gain market research through mandatory registration. Such information can be sold to other companies.

California   A 21-year old college drop-out was found guilty of committing a hate crime in cyberspace. He sent terrorizing email to 59 Asian students at the University of California, Irvine. He also sent threatening email to the campus newspaper staff.

Massachusetts   A woman began frequenting chat rooms and struck up an online correspondence with another user. Feeling safe, she gave out detailed information to her new friend, including her real name, town, and employer name. Shortly after, the new online friend sought to make the relationship a sexual one. Within days, she received an email from him mentioning an item she had purchased at her local deli only the day before, as if the man had stood in line with her. Needless to say, she felt frightened and contacted authorities.

Florida   A Minneapolis man met a 13-year old girl in a chat room and traveled all the way to Tampa, Florida to have sex with her. Turns out, the girl was an undercover FBI agent, and the man was arrested and convicted.

Sound scary? Welcome to the world of online crime, also called *cybercrime*. As if you aren't already overwhelmed by email, e-commerce, e-news, e-this, and e-that, now you've also got to worry about e-crime. Cybercrime includes everything from hacking and theft to stalking and terrorism. And guess what? Cybercrime is on the rise. With more and more Internet users added each day, the percentage of criminal usage goes up.

What sort of crimes are we talking about? Here's a tiny list:

➤ Hacking (breaking into other computers)

➤ Email terrorism

➤ Cyberstalking

➤ Child pornography

➤ Credit card theft

➤ Fraud

➤ Hate crimes

➤ Computer viruses

So what does all this have to do with children? Plenty. If your child uses the Internet, whether at home or school, whether through a commercial service (like America Online) or an Internet service provider (ISP), he or she is susceptible to online crime. It's up to you to educate your kids about the bad side of cybertown and prepare them for what they might encounter. It's also up to you to decide what methods of protection your child needs when it comes to Internet usage.

Other Annoyances

In addition to the major crimes listed previously, you and your child are bound to encounter other annoyances on the Internet, such as spamming, email hoaxes and schemes, and so forth. Although these things are not quite as serious, your children need to be aware of them. These annoyances are discussed at various times throughout the book. Check out Chapter 6, "Evil Email," for more information about kids and email.

Hacking

Cybercrime is everywhere on the Internet—even in places you might think are relatively safe. In February 2000, hackers found ways to shut down several popular Web sites (such as Yahoo and eBay) for several hours, disrupting usage and business. The hacker (or hackers) did not infiltrate internal data, but seemed focused on disrupting commerce. The culprits used a program to direct hundreds of computers around the globe to simultaneously send Web traffic to the sites attacked. As a result of the intense traffic, these sites were virtually shut down for normal business.

Such an attack could be used as a decoy to access sensitive data while the Web site's technical staff addressed the decoy issue.

Hacking

Hacking is when someone illegally infiltrates another computer system.

According to the FBI, 30 percent of businesses, universities, and institutions have been hacked. What's scary about hacking is that it can lead the hacker to classified information: credit card numbers, personal information, account numbers, passwords, and so on. For example, in February 2000, a student at Northeastern University was charged with hacking into federal government computers. The 28-year old man allegedly hacked into the computer systems at the U.S. Defense Department and NASA, read and altered files, and viewed logon names. Fortunately for the government, the affected servers didn't contain classified information. However, the man is also charged with defacing the Interior Department's Web page and hacking an ISP's server out on the West Coast, causing damage there as well. And he supposedly did it all from his home computer. If he's convicted, he could face 10 years in prison and a $250,000 fine.

Don't Use a Debit Card

A word of warning—it's not a good idea to use a debit card to purchase items on the Internet. Unlike credit cards, which hold the user responsible for no more than $50 of purchases made when the card is stolen, a debit card doesn't always offer such a buffer.

Fraud

The Internet is made up of information, and information can be used illegally by others. This is especially true with online commerce. Web site promoters have an uphill battle convincing people that exchanging credit card information over the Internet is safe. Despite their claims of safety, nothing is ever 100% safe on the Internet.

Take the story of Don. He noticed his bank account had been cleaned out, and the course of the investigation led Don online. Someone had used Don's debit card number to purchase $1,400 worth of merchandise at the popular Amazon.com Web site. The card number had been stolen. What wasn't known is how it was stolen. Don had purchased items from Amazon.com before. Did the thieves access the card number by hacking the Amazon.com site, or did they get the number someplace else?

As the investigation unfolded, the theft was traced to a ring of hackers in Thailand. Don wasn't the only one affected; 20 other credit cards had been used to buy merchandise at Amazon.com, and all the merchandise was shipped to Thailand. The ring used the stolen cards to set up separate accounts at Amazon.com.

On the plus side, Amazon.com did eventually pay back the amount billed to Don's account.

Online fraud doesn't stop at stolen credit cards. It also includes email pyramid schemes, long-distance telephone schemes, and other fraudulent practices.

Have You Fallen for a Hoax?

Internet hoaxes happen all the time, and they happen particularly often with email. People start passing around email detailing free stuff, easy money, or scary viruses. Most of these are hoaxes. For example, one famous email hoax is supposedly from Disney and Bill Gates. The email letter says they can track the message, and if you forward the letter to so many people, you might win $5,000 and a trip to Disney World. Not true. There's no such giveaway, and there's no such program to track how many times a message is forwarded.

Another famous email hoax warns you about receiving an email entitled "Penpal Greetings" or "Good Times." Supposedly, the message contains a virus that will destroy your hard drive. Not true. You can't get a virus reading email, but you can get a virus by opening an attachment that contains a virus and comes with the email message. To learn more about email hoaxes, check out `ciac.llnl.gov`. Teach your children about email hoaxes, and be sure to read Chapter 6, "Evil Email," and Chapter 15, "Downloading Do's and Don'ts."

Computer Viruses

There are hundreds of computer viruses floating about, and many can do serious damage to your computer files. A *virus* is a computer code written to cause interruption or damage when executed. Such codes are often contained within another program. Your computer can catch a virus from a downloaded file or from an infected file on a floppy disk if you don't have an active antivirus program on your PC.

Computer viruses are particularly prevalent in the world of Internet email. People send file attachments with email messages and hide viruses in those attachments. For example, many people pass along a cute little program file, sheep.exe, that puts a small, animated sheep graphic on your computer desktop. Fun yes, but one of the versions of this program has a virus.

Many people weren't too happy about the Happy99 worm virus of 1999. Also called w32/Ska, Happy99.exe, I-Worm.Happy, or W32/Skanew, this virus began circulating at the beginning of the year and spread all over the Internet. If you open the file—which comes as a file attachment to an email or newsgroup message—you see the message, "Happy New Year 1999," on your computer screen, along with a graphical fireworks display. While you're watching the display, the program extracts itself, altering your computer's winsock32.dll file, which is the file your computer uses as a doorway to the Internet. Next time you send email or a newsgroup posting, the Happy99 virus copies itself to the recipient(s).

To keep your system safe, get a good virus protection program for your computer and be sure to check files for viruses before you open them. Learn more about viruses in Chapter 15, "Downloading Do's and Don'ts."

Techno Talk

Newgroups? Email Messages?

If you're a new computer user, you might be a bit confused by terms like *newsgroup*. You might want to stop by Chapter 4, "What to Do If Your Kids Know More About Computers Than You Do," for an overview. Or start with a beginners' book that introduces you to the Internet, such as *The Complete Idiot's Guide to the Internet*, by Peter Kent.

Hate Crime

Free speech is all over the Internet, which means you can easily find dozens of sites focused on the practice of hatred, including racial, ethnic, and gender-based hatred. Everyone with an agenda has a Web page these days, and many of the more serious hate groups target children (see Figure 2.1). Their agenda are often disguised and appear like regular Web sites. Some organizations, such as Hatewatch.org, monitor the growth of such sites on the Web.

Most hate sites are quite happy to engage in philosophical debates with users who visit their Web pages. However, it doesn't do any good trying to convince the operators of these sites to change their tune. Unfortunately, some people end up responding to these sites with even more hatefulness and harsh language, which only ends up making the hate group look like the good guys. Don't fall for that sort of carrying on.

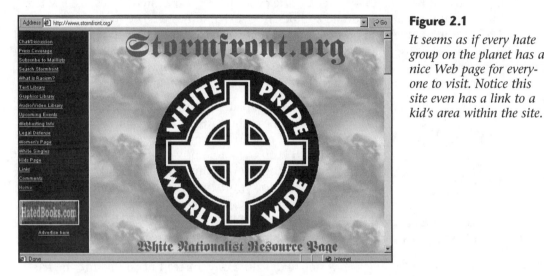

Figure 2.1

It seems as if every hate group on the planet has a nice Web page for everyone to visit. Notice this site even has a link to a kid's area within the site.

As mentioned at the beginning of this chapter, hate crimes are starting to happen on the Internet, such as the case of the California man who sent terrorizing email to Asian students.

Cyberstalking

Let's delve a little deeper into a scarier aspect of Internet crime…cyberstalking. There really isn't a universally accepted definition, but the word refers to using the Internet to harass, intimidate, or threaten another person repeatedly. It encompasses following the person in real life, appearing at the person's home or business, vandalizing property, threatening the person's immediate family—in other words, stalking the victim, both electronically and physically.

Cyberstalking might not initially involve physical contact, but the potential is there, and it can lead to violence. For that reason, it's a serious crime. According to the Justice Department, there have been tens of thousands of victims of cyberstalkers, but the phenomenon is so new, no hard statistics are available. In most of the cases reported, the majority of stalkers are men, and most victims are women.

Cyberstalking can happen to anyone. Here's an example. A Maryland woman spoke out in a newsgroup about the nefarious practices of a literary agency. The agency had started posting advertisements to the newsgroup, which is usually a no-no.

(Newsgroups are focused on topics, and advertising isn't generally welcome.) She checked out the agency and quickly decided it was not on the up-and-up. Online harassment began immediately. She turned to the New York state attorney general (because the agency is based in New York) and filed a grievance. Shortly afterward, she was besieged with lewd email messages, and she noticed newsgroup messages being posted in her name. Apparently, the cyberstalker also posted a message inviting people to call the woman's home and describe sexual fantasies. The message included her telephone number and address. She started receiving 25 to 30 calls a day. Eventually, the messages were traced to three people connected to the nefarious literary agency. The woman began a lawsuit against them, but the harassment did not stop. The suit is still pending and the harassment has gone on for three years.

Newsgroups? Posting? What Are You Talking About?

If you're at all confused about these terms, or others used in this chapter, don't worry. Chapter 4, "What to Do If Your Kids Know More About Computers Than You Do," can help set you straight. Just hang in there.

Think that's bad? Here's another from Illinois. This story appeared on ABC's *20/20 Downtown* and on MSNBC news. For two and a half years, the B family (we'll keep the name private) was harassed, starting online then developing offline. The harassment was directed toward their 9-year old daughter. It began with online postings soliciting sex with the girl and progressed to phone calls in the wee hours of the morning. It turned out to be their neighbor. The little girl had used chalk to scribble "hello" on the neighbor's driveway. Instead of contacting the parents with his disapproval, the neighbor posted messages online in the little girl's name soliciting sex and inviting others to contact her. The B family's home phone number was in the messages. Their phone rang night and day with men requesting to speak to the girl. The situation escalated when a man showed up at their house one night. Detectives traced the message postings to the neighbor and he was subsequently prosecuted. The B family had to move away, but are now using their experience to help pass laws against harassing children online. Spooky story? You bet.

Child Pornography and Pedophilia

If you thought cyberstalking sounded bad, there's more. It turns out the Internet is fertile ground for all manner of child predators, particularly pedophiles and pornographers. There are literally tens of thousands of pedophilia-related Web sites on the Internet. They have their own support groups online, and access to zillions of pornographic materials depicting children. Studies in the United States in 1995 documented one million online images involving child pornography. What do you suppose that number is now? I shudder to guess.

Several years ago in Fort Worth, Texas, police conducted an eight-month investigation of a subscription-based (meaning money was charged) Web service that enabled users to download pornography. Mind you, regular old pornography is legal, but the Web service was offering child pornography as well. According to Texas law (and the laws in any other state), to knowingly possess pornographic material featuring minors, electronic or otherwise, is a felony. The man who ran the site was arrested and charged with possessing child pornography and promoting obscene material on the Internet.

About the same time as the Texas arrest, a woman in Florida brought a lawsuit against America Online, saying the service had allowed a subscriber to market pictures of her 11-year old son and his friends. Apparently, their teacher befriended the boys and eventually took pornographic pictures of them, including pictures of the boys in sexual acts with himself. He then used AOL's chat rooms to distribute the pictures to others. The chat rooms had titles such as "Trading Teen Pics," and "Young Boys for You." The lawsuit stated that AOL had created a home shopping network for pedophiles and pornographers.

Just a year before the AOL suit, the FBI nabbed a man who used AOL to send sexually explicit pictures of children to other computer users. Many of the children in the pictures were under the age of 12. The man was sentenced to three year's probation and six months of home confinement. He is also barred from using a computer for anything but work.

Image Manipulation

In case you aren't aware, people can manipulate images quite easily with graphics software programs today. It's a simple thing to take the head of a person in one digital photograph and place it on the body of another. Unfortunately, it's used frequently with nude pictures, and it happens to celebrities all the time. As a parent, you need to know it happens with pictures of children. A savvy Internet pedophile can take an innocent photo of a child and digitally place the child's head onto a picture of a nude child, and then distribute it to others.

In 1999, police in 12 countries busted an Internet child pornography ring, arresting more than 100 people. Police found a database of over 100,000 pornographic images of children as young as 2 years old. The arrests took place on three continents: Australia, North America, and Europe. The ring originated in the good old U.S.A.

Just like cyberstalking, the threat from pedophiles extends beyond the online world and enters our own communities. In the past, pedophiles used to hang out near playgrounds and parks; now they're online, lurking in chat rooms and on message boards. There are dozens of stories ripped from the headlines about pedophiles who befriend children online and then set out to abduct them.

A grandmother in New Orleans, Louisiana, contacted authorities after her teenage granddaughter received email of a sexual nature that eventually became threatening. The authorities stepped in and set up a sting. Using a female police officer to pose as the girl, they arrested the molester when he showed up at the girl's home trying to kidnap her. Where did the teenager meet the man? Online, of course.

A young Connecticut girl named Katie (now 17) has just written a riveting book about her online seduction and eventual offline meeting with a California man. Her book is entitled *Memoir of a Pedophile's Victim,* and in it she describes how she met a guy, named Mark, online in an AOL teen chat room (Mark claimed to be 23 years old). Katie was 13 at the time. The man befriended her, and Katie came to see him as her best friend. He listened to her problems with parents and school, told her she was special, and eventually told her he loved her. After a six-month relationship online, Katie agreed to meet Mark while on a swim team trip to Texas. Sadly, her online beau turned out to be a 41-year-old investment funds company president named Frances with a history of pedophilia. He immediately molested Katie in the hotel room. Two agonizing years later, he was the first pedophile prosecuted under the 1996 Communications Decency Act (an act passed by Congress to protect children from online pedophiles). He served only 18 months in jail.

The Statistics (The Really Scary Stuff!)

Now that you've read some of the stories, take a look at some of the statistics.

As of August 1999, an estimated 80 million adults and 10 million children access the Internet.

In 1999, the Justice Department studied cases from the Manhattan (New York) district attorney's Sex Crimes Unit and found 20 percent of the cases involved cyberstalking. The Los Angeles district attorney's Stalking and Threat Assessment Unit revealed the same percentage of cyberstalking cases.

The FBI has formed a task force, called Innocent Images, devoted exclusively to fighting child pornography and child predators on the Internet. Their caseload has increased 1,200 percent since 1996. As of December 1998, the initiative had resulted in 232 convictions. There are hundreds of open FBI cases involving adults who traveled to see children that they met online.

All of this proves what you already know to be true—more people online equals more online crime. But what do parents think of all this? In 1999, a survey conducted by the Roper polling organization revealed some eye-opening findings. The survey consisted of 500 online households with children between the ages of 8 and 18. Check out what the parent participants said:

➤ 20 percent say they do not supervise their children's use of the Internet.

➤ 52 percent say they moderately supervise Internet usage.

➤ 48 percent say they allow everyday Internet usage without time restrictions.

Many parents simply aren't aware of the dangers that lurk on the Internet and are ill equipped to deal with them. Worse yet, they are not preparing their children to deal with them either.

A Reality Check

If you're like most protective parents, you might be thinking, "There's no way I'd allow my child online after reading all this." But before you panic, stop and put things in perspective. The vast majority of online users are perfectly normal people, like you, who would never think of visiting the bad side of the cybertracks. Just because you have an Internet connection doesn't mean another user is going to start stalking you or that pornographic material is going to suddenly download onto your computer as soon as you go online.

In this day and age you can't walk out the door without encountering someone spittin', swearin', or brandishin' a gun at some time or another. It's the same thing online, except for the gun part...and the spitting. From time to time, you and your child will encounter something not so pleasant on the Internet. It might be unsuitable language, a crude response in a chat room, or a racy email. What's important is how you educate your children to deal with such things. Just as you teach them not to roam around alone in the seedier parts of your town—particularly when you know there are predators about—you must teach them the same principles about the Internet.

Unlike real life, the Internet makes it very easy to be anonymous, faceless, and deceitful. After all, no one can really "see" you online. Cyberspace, for some people, is about pretending to be someone else. The anonymity enables users to say things they wouldn't ordinarily say. Children need to know that not everyone on the Internet is who they say they are.

Don't forsake the good things about the Internet just to avoid the bad. Instead, prepare your children; and by reading the remaining chapters of this book, prepare yourself.

The Least You Need to Know

It's a scary world out there in cyberspace, and most parents don't fully understand the extent of trouble children can get into online. Here's what you learned in this chapter:

➤ The more populated the Internet becomes, the more quickly the rate of cybercrime will rise.

➤ Cybercrime includes hacking, cyberstalking, and child pornography.

➤ The Internet is populated with the same people you find in real life. There are good people and bad people, it's as simple as that. The bad people are in the minority and they're the ones you need to watch out for. This includes con artists, hatemongers, pedophiles, psychopaths, and the criminally insane. You must teach your children to watch out for these people, and you must watch out for them yourself.

➤ Remember to keep things in perspective. Not everything on the Internet is bad.

Chapter 3

How Did This All Get Started? And Where Is It Going?

In This Chapter

➤ The history of the Internet in a nutshell

➤ A look at who's in charge of the Internet

➤ Details about the Communications Decency Act and other attempts to regulate the Internet

➤ A peek into the future of the information superhighway

To fully understand what all the fuss is about concerning the Internet, start by taking a look at its history and its potential future. This chapter offers you a glimpse at how it all started and where it's going. More importantly, you find out who's in charge of it all. This information is bound to impress not only your kids, but your friends, family, neighbors, and coworkers. Who knows, it might also come in handy if you find yourself on a quiz show with Regis Philbin.

In the Beginning

There you were, going along in life minding your own business, when suddenly, out of the blue, comes the personal computer. Supposedly, this nifty gadget was destined to make your job easier, help you get your life organized, and open up a brand new

More Brands

The IBM PC and Apple computer weren't the only games in town. Companies such as Commodore and Radio Shack also had computers for sale. Unfortunately for them, they didn't succeed in the marketplace as well as the PC and Mac did.

world of information. As it turns out, the Internet did much of what it promised to do, and it continues to do so.

Computers have been around awhile now, but they really became popular in the '80s and '90s. IBM introduced its first personal computer in 1981. Shortly afterward, the PC clones (affordable versions) were everywhere. The computer manufacturing industry saw the number of users more than double between 1981 and the end of 1982. In 1984, Apple's Macintosh line of personal computers was introduced. By the end of the '80s, 65 million personal computers were scattered about homes and offices around the globe.

The Interface Race

Perhaps you'd like to know how computers got to be so easy to use for the masses? The Macintosh line, introduced in 1984, was unique in presenting a user-friendly interface, which made it much easier to control and command the computer. Up until then, most computer users had to wade through a very dull menu system to get anything done. (IBM PCs and their clones used DOS as their operating system.) Microsoft introduced its first version of Windows in 1985, a user-friendly interface for the PC that was similar to the Mac interface. Instead of using menus, the user could click icons to open programs and files. The onscreen environment was visual and intuitive for users. Needless to say, there were skirmishes between both companies over the idea. The dust eventually settled, and both companies continue to churn out improvements. No doubt about it, the user-friendly interface has benefited us all, particularly kids. Pointing and clicking onscreen items is a lot simpler than memorizing complex commands and typing them into a text-prompt.

For much of the populace, the early excitement of personal computers focused on software and operating system developments. But even in the early days of personal computers, the Internet was steadily growing in the background.

New to Computers?

If you're really unfamiliar with computers and Internet terms in general, check out Chapter 4, "What to Do If Your Kids Know More About Computers Than You Do." The basic computer and Internet terminology is presented there. And if you're interested in further research, try the *Complete Idiot's Guide to Computer Basics* or the *Complete Idiot's Guide to PCs*, both by Joe Kraynak.

Where Did the Internet Come From?

The Internet began out of the efforts of the U.S. Department of Defense to create a computer network that would reroute data in the case of a nuclear attack. It was the 1960s, and the cold war was still going strong. The idea was to create a network that could withstand the loss of one or two computers due to a nuclear war disaster and still manage to send and receive data among the remaining computers. This early network was called ARPANET (Advanced Research Projects Agency Network).

Name Dropping

J.C.R. Licklider of MIT is credited as the first man to propose the global network of computers that is now the Internet, contrary to what Al Gore claims. This was back in 1962. Men such as MIT's Leonard Kleinrock (the guy behind the theory of packet switching, which is how the Internet communicates) and Lawrence Roberts (he came up with connecting computers through ordinary phone lines) joined Licklider at ARPANET and, along with many others, were the early visionaries of the information superhighway.

The scientific and academic research community began linking to the network in 1969. Universities and libraries soon followed. In the '70s, TCP/IP architecture was developed. TCP/IP stands for Transmission Control Protocol/Internet Protocol, the rules by which all computers connected to the Internet must exchange data. By the '80s, most networks—particularly those that enabled users to research databases—were using TCP/IP protocols. By 1983, all TCP/IP based networks were connected to the original ARPANET network, and the stage for the Internet boom was set.

In those early days of ARPANET, the network was used primarily by computer experts, engineers, scientists, researchers, and librarians. This was long before the advent of the personal computer, and the methods of using the Internet were very complex. However, the network had much to offer, allowing users access to databases across the country, email, discussion groups, file transfer, and more.

Things really started hopping in 1990 when HTML was introduced. (Don't forget, by this time, the personal computer was well on its way to taking over desktops.) HTML, which stands for Hypertext Markup Language, is a protocol that allows documents to be linked and graphics to be displayed in the documents. This was the birth of the World Wide Web, also known as WWW or simply the Web. The hypertext protocol is a system of embedding a link in the text of one document to text in another document. But the Web wasn't considered cool until someone invented a better way of viewing its pages. When the first Web browser was introduced in 1993, the HTML protocol burst loose on the Internet and it hasn't stopped since.

The Very First Browser

For those of you preparing for a quiz show appearance, here is a bit of trivia: The very first Web browser was developed by Marc Andreessen and the gang at the National Center for Supercomputing Applications (or NCSA for short). The browser's name was Mosaic. Andreessen took his idea and turned it into Netscape Corp.—heard of them? Netscape went on to become the most widely used browser in the world—until Microsoft entered the race with its Internet Explorer. And so the browser war continues to this day.

The Web is only a section of the Internet, a section that focuses on linked documents. You can view a page located on a server in your office, click a link on the page, and suddenly view a page located on a server in another country. It's a beautiful thing, isn't it? Not only can you click a link that leads you to another document, but you can also click links to multimedia features, such as audio or video. Before the advent of the Web, you had to know the exact location of the file you wanted to view, or jump through an exhaustive menu system to find an Internet document. On the Web, a click is all it takes.

Next time you're clicking links, be sure to say a word of thanks to the researchers at CERN (the European Lab for Particle Physics) for coming up with the whole World Wide Web concept, as well as to Tim Berners-Lee for inventing HTML.

What Exactly Is the Internet, Anyway?

Technically speaking, the Internet is a global network of computers—it's an "inter-network," hence *Internet*. A network means connected computers, whether they are computers in an office environment that are connected to share files, programs, and printers, or computers scattered across the world. In the case of the Internet, it's a collection of networks as well as individual computers. These computers are linked by telephone lines, coaxial cables, and even satellite links.

Do you wonder how it works? Allow us to clear that up as well. The Internet works by sending data around in small packets. Hey—don't doze off yet, it's just getting interesting. Large quantities of data are broken down into small units (the packets) to be sent, and then are reassembled at the destination point. During the transmission, the packets zing around the network via computer routers (computers whose main purpose is to find fast routes for packets). If a router determines a heavy traffic area on the network or a sudden loss of a network computer (we hope not because of a nuclear war), it routes the packets another way. Ingenious. Now if only they could figure out how to do this with morning traffic, eh?

Internet Versus Web

Many people use the terms *Internet* and *Web* interchangeably. Technically, the Web is just one section of the Internet. It happens to be the most popular, most used, most talked about section, but it really is only a piece of the whole.

What's the Internet Today?

When we refer to the Internet today, we include all the computers connected to the network, such as personal computers, routing computers, client computers, and server computers (computers that store files for others to access). The Internet is all about sharing information via these computers and the technology that connects them. As mentioned previously, it wasn't so easy to swap information online during the early days of the Internet. You had to know about things like FTP, Gopher, WAIS, Archie, Telnet, Usenet, IRC, and other various services or tools used to share information. Remember, the Internet was populated by technical people, so the tools weren't exactly user-friendly, and they certainly weren't kid-friendly.

In the '90s, commercialism was loosed upon the Internet. Until then, the Internet was pretty much the domain of researchers, educators, and the government. Commercialism was a no-no (unless it aided in research, education, and governing). This changed when independent commercial networks started popping up and joining the online party.

Commercialism, combined with the sudden popularity of the Web and Web browsers, has made the Internet the free-for-all it is today. Reminiscent of the California gold rush of the late 1800s, everybody and their cousin has a Web page and an eye on possible profits, too. Businesses are tripping over themselves to join the zillions already advertising their services and wares online. Why the rush? There are 65 to 100 million Internet users (estimates vary), which makes for quite an online market to tap into. By the year 2003, experts estimate there will be more than 177 million Internet users, and electronic commerce (or e-commerce, for short) will grow to more than one trillion dollars.

Professional Hermits Rejoice!

With today's Internet, you can shop online for just about anything you could ever need. I suppose you've heard of that Dot.com guy who's holed up somewhere in Texas trying to survive for a year by getting everything he needs off the Internet? (I'm not making this up; you can check it out yourself at www.dotcomguy.com.) The online marketplace is a burgeoning thing.

Who's in Charge?

Would you believe *nobody* is in charge of the Internet? It's true. Your kids might think that's pretty cool. The Internet is a collaborative effort. No one organization or institution runs the Internet. Not the government, not the guys who started it all with ARPANET, not the commercial online services—nobody owns the Internet. Interesting to find out, isn't it?

That's not to say nobody has any influence over this beast. There are organizations made up of technical people that help shape the Internet and its protocols. Here are a few you might like to know about:

The Internet Engineering Task Force (IETF)   This group keeps an eye on the Internet's ongoing evolution, helping to ensure that everything progresses smoothly, technologically speaking.

The Internet Architecture Board (IAB)   This group helps define and refine the overall structure of the Internet and provides input to the IETF.

The Internet Engineering Steering Group (IESG)   This group manages the Internet standards process and the activities of the IETF.

The Internet Society (ISOC)   This group is made up of corporations, organizations, government agencies, and individuals taken from the Internet community. Its purpose is to oversee the IAB and IESG and handle Internet policies and practices.

The Internet Network Information Center (InterNIC) and The Internet Assigned Numbers Authority (IANA)   Both of these groups help with the assignment of domain names and IP addresses.

The World Wide Web Consortium (W3C)   This group sets Web protocols and HTML standards.

Plenty of groups contribute to the Internet, such as the government, the telecommunications industries, Internet service providers, and the like. Many of these groups find ways to make money by providing access to the Internet to others. With certain Internet issues, some of these groups have come together to solve technical problems that affect the industry as a whole. But no one group controls the Internet.

Knowing that no one is charge perhaps explains much of what you currently see going on with the Internet and the Web. Keep in mind that the Internet pioneers conducted things a lot differently than you see on the Internet today. They were pretty scientifically and academically minded, and didn't allow all the silliness you see online today. They certainly didn't have to contend with the criminal element. Now, with the growing dangers online, many people are concerned about the direction the Internet is taking, especially as it relates to children. This leads us to our next topic: Is anybody going to regulate the Internet?

Regulating the Internet

In 1996, Congress enacted the Communications Decency Act (CDA). The act was part of a larger bill that was directed at deregulating the telecommunications industry. The CDA sought to ban any online material deemed indecent or patently offensive and that is accessible to minors. This alarmed the Internet community, mainly because the wording is broad enough to include conversations in chat rooms, newsgroup postings, and even data exchange on educational topics, such as rape or safe sex. Needless to say, no one wants to be arrested for typing a curse word in a chat room.

The CDA also sought to make it a felony to knowingly send indecent material to a child (anyone under 18). Although everyone agrees (at least they should) that children need protection from the Internet's more dangerous aspects, figuring out how to protect them has proven quite a challenge. The CDA created a huge uproar at its introduction, and the American Civil Liberties Union filed suit to block the CDA on behalf of free-speech advocates, Internet companies, publishers, civil rights groups, and Net users. Their claim was that the law was too broad and it violated the right to free speech.

A year after the introduction of the CDA, it was ruled unconstitutional. Deeming the Internet the most participatory form of mass speech ever, the judges agreed to protect the First Amendment right to free speech. The CDA failed to pass largely because it broadly tried to regulate indecent material on the Internet, rather than focus on obscene material. What's the difference? Obscene material is already illegal.

For many of us, there's not a lot of difference between indecent and obscene—bad is bad, and bad is certainly bad for children. But in the eyes of the court, there are different levels of "badness" when it comes to indecent or obscene material. According to the United States Supreme Court, something is obscene if it meets *all three* of the following criteria:

> Applying community standards, the average person finds the work appeals to prurient, or base, interests...

> *And* the work describes or shows patently offensive sexual conduct defined by state law, or is offensive to local standards of decency...

> *And* the work lacks serious artistic, literary, scientific, or political value.

Indecency, on the other hand, is merely what makes material off limits to minors but available to adults; pornography falls into this category. So according to law, child pornography is obscene and regular pornography is just indecent (and sometimes downright tacky, but there's never been a law against tackiness—which is really unfortunate if you ask me).

In 1998, Congress tried again with the Children's Online Protection Act (COPA), dubbed "CDA II." This bill attempted to narrow the online focus and pass constitutional muster. It hoped to make it illegal for commercial Web sites to allow minors access to harmful material that is deemed obscene. Commercial Web pornographers would require adult verification or a credit card for users to access the sites. It's widespread practice for such sites to place free "teaser" images (pornographic pictures) on their site's home page, which anybody can access. After you pass verification or use your credit card number, only then can you enter the site and see all it has to offer. The COPA bill would end such practices.

Interestingly enough, commercial Web pornography sites are saying that mandatory age checks are too costly to implement and would deter Web surfers. They want their pornography easy to access, darn it, and a law commanding them to regulate who uses their sites is just too restrictive. Besides, how are they supposed to make any money if they're in jail for letting minors view obscene graphic files?

COPA was signed into law by President Clinton in October, 1998. Opponents say the law is still too vague. Those opposing the law aren't so much worried about the accessibility of pornography, but are more concerned the law will cross over to include other online areas, not just pornography sites. Enforcement of the law was halted in January of 1999, and both sides continue to duke it out in the courts.

The battle to protect children online rages on in the courts and among lawmakers. You can be sure that advocates are online and investigating ways to regulate what children are exposed to on the Internet, as well as offering resources for everyone concerned with these issues. For example, in February 2000, the United Nations introduced an initiative, called "Innocence in Danger," to combat pedophilia and child pornography on the Web. Under the initiative, a group called Wired Kids has been formed. It includes participants such as industry giants Microsoft and AOL, as well as government agencies such as the FBI and Interpol. The group is endeavoring to be an online think tank and a clearinghouse for information about online exploitation of children.

Although the Internet is a difficult area to regulate when it comes to obscenity and protecting kids, laws will continue to be hammered out. After all, the safety of our children is at stake.

Check This Out

Electronic Frontier Foundation

To learn more about the prospects of regulations on the Internet, visit the Electronic Frontier Foundation's Web site at www.eff.org.

Check This Out

What If There Was a Law?

Even if both sides finally agreed to an acceptable law concerning the online safety of children, enforcing it poses a completely different problem. The Internet is global—what's illegal in one country might be legal in another. In fact, with some countries, such as Iraq and Iran, the Internet is already heavily censored. That's not to say the world's governments aren't trying to work together; they are. The difficulty lies in prosecuting cases across borders. To learn more about law enforcement on the Internet, check out Chapter 19, "Finding Law Enforcement When You Need It."

The Future of the Internet

What's next for the Internet? The future's wide open. All kinds of exciting things are in store for the Internet. For starters, there's speed: The Internet, particularly the Web, is known for heavy traffic and slow connection speeds. Current modems and telephone lines simply aren't cutting it when it comes to accessing information. Companies are starting to utilize fiber optic lines, which greatly speed up access to data. Cable companies are also in the game of making the Internet accessible via the very same cable that connects your TV. For example, my local cable provider offers Internet access at a cost that's only slightly higher than my regular Internet service provider, and the connection is 100 times faster than a 28.8KBps modem. Not only is it fast, but you're not tying up a phone line, and access is constant and instantaneous because it's through a cable modem and cable line.

We'll be seeing new technologies that increase bandwidth and speed data. We'll also see Internet sites that cater to the higher speeds. Soon, the mid to slow (56.6KBps modems or slower) users will begin to feel left out. As the story goes with computers, the future is all about upgrading.

We're already seeing a market for pagers and cell phones that can access the Internet, view Web pages, and send and receive email. You can expect to see more gadgets with Internet-enabled devices, such as cars and kitchen appliances. How about ordering groceries from a screen on your refrigerator? Electrolux (the vacuum cleaner makers) has already developed the ScreenFridge. It's an Internet-enabled refrigerator that helps you organize your pantry as well as schedule a grocery order online.

What's Bandwidth?

Bandwidth is the range of frequencies a transmission line, such as a telephone line, or channel can carry. Telephone line bandwidth is low. Web pages that use lots of graphics are often referred to as "bandwidth hogs," which means it takes longer to download these pages onto your browser because the graphics are large and take a long time to transfer.

The Web is expected to continue to grow at a rapid rate (see Figure 3.1). Very few people suspected that the Web would become as popular as it has. Some estimate it's growing by two million pages a day, and as many as 4,400 Web sites are added daily. In 1999, experts estimated there were 3.6 million Web sites. The number continues to climb at a phenomenal pace. You can expect to see an explosion of e-commerce and e-banking. Businesses will videoconference and collaborate online as never before. Online shopping will continue to grow. Some estimate that 70 percent of Internet users have shopped online. That percentile is expected to increase.

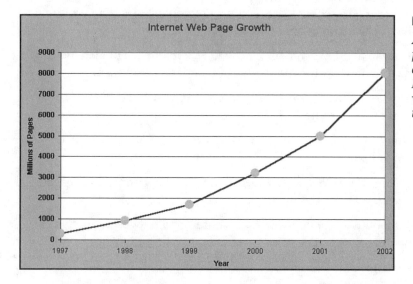

Figure 3.2

According to statistics from The Standard (a company that tracks Internet commerce), there will be more Web pages than people by 2002.

The future of the Internet is already in the works. Back in 1996, the University Corporation for Advanced Internet Development (UCAID) began an experimental network formed by universities, corporations, and government agencies. Called Internet2, this network is a collection of networks utilizing high-speed fiber optics. The next phase of the project went online in February, 1999. Scientists, engineers, and researchers can transmit data over the network at speeds of up to 2.4 gigabits per second. Yowsa! That's 45,000 times faster than my 56.6KBps modem!

Just think of the potential: interactive television, 3-D conferencing, and so much more. And get a load of this: NASA has developed a very cool Virtual Collaborative Clinic that connects hospitals and other medical facilities. Using the virtual clinic, doctors can confer, diagnose, and even simulate surgery. This environment can give surgeons opportunities to practice procedures and access skills that were previously available only in large medical facilities. What does NASA have to do with medicine? Astronauts need doctors and health care, too—especially when they're millions of space miles away from the nearest hospital.

As you can begin to see, the future of the Internet is bright and bountiful. It's going to offer much more for your children, so train them well and help them in their quest to make use of it.

The Least You Need to Know

For most of us, the Internet burst onto the scene soon after the advent of personal computers. With it came new technologies and new responsibilities. Here are a few tidbits to know about this growing phenomenon:

➤ The Internet began as an experiment by the U.S. Department of Defense to establish a reliable network for communication and data exchange.

➤ The Web is a subset of the Internet; however, it happens to be the most popular section of the Internet.

➤ The Web is based on pages written in HTML protocol, a system by which documents are linked.

➤ The invention of the Web browser, a special program for viewing Web pages, made the Web popular for the masses.

➤ The Internet is a network of connected computers and networks—an "inter-network."

➤ No one is in charge of the Internet.

➤ The United States government has made several attempts to pass laws to protect children online, the first being the Communications Decency Act.

➤ The Children's Online Protection Act is the second attempt to regulate online pornography as it applies to minors. It's currently being contested in the court system.

➤ The future of the Internet will include faster high-speed connections, more Internet-enabled gadgets, and explosions in online commerce.

Chapter 4

What to Do If Your Kids Know More About Computers Than You Do

---

In This Chapter

➤ Learn how to refer to your computer's components by their proper names

➤ Find out the many ways to access the Internet

➤ See what sort of things you can do on the Internet

➤ The compressed version of everything you need to know for navigating the Web

---

Do your children babble about ZIP files, URLs, and streaming audio while you just stand there and scratch your head? When you have a question about the family PC, is your child the first person you consult? It's a humbling experience when you realize your kids know more about computers than you do. If you're like a lot of parents these days, computer technology sort of snuck up on you, but your children have grown up with it.

This is your chance to turn the tide. Knowledge is your greatest ally when it comes to protecting your kids online. For that reason, it's important that you know the basics, and a bit more important if you want to stay ahead. If you feel you're lagging behind your kids technologically, this chapter is just for you. If you're already immersed in the world of computers, at work or at home, then you can skip this chapter.

Free Your Mind and Your Fears

Many adults are fearful of computers. Why is that? Because computers, like other gadget-like appliances, can be extremely intimidating and anything can go wrong. When it comes right down to it, you don't understand a lot of the gadgets around the house, right? Take the classic example of the VCR—you already know where this is going, don't you? How many of you still haven't figured out how to get rid of that flashing 12:00 on your VCR? We rest our case.

Check This Out

You Were Afraid to Drive, Too

Don't forget, learning to drive a car the first time was intimidating, too. But after several years and a few scrapes or tickets later, driving became second nature to you. It's the same with computers, but without the scrapes or tickets.

Computers are much worse than VCRs. You've got to start them, enter commands, coordinate that darn mouse pointer thingy, and make them spit out a printed copy of a document. There's always that nagging feeling that you're going to hit the wrong key and the whole thing's going to explode.

Kids, on the other hand, are fearless about computers. They delight in pressing keys and clicking the mouse. Kids love to explore and play on the computer. This really shouldn't surprise us. It's a lot easier to understand computers when you're introduced to them as a child than it is when you're an adult. It's similar to learning a second language, such as Spanish—it's easier to learn it as a child than as an adult. Because computers are relatively new on the scene (PCs were introduced in the 1980s, and became really popular in the 1990s), you might not have had opportunities to acquaint yourself as fully with the technology as your kids have.

The best thing you can do for yourself and your kids is to make like a sponge and soak all this in. If you can manage to absorb the basics of how computers compute and how this Internet thing works, you're well on your way to being technologically savvy and impressing your kids. In case you're worried, such knowledge will not turn you into a computer geek, at least not immediately. It might, however, force you to tap into some brain cells that are currently storing other important information, such as how to program the VCR.

Computer Basics

This isn't going to be a long, detailed discussion of the inner workings of your computer. If that's what you need, there are plenty of other books that cover that. Let's just give you enough of the basics to make you dangerous, eh?

The PC (aka personal computer) is typically made up of *hardware* and *software*. Hardware is the flesh and bones of the computer; software is the instructions that tell the hardware what to do. With that said, allow us to present to you three topics of discussion: hardware inside your computer, peripherals you use with the computer, and software that makes the computer do what you want it to do.

Hardware

The skeleton of your computer is the *system unit*. It's the box or console that holds all the guts of the computer—the wiring, chips, drives, and so on. The system unit is the case you can see. Depending on the type of computer you own, it might be a box on which your monitor sits, or a *tower unit* that sits on the floor, or it might even be built into the monitor as one big unit. If you have a laptop, it's the base beneath the keyboard. Figure 4.1 shows a typical, run-of-the-mill computer setup. Hopefully, you can recognize a few objects in your own setup, particularly the system unit.

Check This Out

Shameless Plug Here

For more help learning about computers, try reading *The Complete Idiot's Guide to PCs Seventh Edition* by Joe Kraynak.

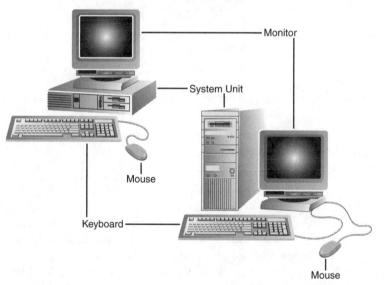

Monitor

System Unit

Mouse

Keyboard

Mouse

Figure 4.1

Most PCs include a monitor, system unit, keyboard, and mouse.

On to things you can't see. That is, you can't see them unless you open the system unit, and who would want to do that without the supervision of a qualified computer geek? Let's start with the *CPU*. The brain of your computer is the *central processing unit,* or CPU for short. It's a smallish sort of chip that commands everything else in the computer. The faster the chip is, the more powerful your PC is. For example, a computer with a 100MHz 486 CPU is faster than a computer with a 66MHz 486 CPU. See if you can find the CPU in Figure 4.2.

Figure 4.2

This is sort of what the inside of your computer looks like.

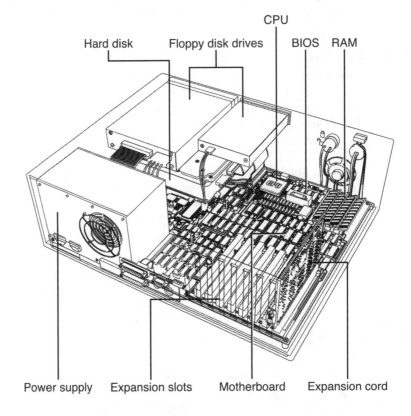

The CPU is plugged into the *motherboard*, the floor of the system unit. The motherboard is an electronic circuit board that connects all the other parts of the computer, such as the CPU. The motherboard is your computer's nervous system.

Also plugged into the motherboard is *RAM*. Amazingly, this has nothing to do with sheep, although talking about it can make you drowsy. RAM is short for random access memory. RAM temporarily stores instructions and data while you're using the computer. When you turn off the PC, RAM is cleared. Next time you turn the computer on, RAM starts out all fresh and ready to store more temporary data. If you have an older computer, your techno-savvy kids might be whining to you about the need to upgrade your computer's memory. The larger the memory capacity is, the zippier your computer is, because it can swap data in and out of RAM. This means your computer can handle more and bigger tasks (such as memory-hogging computer games).

BIOS (Basic Input/Output System) keeps everything working in sync. It's the interface between software and hardware, keeping both sides speaking to each other. The system BIOS handles all the menial tasks that the CPU thinks itself too important to handle, such as prodding the keyboard to pay attention to the next command.

Speaking of paying attention, hang in there. We're almost through with the computer guts.

All the data zipping around inside your computer travels on the *system bus*. Any data you want to store is routed to the hard disk drive or a floppy disk drive. The *hard disk drive* is

Restart Occasionally

To refresh RAM and speed up how your computer works, it's a good idea to restart (also called reboot) the PC from time to time. Just a tip for you and the kids.

where your computer programs, as well as files you create, are stored. The *floppy disk drive* lets you store files on floppy disks. A *CD-ROM drive* lets you work with CD-ROMs. (You never would have guessed that one, would ya?) Also on the motherboard are *expansion slots* into which you can plug upgrades, such as an internal modem or a graphics card for better display of graphics on the computer. Finally, juicing up all these lovely electronic components is the *power supply*.

It's Electric!

Your computer is a delicate system of circuits and wiring powered by electricity. Keep that in mind when setting rules in your house about computer usage. It's not a good idea to have food and beverages around the computer. A spilled drink can cause great damage, and crumbs can really gum up a keyboard. Besides, who wants to use a mouse smeared with peanut butter and jelly?

The computer is also susceptible to power surges and lightning strikes, so another good idea is to invest in a surge protector, a special plug-in power strip. Plug your computer into the strip, and plug the strip into the wall outlet. If your house is zapped electrically, the surge protector sacrifices itself, diverting a surge or spike from entering your computer. Without such a sacrifice, your computer is fried—that means it's time to talk to your insurance agent and find out if you remembered to have your home computer covered in your homeowner's policy.

Peripherals

Let's move on to peripherals. Peripherals are hardware too, and they include all the nifty gadgets you can plug into your computer to do things such as type, print, or talk to another computer. Your keyboard, mouse, and printer are all peripherals. Here's a list of basic peripherals you might have:

Monitor   You can't see what your computer's doing or see what commands you're entering without a screen to view them on. The monitor is that box that looks like a TV. It connects to the system unit and usually has to be plugged into an outlet as well. Monitors come in all shapes and sizes these days. Monitors tend to take a lot of abuse from kids—how many times do you have to wipe the fingerprints off the screen at your house? If you and your family use the PC quite a bit, you might consider investing in a larger screen. The bigger screens make it much easier to see things, particularly if you and your child sit down to use the PC together.

Keyboard   Like the monitor, this one's pretty essential, too. You use it to type in commands or data. You're really not supposed to pound on it, so make sure younger kids know that.

Mouse   This is another device for issuing commands. It's also used for drawing, navigating, and playing games. It's not supposed to be used to swing at your younger brother or sister, conking them on the head.

Printer   You gotta have a printer if you want a hard copy of your computer data. You use this peripheral to print letters, drawings, and such.

Modem   This device lets your computer communicate with other computers. You can't get on the Internet without this little baby (or something like it). Most newer computers have internal modems, a card that fits into the motherboard inside the system unit. External modems are also available. These devices are boxes that plug into your computer's system unit as well as your regular phone line, and sit on the desktop somewhere.

Tape Backup   This is an external or internal storage device for storing important data files.

Joystick   Like the mouse, this peripheral lets you navigate in computer games and shoot the bad guys.

For your sake, and for the sake of your kids, try to refer to these hardware items by their proper names. It makes you sound smart, even if you still don't understand exactly what the devices do.

Check This Out

Got a Cable Modem?

If you're really lucky and your local cable provider offers Internet access, you can get lightning fast Internet access using a cable modem device. It, too, is considered a peripheral.

Software

Software serves as the instructions that tell your computer what to do. You can get all kinds of software to make your computer do stuff, such as process words, calculate numbers, or play games.

Microsoft Word is an example of word processing software. *Myst* is an example of game software. Both of these examples are application software. Application software is task-oriented. The instructions are specialized. You can't tell a word processing program to suddenly act like a video game. So when your kids ask if they can buy the latest version of *Doom,* you're actually buying a set of instructions that tell your computer what to do.

Another type of software is operating system software. Most users are familiar with the Microsoft Windows operating system. Windows is an operating system that tells the computer to display an interactive desktop environment (an environment that lets users point and click on items instead of typing in commands). Operating system software is more complex than application software. Instead of focusing on one kind of task, it tells the computer how to do all kinds of jobs, such as store files, use memory, display data, that sort of thing. One of the coolest things about Windows is that you can perform several tasks at once, commonly called *multitasking*. Put simply, this means you can run two or more programs at the same time. In real life, this is like walking and chewing gum at the same time, or changing a diaper while yelling at your toddler to stop climbing on the bookshelves. How about that—you multitask all the time. See? Computers aren't so hard to understand after all.

Check This Out

A Word About Operating Systems

Microsoft Windows is by far the most popular operating system today, but you might also be familiar with Linux, DOS, UNIX, or even Apple's Macintosh system. Windows itself has evolved through several versions, but all versions offer the same window-themed environment. If you really want to impress the kids, tell them about the good old days of DOS, when you had to type text-based commands into the cold, dark void of a black screen to get the computer to do anything. Ah, those were the days...

That wraps up the basics of computers. At least now you know what everything is called. But don't rest on your laurels just yet. The next thing to tackle is the Internet.

Internet Basics

Internet, Internet, Internet. It's the Jan Brady complex (warning: obscure "Brady Bunch" reference) of the new millennium. Everybody's talking about it, everybody's focused on it, and unless you're surfing it, you're feeling pretty left out. To help you assimilate, the following sections teach you what you need to know about the Internet.

How Do You Access the Internet?

As you learned in Chapter 3, "How Did This All Get Started? And Where Is It Going?," the Internet is actually a vast network of connected computers. As long as your computer has a modem and a phone line, you can connect to the Internet and rule the world (or something like that).

Most of us need to use a middleman to get to the Internet. The middleman, for a small fee, lets you connect to his computer, which in turn is connected to the Internet. These middlemen are called Internet service providers, or *ISPs*, and this type of connection is called a dial-up account. (You must dial up the service with your modem and phone line to connect.) For a nominal monthly fee, you can access the Internet through the provider's computers. Along with access, you get an email address, and sometimes they even let you store your own Web page on their server (more on the Web coming up).

Are You Hardwired?

Some lucky individuals are hardwired to the Internet, which means they don't have to use a modem. This might be the case with your computer at work. Network connections are generally faster than the dial-up method.

Another popular way to access the Internet is through a *commercial online service*, such as America Online or CompuServe. The commercial service middleman also charges a fee. However, unlike ISPs, you must go through the service's interface to get to the Internet. For example, with AOL, you must install their software on your computer, and when you log on, you must jump through several hoops to reach the Internet portal. Commercial services throw a lot of advertisements your way, but they also offer a lot of great features in one spot (so to speak), kind of like a mall. There are currently four big commercial services competing for your dollar: America Online (called AOL for short), CompuServe Interactive, Prodigy Internet, and MSN (Microsoft Network). AOL offers the most kid-related content and boasts the most kid users. All of these services offer parental controls you can use to regulate what areas of the service your child has access to.

Commercial Versus ISP

When deciding whether to use a commercial online service or an ISP, consider how you want to use your time online. If you've never been on the Internet, a commercial service is a good way to begin exploring. Commercial services offer specialized content that's easy to find, tons of content for kids, and lots of parental control features. Unfortunately, you must deal with oodles of advertising, busy lines, and slower Web surfing. If you're looking for speed, quick access, and whiz-bang Internet tools, ISPs are a good way to go. They're a bit difficult at first for absolute beginners, and any parental control to filter out content is left to you, but you don't have to deal with all the advertising.

Depending on availability, you might also be able to access the Internet through a cable company. Such connections promise lightning speeds, but they are also two to three times more expensive than regular modem connections. If patience isn't your virtue and you don't mind paying a bit more, you and your family can access the Internet several hundred times faster than a 28.8 KBps modem.

The first step in getting online is to set up an account with an ISP or commercial service. You can find ISPs in the yellow pages, advertised in computer magazines or computer stores, or just ask a friend who happens to be a computer geek. Commercial services are also easy to come by. With AOL's intense marketing, practically everybody in the United States has received a disk or CD in the mail containing the AOL software and offers of free limited-time usage. You can find commercial services advertised in magazines and computer stores, too.

After you find an ISP or commercial service you want to use, prepare to shell out some dough to establish an account. Setting up an account typically involves installing some software, telling your modem which number to call to connect to the computers, and figuring out a username and password. (The ISP will tell you how to do all this.) After you've got that all set up, you're ready to hit the information superhighway.

The Woes of Local Access

Most of us use an access telephone number to log on to an Internet account. Depending on where you live, the number of access numbers might be limited, or you might have to dial long distance. This can seriously affect how much time you spend online. Be sure to check with the online service or ISP to see what's available and affordable for you.

Server

This is a computer that is used to store a large number of data files (documents). Network servers are used on the Internet or in corporate intranets (internal Internets).

Kids' Browsers

Parents can rest easier about children surfing the Web if they use a kid-specific browser. Kid Browsers, like Kiddo Net or Crayon Crawler, let kids surf safely from a predetermined list of safe sites. Check out Chapter 13, "All About Filters," to learn more.

What's on the Internet?

Everything is on the Internet. You name it, it's out there. It truly is the information superhighway. Mind you, not all the information is reliable, true, or updated, but if it's info you want, it's info you'll find. Information can be viewed, downloaded, posted on message boards, or emailed back and forth. Information takes the form of text, graphics, and multimedia.

There are actually several different ways to access information on the Internet. This section introduces you to several of the more commonly used methods of viewing and exchanging information.

The Web

The World Wide Web, or *Web* for short, is the most popular aspect of the Internet. It's actually the easiest way of viewing information on the Internet. It's based on a hypertext system that links documents. You can click a link on one page that jumps you to another page. The page might be on the same server or on a completely different server located somewhere around the globe. Figure 4.3 shows an example of a typical Web page.

To view Web pages, you need a special program called a *browser*. The most popular browsers are Microsoft's Internet Explorer and Netscape's

Navigator. If you don't already have a browser installed, you can find both of these on the Web and download them free. (However, the files are really big, so they may take awhile to download depending on the speed of your modem and connection.) After you log onto your Internet account, you can open your browser window and start exploring the Web. Commercial services, such as AOL, offer their own integrated browsers to view Web pages. You learn more about using a Web browser at the end of this chapter.

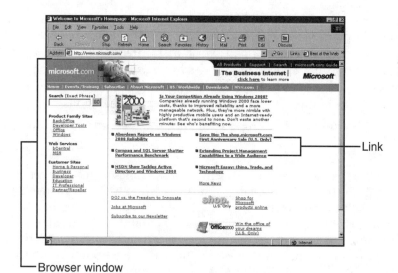

— Link

— Browser window

Figure 4.3

Use links to jump from page to page and view information.

FTP

File Transfer Protocol, or *FTP*, enables Internet users to transfer files. This little trick is called uploading and downloading. You can log onto FTP servers that are open to the public to access certain kinds of software files or large document files. Kids might be interested in FTP sites to download games.

To learn more about downloading files, visit Chapter 15, "Downloading Do's and Don'ts."

Techno Talk

Upload/Download

When you transfer a copy of a file from someone else's computer onto yours, you are downloading. When you transfer a copy from your computer to theirs, you are uploading.

Zipping Files

When you hear your kids talk about zipped files, they're referring to files that have been compressed so they take up less storage space on the computer. Many files you download off the Internet are zipped, which makes transferring them go a bit faster. After you download a zipped file, you need to unzip it—that is, decompress the file, kind of like unpacking it. There are special programs available, such as WinZip and PKZip, that are used for compressing and decompressing files.

Gopher

Introduced by the University of Minnesota and named after its mascot, *Gopher* was one of the very first tools for finding information on the Internet without the need for a degree in Geekology. It indexes Internet databases and uses a text-based menu system (no Web-friendly graphics here). There were once numerous Gopher servers on the Internet that were great for finding certain types of technical information on the Net, but the average consumer prefers the user-friendly Web environment to view and search for information. As a result, Gopher servers are becoming an endangered species.

Usenet

Short for the "users network," Usenet is simply a large network of discussion groups connected to the Internet.

Newsgroups

Have you ever been a member of a club? That's what it's like to be involved in a newsgroup. Usenet *newsgroups* are a global collection of online clubs or discussion groups. They typically focus on a particular topic, such as gardening, computers, or current events. Participants contribute to the discussions by posting messages to the newsgroup. It's a lot like email messages, but everyone who accesses the newsgroup can read them. Some newsgroups are moderated; that is, someone is in charge of keeping the messages updated, archiving old messages, screening postings, and so on.

Newsgroups are great for interacting with people who have the same interests as you. Be warned, however, the discussions can be very opinionated and might contain language unsuitable for children, and participants can be abusive to each other. This isn't exactly the kind of environment in which you want your kids wandering around without strict adult supervision. Learn more about this topic in Chapter 9, "The News on Newsgroups."

Mail List Servers

Much like newsgroups, *mail list servers* are email lists to which you can subscribe. After you've subscribed, all the newsgroup's messages/responses are emailed to you instead of posted somewhere. The downside to subscribing to a list serv is that some send out 30 emails a day. That's a lot to encounter in your email box, isn't it? Fortunately, some mail list servers offer a digest—a single email that contains the text of all the day's traffic.

Be careful subscribing to a mail list server. Always make sure you have the mail list server's instructions for unsubscribing.

IRC and Chat

Before there was chatting on AOL, CompuServe, and the like, there was *Internet Relay Chat (IRC)*. Special IRC servers offer chat rooms where users can log on and conduct live conversations (with the help of IRC-client software installed). How do you talk on the Internet? You type, of course. Anything you type and send to the server is immediately entered into the chat window and read by everyone else in the virtual "room." There might be a slight lag between when you type and send your text and when it appears in the chat window, but the conversations are truly live.

Check This Out

Chat Dangers for Kids

In the beginning of the Internet, chat rooms were focused on topics, many of a technical nature. The conversations were polite, civilized, and informational. Today's chat rooms are far from civilized. I stress the word far. Most rooms are not monitored, which means anything can go on. They are definitely not a suitable environment for children.

Users of commercial online services have truly glommed on to the concept of chat. Unfortunately, most chat rooms are chaotic and the participants are unruly. Check out Chapter 5, "Chat, Chat, and More Chat," for the low-down on the chat phenomenon.

Email

Electronic mail, known as *email*, is a fantastic way of communicating online. It's fast, reliable (most of the time), and puts you in touch with every other Internet user on the face of the planet, providing you know their email address. Email works similarly to real mail (now called "snail mail" by Internet denizens, with good reason). You can use an email program to create messages, or use the email program that's part of your online service. There are good points and bad points to email, which you will learn all about in Chapter 6, "Evil Email."

Web Navigating Know-How

Surfing the Web is the number one Internet activity. If you've got a computer and an Internet connection, you've probably surfed the Web. It's the easiest way to view information on the Internet. Chances are, your kids do this at school with assignments and research. In the quest to keep kids safe online, it's imperative that you know a few things about navigating the Web yourself.

How Do You Find the Web?

First of all, how do you get to the Web? If you're using an online service, look for a button or feature that takes you to the service's Internet portal. For example, if you're using AOL version 5.0, you can click the **Internet** button on the button bar, and then choose **Go to the Web**. This opens AOL's browser window, shown in Figure 4.4. Now you can start exploring!

If you're using an ISP, you must log on to your account and open your browser window, such as Microsoft Internet Explorer or Netscape Navigator. When you first open a browser window, the home page appears. It's the starting point for your online session, and it's usually the provider's or online service's promo page. You can make any of your favorite Web pages into your home or start page. The Netscape Navigator's browser window looks like the one shown in Figure 4.5.

Techno Talk

What Is Surfing?

To surf the Net is to navigate from Web page to Web page. The term is commonly credited to Jean Armour Polly, known as Net-Mom on the Internet. She first used the phrase in a 1992 article entitled "Surfing the Internet."

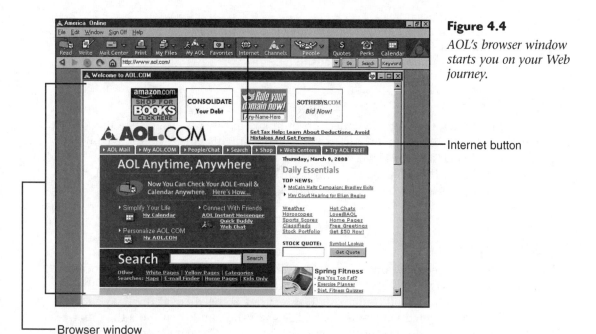

Figure 4.4

AOL's browser window starts you on your Web journey.

Internet button

Browser window

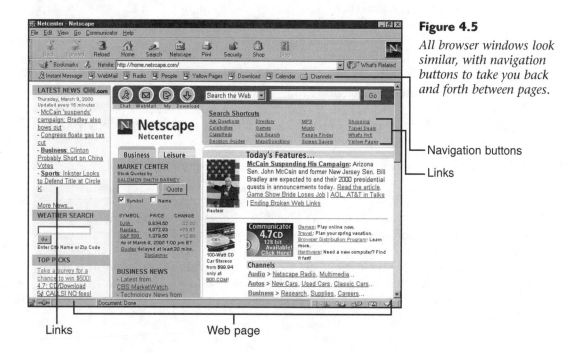

Figure 4.5

All browser windows look similar, with navigation buttons to take you back and forth between pages.

Navigation buttons

Links

Links

Web page

Use the browser window's navigation buttons to move back and forth between pages you've viewed. For example, click the **Back** button to see the page you previously viewed. How easy is that? No wonder kids like it, too.

Clicking Links

As explained earlier, the Web is a collection of linked pages. You can click a link on one page, and it takes you to another page. Web documents are written in a computer code called *HTML* (for Hypertext Markup Language). Links, or hyperlinks, appear as underlined text on the Web page. Links can also be graphics, buttons, or other Web-page items. Move the mouse pointer over a link and click. That's all there is to it.

What's an URL?

Every page on the Web has a unique address, called an *URL* (Uniform Resource Locator). Another way to navigate the Web is to type in the URL (pronounced "Earl") of the page you want to visit. You'll find an address text box somewhere at the top of the browser window in which you can click and type an URL, and then press the Enter key to view the page. URLs are everywhere these days: in magazines, on TV, on the radio. You've probably heard them hundreds of times and not even known it. Perhaps your kids have rattled off a few to you as well. An URL generally looks something like this:

    www.mypage.com

Officially, an URL starts with a content identifier that indicates the type of protocol you're connecting to, such as http:// (standing for hypertext transfer protocol) or ftp:// (standing for file transfer protocol). Most browsers today don't require you to enter the identifier when typing in an URL.

Take a look at this book publisher's URL:

    www.mcp.com

This URL points you to the Macmillan USA Web site. The *www* prefix indicates the Web-managing portion of the site's server, the *mcp* part is the company name (abbreviation for Macmillan Computer Publishing), and the *.com* extension identifies the server as a commercial server. There are all kinds of extensions you might run across, such as *.gov* (government), *.net* (Internet networks), and *.edu* (education).

By the way, the periods that separate the parts of an URL are called *dots*. Don't call them periods, unless you want your kids to laugh at you. So if you want to send your kids to Disney's Web site, tell them to type in "www dot disney dot com" (`www.disney.com`), okay? This is crucial if you want your kids to think you know at least a few things about the Internet.

Additional slashes added to an URL designate the exact path of the Web page document and its location on the server. For example, let's look at `www.mcp.com/que/new_users/new.html`. Notice the path includes directories and subdirectories. URLs can take you to a page or an exact file. They are case sensitive, which means you and your kids need to be careful when typing them in. This is one of the scariest things about kids and computers. Kids aren't always the best typists, and one misplaced character can take them to an unsuitable Web site.

Web Page or Web Site? What's the Difference?

A *Web page* generally refers to a single document. A *Web site* is a collection of related documents. For example, Nickelodeon's Web site (`www.nick.com`) has more than one page, and you can spend a lot of time viewing pages without ever leaving the server that stores the Web site.

Searching for Stuff on the Web

If following links or typing in URLs doesn't take you to the information you want to view on the Web, you can always conduct a search. There are dozens and dozens of *search engines* you can use to look up information. A search engine is a database of Internet content. You fill out a form—typically a text box where you enter the word or words you want to search for—and then command the search engine to look through its index of Web pages for matching data. Within moments, it lists any matching data (called *hits*) it finds. You can then click a listed match that links you to the actual page. You can learn more about using various Internet search tools, particularly those that are safe for kids, in Chapter 14, "How to Search the Web Safely."

More Browser Stuff to Know About

You probably think you can't possibly digest one more concept, but we've got to cover a few more things. To make it easy, we've compressed this information into nuggets. Enjoy!

Saving Web Pages   Did you know you can save Web pages you visit? You can save them as files and store them on your hard disk drive. You can print them out, too.

Refresh/Reload   If you ever experience trouble getting a Web page to display, click the **Stop** button on the browser's Navigation bar. Click the **Refresh** or **Reload** button to try viewing the page again.

Marking Favorite Sites   Most browsers have a feature for marking your favorite Web sites so you can easily return to them the next time you log on.

Web Traffic   There are certain periods during the day when Web traffic is really heavy and the surfing is slow. You get better results after business hours or in the wee hours of the morning.

Graphics   Graphics take much longer to display in your browser than text-only pages. For that reason, you might want to turn off the graphics-viewing feature on your browser.

Plug-Ins and External Apps   There are oodles of applets (small programs) on the Internet that you can download and install to help you with your Web surfing. Some work directly with your browser, and others activate on their own. For example, to see some of the multimedia content on the Web, you might want a program like Shockwave; to hear music, you can download an MP3 player.

If you're learning about the Web for the first time, you might want to invest in a good book on the subject. You can find lots of books for beginners at Macmillan USA's Web site (www.mcp.com). You can also glean a lot of information from your techno-savvy kids, and they might really enjoy teaching you a few things for a change.

The Least You Need to Know

Lots of parents (and adults in general) wrestle with the ever-changing world of computer technology, and in many families, kids know more about it than parents do. This chapter helps balance the situation by teaching you, the parent, the rudimentary terms and concepts for understanding computer components, the Internet, and the Web. Here's what you learned:

➤ You ought to at least know the proper names of the major components on your computer system. They typically include the system unit (which houses all the chips and wiring, such as the CPU, RAM, and system bus), monitor, keyboard, mouse, printer, and modem.

➤ The CPU is the brain of your computer, but you're the brains behind using your computer (or something like that).

➤ Windows is an operating system, not something you look through into your backyard.

➤ Most people access the Internet in one of two ways: an Internet service provider or a commercial online service (such as AOL or Prodigy).

➤ The Web is the most popular aspect of the Internet, which is precisely why your kids will want to go surfing on it.

➤ Other areas of the Internet include FTP sites for downloading files, newsgroups (online discussion groups), and chatting (live conversations via your keyboard).

➤ To access the Web, you need a Web browser, a special program for viewing and navigating Web pages. Popular browsers include Microsoft Internet Explorer and Netscape Navigator. If you're using an online service, you can use its integrated browser to view Web pages.

➤ Follow links to move from one Web page to another. Links are usually underlined text, but they can also be graphics or buttons.

➤ Every Web page has an address, called an URL. (Remember, it's pronounced "Earl.")

➤ Use search engines to find Web pages.

Part 2

The Real Dirt on Online Dangers

How dangerous is the Internet? Ask some people and they'll tell you it's the tool of the Devil, or that any time your kids head online, they'll be stalked, harassed, and subjected to pornography, hate sites, and worse.

Ask other people, and they'll tell you there's nothing to worry about, the Internet is a beautiful place, and your kids never need to worry their pretty little heads about a single thing when they go online.

What's the truth? Of course, it's somewhere in between.

In this part of the book, we show you what you really need to worry about, as well as what needn't concern you. And we do more than just tell you what you need to worry about. We also show you how you can keep your kids safe. Chatting, email, newsgroups, pornography, marketing scams, hate sites—we talk about all that and more. So let's get started. The truth is, the Internet is a great place for kids as long as you make sure they're safe. And here's where we start helping you make sure they're secure whenever they head online.

Chat, Chat, and More Chat

Kids are chatterers. Blabbers. Yakkers, talkers, yentas, and more. Kids of all ages, and especially teenagers, love to talk. In previous generations (and that means *you*, old-timer!) teenagers and kids chatted on the telephone for hours. Today, they spend their time chatting online.

Chatting is a great way for kids to keep in touch with their friends, family, and long-lost friends. And it's a great way for them to make new friends as well. But there are also dangers in chats. Your kids can be stalked or harassed, or tricked into meeting someone who is a predator. And there are other dangers as well. In this chapter, I show you all the ways kids chat, and clue you in on the dangers. Most important, though, I show you how you can make sure your kids are safe when they chat. So they can yak away to their heart's content, when all the while you know they're safe and sound.

What Ways Are There for Kids to Chat on the Internet?

You might not be as clued in as the wired generation is about chat, so let's start off by telling you what it means.

When your kids chat on the Internet, they don't actually speak to someone else or hear what the other party is saying. Instead, they type messages on their keyboards, and other kids can see what they type. In turn, other kids type messages on their keyboards, and your kids see what's typed. It's all done live—in other words, everyone who's chatting is online at the same time.

What Does Real Time Mean?

You might sometimes hear the phrase *real-time chat*. No, it's not another word for that hackneyed, meaningless phrase *quality time*. It just means you're chatting live—you see what people type the moment they type it, and they see what you type at the moment you type it. And because all chat is live, the term *real time* doesn't really add any meaning to the term *chat*.

Chatting is like a giant free-for-all. Your kids can talk to the entire group of chatters, or they can carry on a side conversation, one on one. In fact, they often do both simultaneously. Most chats are focused on a topic, such as schoolwork, MTV, pets, or just about any other kind of topic you can name. Often, a chat area is called a *chat room*. There are thousands of chat areas on the Internet that go on at the same time, and tens of thousands of kids chatting away. Just thinking about it gives me a headache! If all this is a little confusing for you, don't worry—just take a look at Figure 5.1 to see what a chat is like. This one is being held on America Online, which is Chat Paradise as far as most kids are concerned.

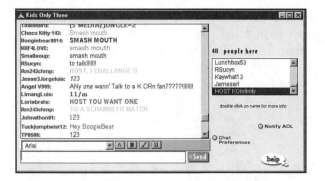

Figure 5.1

Chat Central: Here's a chat going on at America Online. Is this confusing or what?

What's the Difference Between Chat and Instant Messaging?

People often use the terms *chat* and *messenger programs* (usually referred to as "instant messengers") to mean the same thing; in fact, they're somewhat different. Although chat and instant messaging are becoming more alike, there are major differences between the two. Here are the differences:

➤ **When your kids chat, they communicate with a lot of people at the same time.** So there might be 10, 20, or even more people chatting together at the same time in the same chat room or chat area. Everyone can see everything that every other person types—with some exceptions, as is explained later.

➤ **When your kids use an instant messenger program, they communicate one-on-one with someone else.** It's a one-on-one conversation, like a phone call. These programs also include "buddy lists"—they alert your kids when their "buddies" are online so they can immediately start conversations. And they always do! Shown in Figure 5.2 is the America Online Instant Messenger program on the Internet.

Figure 5.2

When kids use an instant messenger program, such as AOL Instant Messenger, they hold one-on-one conversations.

Of course, this is the Internet, so things can get a little confusing. Some instant messenger programs also let kids chat, and chat rooms often let kids have one-on-one, private conversations with others. Still, a chat program or site is one in which the main purpose is to participate in group talk, whereas an instant messenger program's main purpose is to talk one-on-one.

What Does "IM Me" Mean?

When your kids spend time in an America Online chat room, they often have someone send them a message saying "IM me." What in the world does that mean? It means someone is asking them to use instant messenger capability to have a private, side conversation, apart from the rest of the chat room. In some instances, they use an "IM" feature built directly into the chat room, whereas in other instances, they use a separate "IM" feature. In any event, it means someone wants to hold a one–on–one conversation.

What Are the Main Kinds of Chat?

There are a whole lot of ways kids can chat online; some methods are safer than others are. Here are the main ways your kids use to chat. Later on in this chapter, you learn how to keep them safe while they chat.

➤ **Chats on America Online** America Online was built on chat. It's a yakker's paradise for kids. Pick a subject, any subject, and you find kids chatting about it—right now, as a matter of fact. For those who like to chat with others, the joint is jumping. Some chat rooms on America Online are watched over by adults, and they're probably the safest places for chatting on the Internet.

➤ **Internet Relay Chat (IRC)** This is the granddaddy of chat on the Internet. It was the first kind of chatting available on the Internet and is still popular. For kids to chat using IRC, they need special software that they can download free at popular download sites such as ZDNet Downloads at www.zddownloads.com. Generally, IRC chats aren't nearly as safe for kids as other kinds of chat are. There's no way for adults to watch over kids in IRC chats, as there is on America Online. IRC attracts a lot of adults. And there are other kinds of security holes hackers can use to plant viruses on your kids' computer with IRC.

➤ **Web-based chats**   Some Web sites let kids chat right on the site itself. No software is needed—they just head to a site and yak away. Many kid-friendly Web sites have chats that are watched over by adults.

➤ **Private chat rooms**   In some kinds of chats, such as on America Online, kids can create private chat rooms where they and those they invite can visit. Or they might be invited into a private chat room. Kids should never go into a private chat room unless they know the person who created it.

What Are the Main Kinds of Instant Messenger Programs?

As with chat, there are several different kinds of instant messenger programs. Here's the rundown on what you need to know about each:

➤ **ICQ (pronounced "I Seek You")**   Millions of people use this to send instant messages to one another. It can only be used to chat with others who use ICQ. It can be downloaded at sites such as the ZDNet Software Library at www.hotfiles.com or at www.icq.com. You can see it in action in Figure 5.3.

Figure 5.3

The most popular instant messenger program of all: ICQ.

➤ **America Online Buddy List**   This tells kids on America Online when their friends go online, and then lets them send instant messages to each other.

➤ **AOL Instant Messenger**   This instant messenger program lets anyone send instant messages to people on America Online from the Internet. That means non-America Online subscribers can send and receive instant messages to people on America Online. They can also send and receive instant messages from other AOL Instant Messenger users.

➤ **Other instant pagers and instant messengers** There are a lot of other instant messengers out there, including Yahoo! Messenger, MSN Messenger, PowWow, and others.

Check This Out

Instant Messenger Programs Don't Work with One Another

When kids use an instant messenger program, they can only send and receive messages from kids using the same program. So, for example, a kid using Yahoo! Messenger can send and receive messages from other Yahoo! Messenger users, but cannot send and receive messages from ICQ users.

Check This Out

How to Protect Your Kids from Email Harassment

Someone your child meets in a chat room might harass your child via email. To learn how to protect your kids against email harassment, turn to Chapter 6, "Evil Email."

The Dangers in Chatting

There are a number of dangers your kids face while chatting. These include episodes as simple as having to deal with a rude or unpleasant person as well as instances of your child being harassed. And at worst, a predator can target your child and try to meet him or her without you knowing about it. In this section, we show you the main dangers your kids face in chat rooms and while using instant messenger programs.

A Predator Might Target Your Child

There's no real way for your daughter to know whether the person she's chatting with is another 12-year-old girl or a 45-year-old male pedophile. It's easy for adults to pose as children and try to entice children into meeting them in the real world. Adults might even enter into inappropriate online relationships.

Your Child Can Be Harassed

Chat rooms are sometimes free-for-alls. Kids can be rude and can act out. And kids who are having difficulties at home or at school might take out their problems on other kids in chat rooms and instant messenger programs by harassing them. Sometimes they take the harassment further, following it up with harassing email.

Your Child Might Become Addicted to Chat

Usually, kids who chat online are sociable—online chatting is just another way to keep in touch with friends and meet new people. But there's a possibility that for one reason or another—maybe a child is facing real-world social difficulties, for example—a child could become addicted to chat and withdraw from the real world, turning to online conversations instead for social contact.

Your Child Might Be Sent a Virus or "Trojan Horse"

Some chats—notably IRC—allow kids to send files to each other from computer to computer. There's a chance that your child could be sent a virus or *Trojan Horse* program in a chat program. There are several different kinds of Trojan Horses. A common one allows a hacker to control someone else's computer, so he can delete and copy files from it, or even launch hacker attacks against other computers using it.

Your Child Might Have a Password Stolen

One of the most common scams with instant messenger programs on America Online involves someone claiming to be from America Online, asking for a kid's password. After the password is given, the scam artist can log onto the account and do anything he wants, posing as someone else.

Your Child Might Be Sent Links to Pornographic or Other Inappropriate Web Sites

Chat and instant messenger programs allow people to send hyperlinks to kids. When kids click on the link, they're sent to a site in their browser. It's possible that people could send your kids links to pornographic or inappropriate programs.

How to Protect Your Kids While They're Chatting

All this is pretty scary, we know. But here's the good news: There are some basic steps you can take to help make sure your kids are safe when chatting. In this section we show you how to keep your kids safe.

The first piece of advice has nothing to do with computers. It's simple: Follow your instincts. As a parent, you know your children better than anyone does. If you notice odd behavior on their part having to do with when they're using the computer, pursue it. For example, if every time you come into the room when they're using the computer, they minimize a screen, or have a look that appears to show they've been caught in the act of doing something wrong (you know that look well!), something might be wrong. As you know, kids often don't like to be approached directly about problems, so pursue the issue sideways. Start off by asking them where they're chatting and who they're chatting with and move on from there.

Know Where Your Kids Go to Chat

When your children leave the house, you want to know where they're going and who they're going to spend time with. The same thing should apply to chat rooms. Know where they're going. If they're on America Online, what rooms are they chatting in? Are they staying in kids' areas or are they going to other areas as well? Who are they chatting with? Their friends from school or sports teams? With strangers? You should ask these kinds of questions. True, your kids won't particularly want to answer them, but even the act of asking helps keep them safe, because they know you're aware of what they're doing.

> **Techno Talk**
>
> ### Drop In on Your Kids While They're Chatting
>
> It's a good idea to drop in regularly on your kids when they're chatting. If they think no one is watching what they're doing or no one cares, they're more likely to get into trouble than if you're checking in regularly.

Steer Your Kids Toward Monitored Chat Rooms

Some chat areas, such as certain ones on America Online, are monitored by adults to make sure kids aren't harassed or targeted by predators. On America Online, the Kids Only chat areas (keyword, "Kids Only") are monitored. Many other chat areas for kids on the Internet are monitored as well. Popular ones are http://chat.freezone.com and www.headbone.com/hbzchat.

By the way, just because a child is in a monitored area doesn't mean he can't be targeted by a predator. A predator can go to a chat room, say nothing at all, but listen in on conversations, trying to gather personal information about your kids. They can then use that information later to gain your child's confidence via instant messaging or email. So although monitored rooms help keep your kids safer, there are still other things you should do.

Keep Your Kids Away from IRC

I'm not a big fan of IRC chat for kids. IRC is mainly frequented by adults, and there are many pornographic chat channels. The nature of IRC means you can't block your kids from visiting those channels. And IRC also has some very big security holes in it that can allow hackers to send your kids Trojan Horses. We recommend not allowing your kids to use IRC chat. By the way, we don't say this lightly—I can't think of any other Internet service I recommend banning.

Do This If Your Kids Use IRC

If you decide to let your kids use IRC, there is something you can do to help make sure they don't get a Trojan Horse or are attacked by a hacker in another way. Make sure your kids never run what are called *scripts*. These are automated commands that IRC software runs. These scripts can be very complicated and can be used to attack computers. And make sure your kids turn off DCC. DCC is a way files can be sent to other people on IRC. If you turn off DCC, no one can send your kids Trojan Horses.

Block or Limit Their Chats

You can block the way your kids chat—for example, you can limit them to visiting only certain chat rooms or you can stop them from visiting private chat areas on America Online. On America Online, you do this by using Parental Controls. To get to the Parental Control portion of AOL, use the keyword "Parental Controls." In Figure 5.4 you can see how you can limit their use of chat on America Online. There are many ways you can limit chats. You can block chats completely, or block access to private chat rooms. You can also limit chats so they can only visit certain chat areas. You can block kids from viewing and using hyperlinks in chat areas, and you can also block kids from getting instant messages. Turn to Chapter 16, "Playing It Safe on America Online," for detailed instructions on setting these options.

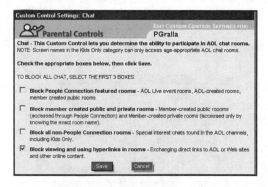

Figure 5.4

Here's how to make sure your kids only visit monitored chat areas on America Online.

You can also use kid-protection software, such as Norton Internet Security 2000, to limit their chats. For example, the program can block children from using any instant messenger programs.

Report Abusive Behavior to Moderators or the Online Service

If someone is abusive to your kids in a chat room, there's something you can do about it—report the abusive behavior.

If abuse occurs on a chat on America Online, report the behavior to the service. On a service like America Online, people can be kicked off the service for abusive behavior. If the behavior bothers you and there is no moderator or it's not a chat on an online service, leave the chat area.

Techno Talk

What's a SYSOP?

People who moderate chat areas go by a number of different names. A common one is SYSOP—short for System Operator.

To report abusive chat or instant message behavior on America Online, go to the Neighborhood Watch area (keyword, "Neighborhood Watch"). Click **Notify AOL**. Next, click **Chat** or **Instant Message Notes**, depending on what abusive behavior you're going to report. Then fill out the form and AOL receives the note about the behavior.

Your kids can also report the abusive behavior while the chat is going on. They should click the **Notify AOL** link in the chat area. Then they should fill out the form. They should cut and paste the portion of the chat with the abusive behavior into the message. That helps AOL put an end to it.

Teach Your Kids to Use a "Bozo Filter" to Block Messages from Bozos

If your kid is being bothered by someone in a chat room or via an instant messenger program, there's something else they can do. They can use a Bozo filter to block messages from anyone they want. Bozo filters are easy to use. Your kids just enter the names of the people they want to block. From that point on, they never see messages from that person. Figure 5.5 shows the Bozo filter on AOL Instant Messenger.

Figure 5.5

Don't let the Bozos get you down. Here's how to use a Bozo filter to block messages from annoying people.

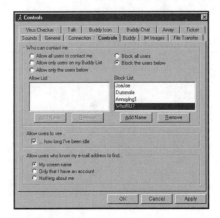

You Can Issue Warnings and Take Away a Harasser's Privileges with America Online's Internet Instant Messenger

America Online's Internet Instant Messenger lets you block people from sending your kids messages, but it goes well beyond that. You can also issue a warning to someone. After you issue a warning to someone, that person can send and receive fewer messages than he could before the warning. If he receives enough warnings from people, he isn't allowed to send or receive messages at all. It's the best way of all to block the Bozos.

Make Sure Your Kids Have a Full Life Apart from Chat

If you start to notice that your kids are withdrawing from friends and family and spending more time in chat rooms, you have a problem. You have a kid who is too dependent on chat for social interaction. To combat this, make sure your kid has a full social life. Make play dates with friends. Get him or her involved in sports or hobbies. Spend more time with him or her. And limit the time allowed online.

Teach Your Kids These Rules for Self-Protection

As you can see from the previous sections, technology can do a lot to help keep your kids safe when chatting. But the truth is, the best protection for kids has nothing to do with technology. The best way for kids to stay safe in chat areas is for them to know the rules for self-protection and to follow them. So make sure your kids follow these rules:

➤ **Kids shouldn't give out identifying information.** Things such as your home address, phone number, and even things like the names of your kids' teachers shouldn't be given out online. Stalkers and predators can use that to track down children. They can also lurk in chat rooms, waiting for kids to reveal personal information, and then use it to insinuate themselves into kids' lives. Using this technique, predators have been able to weave a web of deceit and trick kids into thinking they're their friends. Let your kids know that the most dangerous people are often the ones who appear the nicest. It's sad, but true.

➤ **Kids shouldn't give out their passwords.** If they do, someone can use their account on America Online, another online service, or on a Web site. This restriction applies even to someone who contacts your kids claiming to represent the online service—legitimate employees never ask for passwords.

➤ **Kids should tell their parents about threatening or bad language, or if something someone does online makes them feel uncomfortable.** When you know about the problem, you can alert the service, block the person from contacting your kid, or take similar action.

➤ **Kids shouldn't accept files or URLs from strangers.** Strangers might try to send your kids pornographic pictures in instant messages, links to pornographic sites, or files with viruses in them. If they don't accept those things, they can't get into trouble.

➤ **Kids shouldn't agree to meet someone in the real world that they've met in a chat area, unless a parent is present and it's a public place.** Chatters can easily disguise their ages. They might ask your kid to an innocuous meeting, such as at a movie theater. Your kids should never agree to meet someone in the real world, unless you're present and it's in a public place. And before the meeting, you should send a note to the person, saying that you're coming along. That, in itself, is enough to scare away any potential predators.

The Least You Need to Know

Kids love to chat, chat, and chat some more. It's a great way for kids to keep in touch with one another and make new friends. But you want to make sure they're safe when they chat. Here's what you need to know to make sure they're safe when they start chatting:

➤ Make sure your kids know that people might disguise their identities and personalities when they chat.

➤ Moderated chats are safer to participate in than those that aren't moderated.

➤ Your kids should never give out identifying information in chats. And they shouldn't agree to meet people in the real world that they've met in chats unless it's in a public place and you're along.

➤ Use Bozo filters to block messages from people who are abusive or harass your kids.

➤ Report any abusive behavior to America Online or the Web site where the behavior takes place.

Chapter 6

Evil Email

In This Chapter

➤ What kinds of dangers are in email

➤ What you can do about "mail bombs"

➤ How to handle email stalkers and harassers

➤ How to protect your kids against dangerous email attachments

➤ How to make sure your kids aren't victimized by spam

Kids and email go together like peanut butter and jelly. (And often, email and peanut butter and jelly go together, leaving you with a very messy keyboard to clean.) Kids of all ages live to communicate with one another, and email has replaced the old-time pen pal, and even goes toward replacing the telephone as the major means of talking.

All that is great for kids, and it's healthy for them, too. But there are also some dangers in email—bad things such as unsolicited email that might contain pornographic or inappropriate material, harassing emails, or viruses or inappropriate material in attachments sent to your kids.

In this chapter, you learn how to protect your kids from any dangers caused by email. That way, they can send and receive letters with ease. Just make sure they stay away from the peanut butter while they're typing!

What Are the Dangers in Email?

Let's get the first things first. Before you can learn how to protect your kids against email dangers, you need to know what dangers are out there. Here's the rundown of some potential problems with email:

➤ **Your kids can be sent unwanted email (*spam*) that contains inappropriate material, such as links to pornographic sites.** Millions of pieces of unwanted email—commonly known as spam—are sent over the Internet every day. A surprisingly high percentage of such mail includes links to pornographic sites. To visit the sites, your kids need only click on the links.

Is Spam with Links to Pornographic Sites Legal?

According to lawyers we've talked to, sending spam that has links to pornographic sites to kids is apparently legal. That's because the sender doesn't knowingly send the spam to kids—the spam is sent to many thousands of email addresses, and the spammer doesn't know who's at each address. However, if the spammer actually sends pictures, that might not be legal. But spammers never, if ever, send pictures. Instead, they send links to the site.

➤ **Your kids can be sent spam that ensnares them in a bait-and-switch scheme.** Much of the email sent out is phony, get-rich-quick offers. The only person who might get rich, of course, is the spammer himself. Many kids are gullible, though, and they could be tricked into sending cash through the mail, or using your credit card in response to the offers. Figure 6.1 shows an email account chock full of spam.

➤ **A stalker can target your kids via email, posing as a child.** A stranger can send email to your children, and there's no way for your kids to know that the sender of the mail is really a 35-year-old man, not a 10-year-old boy, as he claims.

➤ **Your child can be sent harassing email.** Someone can target your child and send him or her harassing email—the email might be as dangerous as a threat, or as innocuous as teasing. But even innocuous teasing can seem dangerous and harassing when it's received via email.

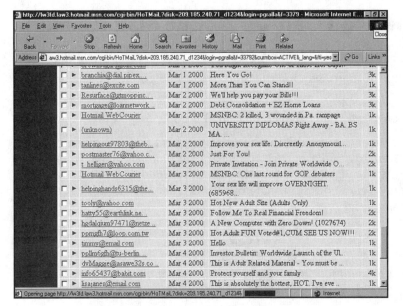

Figure 6.1

Here, there, and every-where...examples of spam in an email box.

➤ **Your child can be sent an attachment that contains a virus or is pornographic in nature.** Files can be attached to email messages. Kids love to send attachments to each other—things such as pictures or funny little pro-grams. But there's a chance that your child can be sent an attachment with pornographic material or a virus in it.

➤ **Your child can be sent a "mail bomb."** A mail bomb isn't a file that blows up a computer. Instead, it's a constant series of emails—possibly hundreds or more—that makes it difficult, if not impossible, for your child to use email or the computer.

Techno Talk

Chain Letters Aren't Mail Bombs

To you or me, an email chain letter is an annoyance. Ah, but to kids it's the very stuff of life. Kids love to send and receive chain letters. So if you notice your kids' mailbox is stuffed with chain letters, don't worry. It's not a mail bomb. Your kids just wanna have fun.

It sounds scary, I know. But you don't really need to be concerned. As I show you in the rest of this chapter, there's a lot you can do to protect your kids from any email dangers.

Defuse It! What You Can Do About Mail Bombs

As I explained, a mail bomb is when someone sends your kids massive amounts of email, so that they get dozens or even hundreds of messages or more all at once. Your kids might have to spend hours deleting the messages, and it could also conceivably crash their computers.

There are things, though, you can do to combat mail bombs:

➤ **Contact your Internet service provider (ISP) and send them a copy of a piece of offending mail.**   They will be able to block messages from the person sending the mail, so that your kids won't get any more mail from the person. Be aggressive and demand that your ISP do this, because sometimes ISPs can be less than helpful.

A Personal Mail Bomb Story

Several years ago my daughter, who was then 11 years old, was mail bombed. She received dozens of email messages from a single sender in a short period of time, all of which were not very friendly, although not specifically threatening. Still it was frightening enough to her that she didn't want to use email anymore.

I first checked the address of the sender of the message. It didn't appear to be forged. From the content and wording of the message, including its poor spelling and grammar, I guessed that the message was coming from a pre-teen or young teen, which made it more likely that the address wasn't forged. First, I sent a note to the sender's ISP, telling about the mail bomb. Next, I used America Online's email filters to tell the service to reject any email to my daughter coming from the offending address. It worked like a charm. After I took action, she never received another message from the bomber.

➤ **Contact the offender's ISP and send them a copy of a piece of offending mail.**   Ask that the ISP take action against the offender. It's often easy to find out someone's ISP—just look at the second part of the email address. For example, evilperson@aol.com uses America Online (AOL) as an ISP. By the way, this doesn't always work, because it's fairly easy for people to disguise their true email address and ISP.

➤ **Use your kids' email software to reject messages from the mail bomber.**
Many email programs enable you to reject messages from certain senders, or at
least flag them or put them into common folder where you can easily delete
them. Check your email software to see how. America Online enables you to
block messages coming from specific email addresses. Chapter 16, "Playing It
Safe on America Online," shows you how to do that.

How to Handle Stalkers and Harassers

Your child comes to you practically in tears and says that she's getting harassing email
from someone, or else she's getting email from someone who wants her to set up a
private meeting. What to do?

First, take heart. These messages usually come from other kids trying to cause trouble.
The great odds are, the problem will go away. But at first there's no way to really
know whether the message is from a kid. So you have to take action.

If the mail is from someone asking to set up a private meeting, have your child send
back a message saying she doesn't want to meet, and doesn't want to receive anymore mail. Then you should send a copy of the email to your ISP and the sender's
ISP, so that each can investigate the person if need be. This will probably solve the
problem. If it doesn't and the emails continue, contact your local police department
and send an email to the sender telling him what you've done. The emails will stop.

Take similar action against harassing emails. Send a message to the harasser asking
that the emails stop. Send copies of the harassing message to your kids' ISP and to
the sender's ISP. And contact the local police if the problems continue.

What to Do About Dangerous Email Attachments

There are several potential problems involving email attachments sent to your kids.
They could contain viruses, or they could be pornographic or inappropriate. Luckily,
this is one of the easiest problems to solve. Here's what to do:

➤ **Tell your kids never to open attachments in email sent by someone
they don't know.**   It's this simple: If they don't open attachments, they can't
be harmed by them. So not opening attachments sent by strangers will solve
almost all problems.

➤ **Make sure your kids use antivirus software on all attachments, even
from files sent by friends and family.**   Antivirus software can scan email
attachments for viruses, and then tell your kids not to open the attachments if
they contain viruses. So this ensures they don't get viruses via email. For information on how to do this, turn to Chapter 15, "Downloading Do's and Don'ts."

Use America Online's Email Parental Controls

America Online gives you complete control over how your kids use email. It can block them from receiving attachments, it can be used to allow only email from certain people to reach them, and allows you other controls as well. Chapter 16, "Playing It Safe on America Online," will show you how to do it.

➤ **Use filtering software on your kids' computer.** Some filtering software will block your kids from opening email attachments. Turn to Chapter 13, "All About Filters," for information on how to use filtering software.

➤ **If your kids use America Online, use Mail Controls to stop them from receiving attachments.** Using America Online Mail Controls (see Figure 6.2) you can stop your kids from receiving attachments. Turn to Chapter 16, "Playing It Safe on America Online," to see how.

Figure 6.2

Here's how to make sure your kids don't receive attachments on America Online.

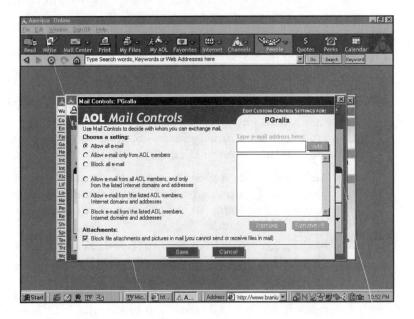

How to Protect Your Kids Against Spam

There's so much spam around the Internet that your kids might well receive dozens of pieces of spam in a day, and sometimes even more. America Online users are particularly targeted by spammers and tend to receive more spam than do people using other Internet service providers. Some spam is little more than an annoyance to kids, and you don't need to worry about it. But you do need to worry about spam that contains links to pornographic sites, or spam that tries to lure them into sending money.

There's a simple way to protect your kids against this kind of thing: Tell them not to read any spam. As long as they don't read that mail, there's nothing for them to worry about.

Of course, it's not always easy to know what's spam and what isn't, because sometimes the subject of the message will make it appear that the person knows who your kids are. It might say, for example, "Just wanted to say hi again..." So there's more you should do to fight spam. The following sections show you what you can do.

Why Is It Called Spam?

No one is quite sure why unsolicited email is called spam, but many people believe it gets its name from a skit done by the old Monty Python comic group on their television series. In the skit, someone asks what's on the menu in a diner, only to discover that every item contains Spam luncheon meat—in fact, Spam takes over the entire menu, crowding everything else out. In the same way, email spam crowds out your regular email.

Use Your Kids' Email Program to Stop Spam

One way to stop your kids from being hit by spam is to use their email program to filter it out so they don't have to see it. Depending on the program's features and how you want to use it, the software can refuse to accept spam, automatically delete it, or put it in a folder so your kids can delete the spam themselves.

I suggest having the email program put all the spam in a folder so your kids can delete it themselves. Software isn't perfect, after all, and the last thing you want is to have them delete a message from their mother (eat your vegetables, kids!) because the email software thought it was spam.

The way to do this in all programs differs, so read the documentation. If you use Outlook, it's easy to turn the spam filter on. Click the **Organize** button at the top of Outlook and, from the screen that drops down, click **Junk E-Mail**. Then, just turn the spam filters on, and Outlook starts filtering your email. You can tell it to shade the suspect spam a certain color, such as gray or maroon, so you can tell at a glance that you've been sent spam. Or you can have it send all suspected spam to a folder, and you can then look at all the spam there. That's how I handle spam. Figure 6.3 shows you how to turn on the spam filter in Outlook. Note that there are two kinds of spam filters. One covers garden-variety spam. The other filters out adult-content spam.

Figure 6.3

Here's how to filter spam using Outlook.

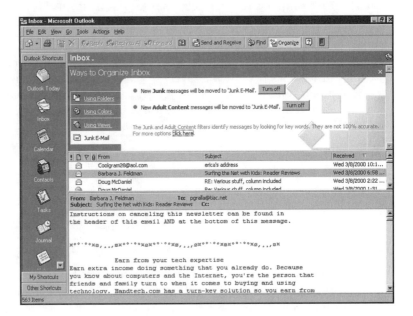

How Do Email Filters Detect Spam?

How in the world, you might wonder, can an email program or spam-killing software automatically know which mail is spam and which isn't? They do it in a variety of ways. Some have a list of known spammers, so all email that comes from one of the spammers on the list is considered spam. Some search for keywords in the header and sometimes the body of the message—words that are commonly used by spammers. And some examine the headers of the messages, looking for certain tell-tale signs that show the sender is a spammer.

Use Spam-Fighting Software to Kill Spam Dead

There's another way to make sure spam doesn't reach your kids—use spam-fighting software. This software works one of two ways: It can work right inside their email software to detect and kill spam, or it can be run before running the email software to detect and kill spam.

There's a lot of spam-fighting software out there. Most offer more capabilities than the filters that come with email software. Some of the good ones include Spam Exterminator, Spam Buster, and SpamKiller. You can try them all out free by downloading them from many download sites on the Internet, including ZDNet Downloads at www.zddownloads.com.

Fight Back! What to Do If Your Kids Have Been Spammed

One way or another, your kids are going to be spammed. You might cut down on spam, but you'll never kill it entirely. Still, if your kids are spammed, there are steps you can take to make sure it doesn't happen again or to track down the spam senders and curtail their actions or even put them out of business. Here's what to do:

Clean Your Kids' Mailboxes

Your kids probably don't like to clean their rooms. They probably don't like cleaning out their email boxes either. Help them delete old, unwanted mail, because if they don't, it could get full and they won't be able to get any new mail.

➤ **Complain to your kids' ISP.** Your ISP hates spam as much as you do—it forces ISPs to spend more money on mail servers and other costly Internet stuff. Many ISPs have an email address to which you can send spam. Forward all your spam to that address—and include the true address of the spammer if you've been able to find it out from the message header. On America Online, forward the spam to the screen name TOSSpam. In all cases, forward the original email, don't copy and paste the spam into a new message. If you forward the original email, it will make it easier for the ISP to track down the offender.

➤ **Complain to the advertiser.**   Sometimes spam mentions the name and phone number of an advertiser sponsoring the spam. Call up the number, complain, and tell them you're going to tell everyone you know never to do business with them unless they stop spamming. A legitimate business might listen to you. Scammers won't.

Never Respond to Spam

When your kids get spam, you'll be tempted to respond to it by sending off an angry note. Or there might be a return email address in the note, saying if you want to get taken off the spam list, send an email message to that return address. *Never* respond to spam. Spammers rarely take you off their lists. By responding, you're only letting them know that your email address is a valid one—and they'll send you even *more* spam.

➤ **Complain to your state attorney general.**   In some states (such as California, Virginia, and Washington), spam is more than a nuisance—it's illegal. Although the laws vary from state to state, increasingly, states are passing anti-spam laws. The state attorney general is responsible for enforcing them. These laws can have some pretty stiff penalties. In Washington, for example, spammers can be fined $2,000 for every piece of spam they send. Considering that most spammers send out millions of pieces of spam, we're talking some big-time money.

➤ **Get more information at these Web sites.**   Web sites can help you complain about spam and learn more about how to track down the true senders of spam. Head to the Fight Spam on the Internet site at `http://spam.abuse.net/`. And the How To Complain About Spam or Put a Spammer in the Slammer site at `http://dlis.gseis.ucla.edu/people/pagre/spam.html` is especially worthwhile for figuring out where to complain.

The Least You Need To Know

➤ Among email dangers for kids are being stalked or harassed, getting viruses or pornographic attachments, "mail bombs" that can clog their email boxes, and spam that might contain links to pornographic sites.

➤ Tell your kids never to open an attachment from someone they don't know—and to always virus-check attachments, even if they're from people they do know.

➤ If your kids are harassed or stalked via email, contact your ISP and the ISP of the offender. If the harassment continues, contact your local police department.

➤ Use antispam software or filters to stop spam from getting to your kids.

➤ Tell your kids to never respond to spam—it only proves to the spammer that their email address is a valid one, and they may get even *more* spam.

Chapter 7

Warning: X-Rated Content

In This Chapter

➤ Find out how widely available porn is on the Internet

➤ Learn some amazing statistics about online porn and its users

➤ See how easy it is to run into online porn

➤ Some practical steps for protecting your family from this online danger

---

One of parents' major concerns is the availability of inappropriate pictures online, namely pornography. This chapter takes a serious look at what's online, how easy it is to accidentally stumble across it, and how you and your family can be on guard.

Is Online Pornography Really a Danger?

You don't have to be a rocket scientist to figure out that pornography isn't exactly a good thing. There's plenty of clinical evidence to tell you it's not. Early exposure to pornography can be the first step in a downward spiral that leads to desensitization and acting out. What's really scary is when it involves children.

Here's a little tidbit for you: According to the *U.S. Attorney General's Final Report on Pornography* (1986), one of the primary consumer groups of pornography is young boys between the ages of 12 and 17. That's right, pornographic publications target our children. Thankfully, there are laws about the display of pornographic material in stores. But what about pornography online?

FamilyPC magazine conducted a study of online safety (published in the March 2000 issue). Out of 693 responses, 51 percent of parents say their top concern is their children's exposure to pornography, and 66 percent say that sexually explicit material is a growing problem on the Internet.

Welcome to the World of Cybersmut

There's plenty of pornography on the Internet, and there's quite a market for it, too. Of course a lot of it is the typical run-of-the-mill stuff you can find in adult magazines and bookstores. Unlike magazines, however, users don't have to duck into seedy adult bookstores to find it. They can view it from the privacy of their own computer without fear of public ridicule. Along with the standard soft-core porn, there's also an abundance of hard-core stuff, and worse.

Pornography on the Clock

People aren't just viewing porn from their home computers. The Xerox Corporation fired 40 employees in October of 1999 for viewing pornography during working hours on company PCs. Xerox installed hardware and software that tracks the Internet use of its employees. Other companies are following similar actions. Non-work related Internet usage is a growing problem among companies today.

Did you know that hundreds of thousands of Internet users have a tendency to seek out sexual material on the Internet? According to a recent study published in the journal *Sexual Addiction and Compulsivity* (March 2000 issue), Internet users are finding such material on Web sites, in chat rooms, and in newsgroups. They're swapping it online through email and downloaded files. What's the big deal? These are grown adults who can do what they want, right? These users are spending more than 11 hours a week seeking out such material, and researchers are classifying such usage as *cybersex compulsive*. Yes, there's a name for it. We're not talking about casually stopping by a site with a few pornographic pictures; we're talking serious time spent in the quest of viewing pornographic material. It's consuming, it's compulsive, and in a loose sense of the word, it's even an addiction.

We don't really need a study to tell us pornography is addictive and destructive. The sheer volume of online porn should tell us it's a problem. And no matter what sort of problems adults have with porn, there's no question that pornography doesn't belong in the hands of children.

So where is all this online porn anyway? Most of it is found in several Internet niches:

Usenet newsgroups   Online message boards that typically focus on a topic or hobby. As you learn in Chapter 9, "The Scoop on Newsgroups," these online discussion groups are a haven for people seeking pornography, including child pornography. Thanks to the practice called spamming, porn can show up in any newsgroup, not just those dedicated to it.

BBSs   Short for *bulletin board services* or systems, these are similar to news-groups in that users meet to discuss similar interests. There are thousands of adult-oriented BBSs and they typically charge a fee for membership.

Chat   Online rooms where users can meet and carry on conversations. Many of these chat rooms are used for people wanting to swap pornographic pictures, a lot like trading Beanie Babies or Pokémon cards.

Web sites   These are sites that target adults and offer anything from your standard soft-core, Playboy-style photos to hard-core, make-you-sick photos. Some sites also offer video clips or access to live video feeds.

Porn purveyors spread the word about their wares through online advertising. Some-times this means banner ads at other sites, message postings on newsgroups, or email solicitation.

Researchers at the Carnegie Mellon University (Pennsylvania) conducted an 18-month study of pornography on the Internet in 1995, surveying over 900,000 images, descriptions, text stories, and video clips. Here's what they found:

➤ Of all the Usenet newsgroups that store and swap image files, more than 80 percent of the pictures were pornographic.

➤ Trading pornographic images is one of the largest recreational applications of Internet users.

➤ A survey of BBS (online bulletin board services) operators found that 98.9 per-cent of online porn consumers are men. (I'm sure nobody saw that coming.)

➤ The adult market for images isn't driven by ordinary pictures of naked women; you can get those anywhere. Rather, it is driven by hard-core pictures not available elsewhere, pictures of pedophilia (chil-dren), hebephilia (youths), and paraphilia (deviant material).

Check This Out

Looking for S-E-X

This probably won't surprise you, but the word *sex* is one of the most often used search keywords on the Internet.

According to Forrester Research, a firm that tracks Internet trends, Web porn sales totaled over $140 million in 1997. They're estimating sales to reach over $350 million by the year 2001. Online pornography accounts for 10 percent of online retail sales and services. There's big money in online porn. Images Inc., an Australian-based porn site, regularly make sales of over $3 million a month. Customers pay $29.95 per month to access the site's collection of pornographic pictures and videos.

According to Researcher Relevant Knowledge, another Internet trend tracker, the top 10 Web sex sites are viewed by 13 percent of an estimated 60 million Web surfers over the age of 12. Playboy.com is the 22nd most popular Web site for teen-age boys. You're not too surprised, are you?

The point in telling you all of this is, simply, don't be naive about how much pornography is on the Internet and who is accessing it. It's out there, there's a lot of it, and it's not going to go away—not as long as there's money to be made.

What's Legal, and What's Not

As explained in Chapter 3, "How Did This All Get Started? And Where Is It Going?" indecent material is legal; obscene material is not. To be considered obscene, the material must meet all three of the following criteria:

Applying community standards, the average person finds the work appeals to prurient interests...

And the work describes or shows patently offensive conduct defined by state law, or is offensive to local standards of decency...

And the work lacks serious artistic, literary, scientific, or political value.

Indecent material is illegal when you let minors see it. The Children's Online Protection Act (COPA) is trying to force commercial porn sites on the Web to verify the age of users accessing the site. COPA also makes it illegal for commercial porn sites to have teaser images—pornographic pictures that are meant to entice users to join the Web site—on their home pages. The matter is still in the courts as of this writing, so teaser images are still out there.

Any pornography involving children is absolutely illegal, on or off the Internet. Here's what's currently illegal:

➤ To depict minors in sexually explicit conduct, in any image, even virtual images.

➤ To coerce or entice children to perform sexual acts.

➤ To transport, send or receive, or import obscenity.

➤ To advertise child pornography, or imply that minors are performing sexually explicit acts.

Unfortunately, the Internet is a haven for pedophilia. Kiddie porn is traded online 24 hours a day, 7 days a week. There are millions of pornographic images online that involve children. Thankfully, there are some very strong laws in place concerning the exploitation of children, and many of these laws cover the Internet as well. It is illegal to produce or distribute any pictures showing children in sexually suggestive poses or minors engaging in sexually explicit conduct. It is also illegal to manipulate an image using computer technology to make it look as though a minor is engaging in sexual activity.

The government can now subpoena ISPs during investigations into child porn to identify perpetrators who use the Internet to lure children. The FBI, the Customs Service, and the Postal Inspection Service, among other agencies, are heavily involved in the fight against child pornography. In 1998, half of the U.S. Postal Inspection Service's cases involved child pornography on computers. As you learn in Chapter 19, "Finding Law Enforcement When You Need It," fighting online crime is a daunting task.

Complicating matters is the fact that although strong laws restrict the production of kiddie porn in the United States and most industrialized nations, some poorer countries host an active sex industry that, unfortunately, involves minors. The Internet makes it easy to access images produced overseas. Nevertheless, it's still illegal for an American to receive, transmit, store, or download such images.

Not a month goes by without a headline about child pornography on the Internet. At the time of this writing, an elementary school teacher was arrested in Los Angeles, California, for trafficking in child pornography. U.S. Customs agents were investigating a porn site operating out of the Netherlands and followed a lead to this California teacher. The man allegedly had downloaded over 60 pictures of children engaging in sexual conduct. Depressing, isn't it?

Watch What You Type

Perhaps you think that if you and your child don't go looking for pornography you aren't likely to encounter it. Ha. I guess you've never mistyped a Web address before. Let's say you or your child is in a hurry to see the White House's Web site. You or your child type in **www.whitehouse.com** without thinking. Guess where this address takes you? Figure 7.1 shows you (minus the naughty parts) where you and your child end up.

Dorothy, we're not in Kansas anymore, and we're certainly not at the White House. The site is actually a commercial porn site. What you should have typed is **www. whitehouse.gov** (.gov, meaning government; instead of .com, meaning commercial). Pretty innocent mistake, but the pictures you're viewing aren't so innocent. Needless to say, the real White House isn't amused by this site. The guy running the site doesn't care; he's making a fortune. The online porn industry makes more than $185 million year.

Figure 7.1

This doesn't look like a government Web page. The naughty bits were edited out for this family-targeted book.

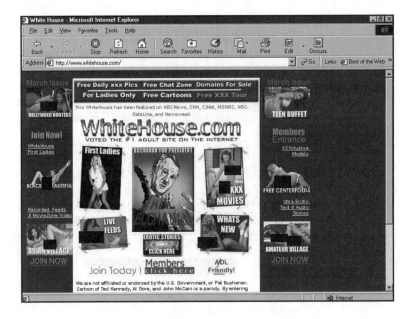

Typos are causing some serious problems on the Internet. A few misplaced characters can send you or your child to an adult Web site, complete with teaser pictures for all to see. For example, up until recently, if a user mistyped several of the major search engine names in an URL, such as www.yahhoo.com instead of www.yahoo.com, they ended up at porn sites. Oops.

Parents and children must also be mindful of what is typed into search engines. For example, my husband was trying to redo a dining room table for me and needed to find some table legs. He decided to try the Web. He used a popular search engine and typed in **table legs**. Figure 7.2 shows what popped up in the results.

Call me crazy, but something tells me we aren't going to find oak table legs at the Bondage Playground. This sort of thing can happen to your kids, too. They might innocently research a topic for a homework assignment, only to end up at the Bondage Playground by mistake.

Sometimes you search for what you think is the right Web site, only to end up on the bad side of the cybertracks. Most browsers enable you type in the name of a company, and the browser automatically pops on the .com part, or maybe you're just guessing at the site name. Be warned, however, that some guesses can take you where you don't want to go. The publishers of the popular *Teen* magazine were shocked to find out the URL www.teenmagazine.com is a hard-core porn site. (The magazine's own site is www.teenmag.com.) The magazine began getting complaints from readers. The average age of the magazine's readers is 15, so the site's content, even if users inadvertently ended up there, was of great concern.

Figure 7.2

A search can inadvertently lead you or your child to porn sites as well.

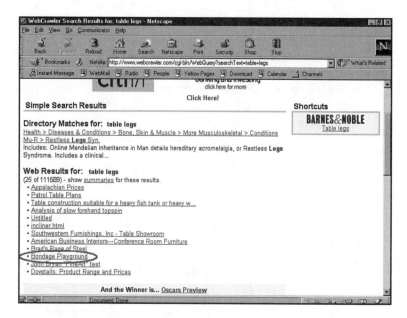

There's a name for this type of mistaken Web identity. It's called *cybersquatting*. A company buys a domain name that is closely related to a recognized name brand with the intention of either forcing the actual company to pay a high price for acquiring the rights to the name, or profiting from the traffic associated with the actual company. Cybersquatting is currently illegal under the Anticybersquatting Consumer Protection Act (there's an act for everything, you know), an amendment to the U.S. trademark law. In the case of *Teen* magazine, they're duking it out in court with the porn company over the URL.

Fake Out!

The more salacious porn sites are onto the whole keyword-search game and purposefully use perfectly normal keywords for search engine indexing. That's why it's not uncommon to see a porn site pop up from time to time among the search results, even for topics that seem totally unrelated to porn.

Search engines can also be fooled into producing a list of porn sites as matches, known as *meta tag theft*—a sort of digital bait-and-switch technique. A hacker finds out the existing meta tag of a site (the tag is a part of the HTML code for a Web page that makes the site easy to find), then turns around and registers it to another site. Some search engines use meta tags as keywords when they index Web sites. A search engine's spider, special software that roams the Internet and indexes keywords, catalogs a page without knowing if the page has been hijacked. It automatically places the URL in its database without knowing that the site is a redirect. This happened to a man in Texas who runs a video game Web site. He checked to see if his site was listed by running a search using the AltaVista search engine. Instead of revealing a link to his game site, the search results link took him to a porn site.

Meta tag theft is a common practice. Hackers are paid to redirect Web sites to a second site. Increased site traffic means you can generate more dollars with advertisers. This trick is quite common among adult content on the Web. For that reason, many search engines, such as Excite@Home, don't use meta tags to index content. Who knew you could be hijacked on the Internet?

Another way your kids might stumble across pornography is through email. As I mentioned earlier, lots of Web porn sites advertise through email solicitation. It's not uncommon for people to get your name from a chat room and email you a solicitation. It can happen to your kids, too. A 10-year-old boy in New York frequented the Treehouse chat room on AOL. One day he got an email message with an attachment from a complete stranger. He followed the directions for downloading the file only to find his computer screen filled with thumbnail pictures of people having sex. His mother, like many parents, had no idea such material was online.

Use Kid Search Engines

One practical solution to misadventures with search tools is to use a kid's search engine, such as the one found at Yahooligans! (www.yahooligans.com). Kids' search engines conduct searches using predetermined safe sites.

It's extremely easy to accidentally stumble across pornography on the Internet, so you and your kids need to be careful what you type, pay attention to URLs, and be cautious about opening email from strangers.

What's to Be Done?

Well, there's no way you're going to get rid of online pornography—not with the millions of dollars it's generating for its purveyors. But there are some practical steps you can take to protect your children online:

➤ The first thing you need to do as a parent is to sit down with your child and set some guidelines about where they are allowed to go online.

➤ You must also specify a plan for them when they do run across obscene images, such as exiting the screen immediately or letting you know about it.

➤ Make it clear that your child isn't to open email from strangers without your approval.

➤ Depending on your child's age and the level of trust in your relationship with them, you should also supervise your child's Web searches.

Setting Guidelines for Kids

To learn more about setting guidelines for computer usage, turn to Chapter 17, "Setting Guidelines for Your Kids."

Other than guidelines you establish with your child, you can also consider installing filtering software. Filters are computer programs you can install to block access to pornographic material on the Internet. Programs such as SurfWatch, McAfee Internet Guard Dog, Net Nanny, and Norton Internet Security (to name a few) help parents block newsgroups, stop family users from giving out personal information online, an even prevent the use of a credit card online. Filtering isn't foolproof, as you'll learn in Chapter 13, "All About Filters," but it can help. Filtering and blocking software can limit access to sites that harbor sexually explicit images, hate groups, graphic violence, and criminal activity.

For example, Figure 7.3 shows what happens if a user types the keyword *sex* into the Yahoo! search site. Notice the teaser ad at the top of the page that, when clicked, takes the user to a porn site. Of course, according to the rules of the site, the user must be 18 to enter, but still—look how provocative the teaser ad is.

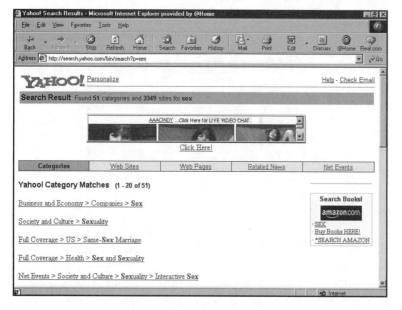

Figure 7.3

The keyword sex is one of the most often typed keywords for online searches.

Now here's what happens if the user types in the same keyword with Net Nanny installed and running (see Figure 7.4).

Figure 7.4

With Net Nanny monitoring in the background, your child can't access a site without a warning like this.

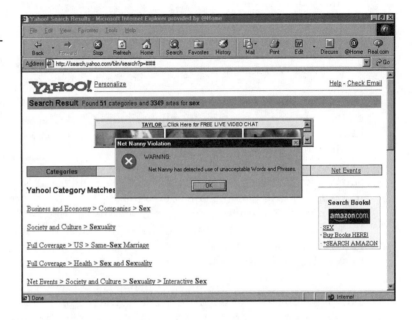

Not only does Net Nanny display a warning prompt, but the filtering program also logs the hit (techno speak for when someone visits a site) in its log book so parents can keep an eye on everywhere a child goes online. Check out the log shown in Figure 7.5.

Figure 7.5

Notice the keyword "sex" is logged in the report.

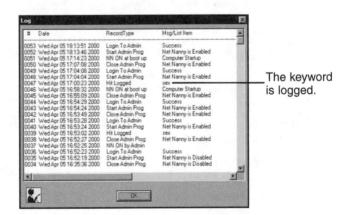

The keyword is logged.

Filtering programs rely on a list of unsuitable keywords children might type to search for pornography on the Internet, such as *nudes*, *porn*, and even the classic *boob*. Can we say *boob* in this book? You get the idea, anyway. Filtering programs also utilize lists of predetermined unsuitable Web sites to help parents control what Internet information comes into their home.

It Takes All Kinds

There are all kinds of filtering software. Some do a variety of tasks, such as filtering keywords as well as logging online activity, as you can see in the Net Nanny example shown. The type of software you choose will depend on your child and his or her protection needs. For example, if you suspect your child is viewing online pornography despite the good intentions of your house rules, you might think about using monitoring software that tracks where kids have been online. Monitoring software alerts parents to online activity. The proof is in the pudding, or however the saying goes.

Today's Web browsers also come equipped with parental control features. For example, more and more Web sites are policing themselves and voluntarily allowing third parties, like RSACI (Recreational Software Advisory Council on the Internet), to rate their content. Browsers can then read RSACI labels found on the Web pages, and based on parental control options, block a child's access to certain unsuitable Web pages.

Watch Out!

Some porn sites are onto the whole keyword-filtering game and purposefully use other spellings (such as phonetical spellings) for search engine indexing. For example, *phun sex* or *phun nudes*. Your kids might hear about this little trick, so if you do use a filtering program that lets you update the keyword list, add these to it.

For example, the newer versions of Internet Explorer have a feature called Content Advisor that enbables parents to specify rating levels based on RASCi labeling. If you're using Internet Explorer on your computer, open the **Tools** menu, select **Internet Options**, click the **Content** tab, then click the Content Advisor's **Settings** button to reveal the Content Advisor dialog box as shown in Figure 7.6. From this dialog box, you can choose a RSACi category and specify a level, ranging from no restrictions to increasingly higher levels of restrictions. Be sure to check out the other tabs in the dialog box for more control options. The nice thing about the RASCi settings options, along with the other controls, is that you as a parent can set a password for the feature so it's locked. This means your potential household juvenile delinquent can't get in and change the controls unless he or she discovers the password.

Where Did RSACi Come From?

RSACi is a nonprofit organization that rates Internet content. Learn more about RSACi and other Internet content rating services in Chapter 13, "All About Filters."

Figure 7.6

Internet Explorer's Content Advisor is helpful for parents who want to set controls for Internet access.

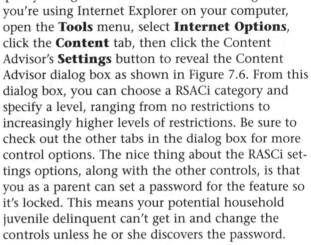

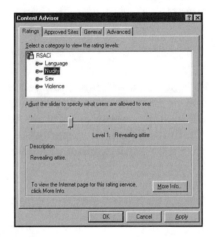

Unfortunately, not all Web sites have been rated, so the browser controls might not filter everything. But at least they're a help.

Other options for preventing porn on the home PC is to make your kids use kids' browsers to search for Web sites. Browsers like Crayon Crawler (www.crayoncrawler.com) can help your kids surf safely without running into online porn. And good news for you, many of these browsers are available free or offer trial versions you can download and take out for a test drive.

Kids' search engines are also handy for filtering out porn sites on the Web. Figure 7.7 shows the results of a search using the keyword *sex* at the Yahooligans! Search engine (www.yahooligans.com). The number of matches here varies greatly from those found on the regular Yahoo! site (shown earlier), and are strictly educational in nature.

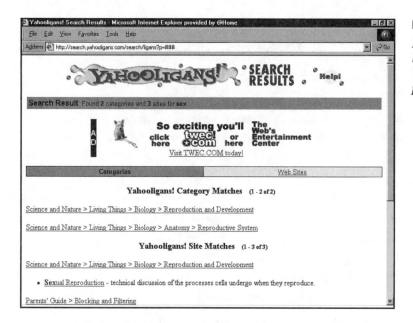

Figure 7.7
*Kids' search engines,
like the one found at
Yahooligans!, keep out
porn sites.*

So there you have it—the porn is out there, but you can take steps to prevent your child from being exposed to it.

The Least You Need to Know

No doubt about, online pornography is a danger to children. Here's what you learned in this chapter:

➤ Your children are the next wave of consumers for online pornography, so don't think commercial pornographers aren't interested in getting your kids hooked.

➤ Online porn can be found on Web sites, in newsgroups, among BBSs, and even traded in chat rooms.

➤ Pornography is legal on the Internet, but not when it's viewed by or given to minors. Child pornography is not legal, online or offline.

➤ Pornography is a booming business online, so don't think it's going to go away. There are millions upon millions of pornographic images on the Internet, and too many of them involve children.

➤ Be very careful when typing in URLs, and warn your children to be careful, too. A simple typo can lead you or your child right to a porn site.

➤ It's easier than you think to stumble across pornography on the Internet. It can happen through a search link or an email solicitation.

➤ Thankfully, there are options open to parents to help prevent the viewing of porn sites online, including using filtering programs, browser control options, and even kids' browsers.

➤ Consider installing a filter program and check out Chapter 13, "All About Filters."

Chapter 8

Internet Marketing: We Want Your Money Now

> ## In This Chapter
>
> ➤ Why you should worry about your kids' privacy
>
> ➤ What dangers marketers pose to your kids' privacy on the Internet
>
> ➤ How Web sites collect information about your kids
>
> ➤ How the law protects your kids' privacy
>
> ➤ What you can do to make sure your kids' privacy isn't invaded
>
> ➤ How you can let your kids shop online safely and without breaking your bank account

Increasingly, the Internet is used for commerce. And that affects your kids.

That's because not only can your kids buy things online, but they can also sign up for free sites, without realizing those sites might be gathering information about them, and possibly selling the information to direct marketers, or aiming ads at your kids.

In this chapter, you learn about all the dangers to your kids' privacy posed by the Internet—and you learn how you can fight back and make sure they don't give up their privacy. You also find out how you can let your kids buy online without breaking the bank.

Why You Should Care About Your Kids' Online Privacy

You look at your children and see innocence and light. (Well, when they're not arguing over whose turn it is to play *The Sims* computer game, or over whose turn it is to use the ketchup, you do, anyway.) But when direct marketers, advertisers, and some Web sites see them, they see something very different. They see dollar signs, and big fat ones at that. Don't believe me? Consider these facts:

➤ The Internet research firm Jupiter Communications says that the number of children 12 and under who use the Internet will grow from 11.4 million in 1999 to 24.3 million by the year 2003. And many of those kids spend money online.

➤ Many advertisers and marketers believe that if children are taught to recognize and use a brand from a young age, these children will become loyal consumers of that brand as adults.

➤ The Internet research firm Forrester Research estimates that one third of 16- to 22-year-olds will have made purchases online in 2000 alone—and these sales will total $4.5 billion.

Making kids even more valuable to advertisers and marketers is that they do more than just spend their allowance money, which amounts to billions of dollars a year. They also influence the spending of many billions of dollars more—and if you don't believe that, take a look in your cupboard sometime. Count the boxes of cereals with names like "Super-Cocoa Marshmallow Sugar Flakes." Or look at the toys littering your living room.

Check This Out

An Oil Company Site for Kids? Why Do That?

How far will companies go to try to imprint their brands on kids' brains? Pretty far, indeed. Take, for example, the site created for kids by the Chevron oil giant, www.chevroncars.com. It offers games, coloring books, cartoon-like cars, screen savers, and other downloadable free stuff for kids. Now, I don't know about you, but I can't remember the last time I've seen a seven-year-old filling up her car at a gas pump. So why create a site like this for kids? Because Chevron, like other marketers, is trying to buy customer loyalty at the earliest possible age. If a company can hook your kids on its brand when they're young, the company gets a lifetime customer.

There are other reasons marketers target your children. Your kids are very susceptible to advertising, and they have a hard time distinguishing advertising from non-advertising. This makes them prime targets. For instance, consider how many children's cartoon shows feature the adventures of a line of action figures.

Because of all of this, your kids are worth a whole lot of money to advertisers and marketers. And when it comes to kids, the Internet is a marketer's and advertiser's dream. The Internet makes it easy for marketers and advertisers to track everything kids do online; they can gather information about kids, their buying habits, and the buying habits of the rest of your family as well.

Other Reasons You Need to Worry About Your Kids' Privacy

Your kids face even bigger privacy dangers than being targeted by marketers. Some Web sites have posted public information about children, including their names, addresses, and email information—so the site could inadvertently provide a stalker with information about your child.

Many Web sites have tried to take advantage of children's innocence and invade their privacy and yours. Children—and you—can end up on marketing lists where exceedingly private details of your life can be tracked. Consider just a few of the facts uncovered by the Federal Trade Commission when it did a survey of Web sites designed for kids:

➤ Almost 90 percent of sites collect personal information about children.

➤ Less than 10 percent of sites that gather personal information try to notify the child's parent to get parental consent to gather the information.

➤ One site surveyed collected information including the child's full name, postal address, email address, gender, and age. It also asked for extensive personal and financial information, including whether the child had received stocks, cash, savings bonds, mutual funds, or certificates of deposit. It also asked for the family's financial information, including whether the parents own mutual funds.

➤ The same site ran a contest and posted the full name, age, city, state, and zip code of each winner.

➤ A different Web site collected comprehensive personal information about children, including their hobbies. The site held a contest and posted the winners' full names and email addresses.

103

Teach Your Kids the Difference Between Advertising and Content

As an adult, you can tell the difference between an ad and unbiased information on a Web site. Kids can't always tell the difference, though. So it's a good idea to sit down with your kids and go through several Web sites with them, pointing out the difference between what's an advertisement and what is unbiased informa-tion. In fact, some entire Web sites may appear to be informational, but in essence are little more than infomercials. If a site recommends only a single product for solving a problem or accomplishing something, that's a dead giveaway that your kids have come across an infomercial.

Even well-meaning sites can cause privacy problems. For example, the well-regarded SurfMonkey site, at www.surfmonkey.com, when trying to comply with Federal Trade Commission rules, sent out an email to parents, asking if it was okay for their kids to have email accounts at SurfMonkey. Sounds fine, right? The only problem was that SurfMonkey accidentally sent to many parents the complete list of the email addresses of the thousands of kids who had registered at the site. Ooops! Sometimes bad things happen to good companies.

As you can see, there's a whole lot you need to worry about as a parent when it comes to your children's privacy online.

How Do They Collect Information About Kids?

Before you know how to protect your kids' privacy, you have to know how informa-tion is collected about them. The first rule for protecting your kids' privacy online is this: Know thine enemy.

Here are common ways that Web sites gather personal information from children:

➤ **Registration**   To enter a site (or to use a special portion of a site, such as a games area, or to get a free email address), sites might require that your kids register and fill in personal information about themselves. For example, at the excellent www.headbone.com kids' site, kids have to register before they can get free email, win prizes, enter chat rooms, and participate in other features. You can see the sign-up page in Figure 8.1.

Figure 8.1

Sites like the very good kids' site www.headbone.com *require that kids register before taking advantage of things such as free email and contests.*

➤ **Contests**   Kids love contests—they love entering, and they love winning. Sites might require that kids fill out a form before entering contests.

➤ **Free gifts**   Sites offer giveaways, such as free screensavers or other gifts, if kids give personal information about themselves.

Just Because a Site Promises to Protect Your Kids' Privacy Doesn't Mean It Will

Promises are easy to make, but they're even easier to break. Just because a site promises never to share information about your kids doesn't mean it never will. The popular page-building site GeoCities, for example, promised never to share information that it gathered about children (and adults, as well). Actually, though, as GeoCities later admitted to the Federal Trade Commission, it turned over that information to other businesses that used it to target thousands of children (and adults) for direct email solicitations.

➤ **Message boards, pen pals, and chat areas**   To participate in discussions with other kids or to find pen pals on a site, the site might require that personal information be given out.

➤ **Surveys and polls**   Put a survey or a poll in front of a kid, and she'll fill it out. So Web sites put them in front of kids—and might require that they supply personal information when filling them out.

➤ **Through technology, without your kids knowing about it**   Web sites can track every click your kid makes. They can track what your kid reads, what your kid's interests are, and what doesn't interest your kid. This is done through a variety of technologies. The most common is called *cookies*. No, we're not talking about the Oreos that all kids love. Cookies are tiny bits of data put on a computer that enable Web sites to track what people do on the Web. But there are other ways that Web sites can track people's online activities as well. They can examine what are called server logs, for example, and they can even put invisible *graphics* on a Web page that only they can see, and use that invisible graphic as a way to track people's activities.

Here's How to Surf Anonymously

If you want to make sure that no information can be gathered about your kids when they surf, head them to the Anonymizer site at www.anonymizer.com. They can visit that site, and then from there surf somewhere else. When they do that, no one will be able to track their surfing activities.

Surprise! There's Good News: The Law Is on Your Side

Reading all this bad news isn't much fun, I know. Well, it's time to cheer up because there's some very good news: When it comes to protecting your kids' privacy on the Internet, the law is on your side.

And the law even has a name. It's called the Children's Online Privacy Protection Act (COPPA), and it puts forward a set of guidelines about what Web sites can and can't do with information they gather from your kids. In fact, it even *prohibits* Web sites from gathering information about your kids without your express approval.

Hard to believe, I know; it seems that Congress never did anything intelligent when it comes to the Internet. But in this instance, the members of Congress were right on target.

The Federal Trade Commission enforces the law, which is pretty strict. Here's what the law says about what Web sites can and can't do with regard to children's privacy:

➤ **Web sites directed at children, or that collect information from kids under 13, have to post their privacy policies.**   They have to spell out, online, what kind of information they gather, how the site will use the information, and whether the information is sent to third parties, such as advertisers or marketing firms. And the sites must post a person to contact at the site about the policies.

➤ **Web sites must get parental consent before collecting, using, or disclosing personal information about a child.**   So that means you must be contacted before any of this happens—and you also must give explicit consent. There's a three-part process for getting parental consent via email, by phone, and by other means. And if the site shares information about kids with others, there's an even more complicated consent process it has to follow. If a site doesn't do this, it's breaking the law.

Some Sites Now Won't Give Kids Free Email

One unintended consequence of COPPA is that some sites no longer give kids free email accounts. That's because they ask for personal information from people who sign up for the accounts, and the sites don't want to have to go through the bother of asking for parental consent. For example, the Web site www.snap.com stopped giving kids free email accounts because of the passage of COPPA. Oh, well. You have to take the good with the bad.

➤ **Web sites must get parental consent again if their information-gathering policies change.**   That means if a site has a set of policies for gathering information and you say it's okay, the site has to get your consent again if its policies change.

➤ **Parents are allowed to review the personal information gathered about their children.**   You have the right to see exactly what information a Web site has about your kids.

➤ **Parents have the right to revoke their consent, and to delete information collected about their kids.** If you change your mind and don't
want information collected, you can do that. And you can delete any information that you want.

You can get more information about all this at the www.ftc.gov Web site. Head to
www.ftc.gov/bcp/menu-children.htm for information about how the FTC protects
kids. The FTC posts information online to help you understand the COPPA, as shown
in Figure 8.2.

Figure 8.2

Head to the www.ftc.gov
*Web site for information
about how the COPPA
protects your kids.*

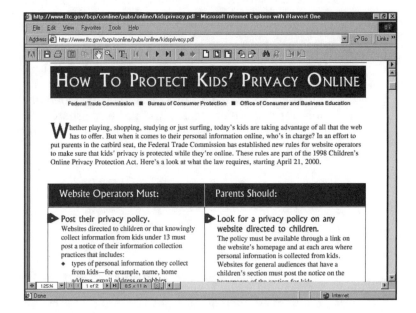

Okay, I Understand the Law. But How Can I Make Sure It's Followed?

As we all know, passing a law is one thing, and getting people to follow it is another.
A law is only as good as whoever is enforcing it.

The good news is that the FTC takes its job seriously. Even before COPPA was passed,
it was using its power to help protect kids' privacy. For example, under rules in effect
before COPPA, it took action against a site called Young Investor. The site asked kids
to give information about their allowance and savings habits, and collected personal
information such as names and addresses. In return, the site said it would keep the
identities of the kids anonymous. The site, however, tracked the identities of the kids.
It didn't sell that information or give it away, but it did keep the identities. In reply,
the FTC took action against it.

If you believe a site is breaking the law, it's easy to ask the FTC to investigate. You can call a toll-free number to complain, at 1-877-382-4357, or send a complaint by mail to the Consumer Response Center, Federal Trade Commission, 600 Pennsylvania Ave, NW, Washington, DC 20580. And you can fill out a complaint form online at www.ftc.gov/ftc/complaint.htm. The form is pictured in Figure 8.3. A site found breaking the law must pay a $10,000 fine. And more importantly, the fine is announced publicly, which means other parents can steer their kids away from it.

Figure 8.3

Here's how to ask the FTC to investigate a site that you believe has invaded your child's privacy.

What Else Can You Do to Protect Your Children's Privacy?

There's a lot more you can do other than complain to the FTC to make sure your kids' privacy isn't invaded online. You can fight back and make sure that information about your children isn't gathered online if you don't want it to be. Here's how to do it:

➤ **Check out a site's privacy policies.** The law says privacy policies must be posted. So read them before your kids use or register at sites. What information do they gather about your kids? How do they use it? Ideally, a site would collect no information—but if it does, you want it to be absolutely minimal, and you don't want it shared with other sites.

What Information Should Your Kids Not Reveal?

The law doesn't govern what kinds of information Web sites can gather from your kids. But there is information that *you* don't want given out, so your kids shouldn't fill it in. For example, they should never give out their social security number, or the number of anyone in the family. They shouldn't reveal information that you'd want kept private, such as your salary, and possibly your occupation, age, and employer. In fact, you should compile a list of all the information you don't want your kids to give out, and make sure they know never to fill that in when they register on a Web site.

➤ **Look for a special children's privacy seal on a site.** Two private groups, TRUSTe at www.etrust.com (shown in Figure 8.4) and the Better Business Bureau online at www.bbbonline.com, have established programs to help protect children's privacy. When a site adheres to these standards—which are quite strict— it gets to put the seal of the group on its page. Look to see if a site has the seal. If it does, it adheres to the privacy rules. Also, the FTC is putting together guidelines for an FTC privacy seal, so look for that one as well.

Figure 8.4

The TRUSTe kids' seal ensures that a site adheres to privacy standards for children.

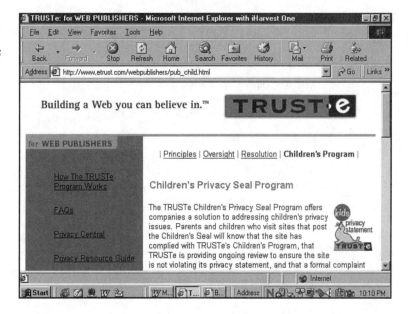

➤ **Tell your children never to give out private information about themselves.** This is one of the surest ways to help protect your kids' privacy. Tell them not to give out their full name, address, and similar information in public areas or in an Instant Message conversation.

➤ **Ask that your children check with you before registering or giving out personal information about themselves to a Web site.** That way, you can check out the site with your children before they give out their information. This also educates them in what to look for to protect their privacy themselves. Sure, the law says you have to give your consent first, but not all Web sites follow the law.

It's Easy for Your Kids to Lie to Web Sites

When it comes to privacy, keep this in mind: It's easy for kids to lie to Web sites about their age. If they really want to register for a site, but worry you won't give your consent, all they need to do is say they're much older than they really are. And a Web site won't check to see if they're telling the truth. So make sure your kids don't lie about their age just so they can register for a Web site. Unfortunately, they can lie about their age when they visit pornography sites as well, so make sure they know they should never lie just so they can visit a site.

➤ **Think hard before giving your consent to allow your child to register at a Web site.** If the privacy policies make you uncomfortable, just say no.

➤ **Use parental control software to block private information from being sent over the Internet.** Parental control software like Norton Internet Security 2000 and McAfee Internet Guard Dog have a feature that lets you block your children from sending personal information over the Internet. You can block your social security number, address, phone number, and any other information you'd prefer to be kept private.

➤ **Ask to see the information the Web site gathers about your child.** The law gives you the right to examine this information. So ask to see it to make sure your kids' privacy isn't being invaded.

➤ **Ask the site to delete information you don't want gathered.** If you see information gathered by a site that you don't want collected, inform the site so it can delete the questionable information.

111

How to Let Your Kids Shop Online Without Worrying About Breaking the Bank

If you have a pre-teen or a teenager, you know that shopping seems to hold an unholy attraction for kids. Whether it be music, sports equipment, makeup, clothes, toys, or almost anything else, kids love to buy things. And increasingly, they love to buy online.

The only safe way to buy online is with a credit card. And as any parent in their right mind knows, you should never hand your credit card over to your kids and let them run wild.

So what to do? You want to allow your kids to make their own decisions about money, but you don't want them breaking the bank. How can you let your kids buy online?

There's an easy way to do it—you can let them use one of several sites created just for that purpose. At these sites, parents create shopping accounts for their kids. Generally, the sites all work on a similar basis. At the site, you register yourself and your kids, and you can set up a separate account for each child. You can give them each a lump sum of money (usually a minimum of $25) using your credit card or some other means of payment, although a credit card is the most common. You can also give them a shopping "allowance" every week or month—you can have a certain amount of money automatically taken from your credit card and put into their account. One of the sites that works this way is RocketCash, pictured in Figure 8.5.

Figure 8.5

The Rocket Cash site enables parents to set up shopping accounts for their kids.

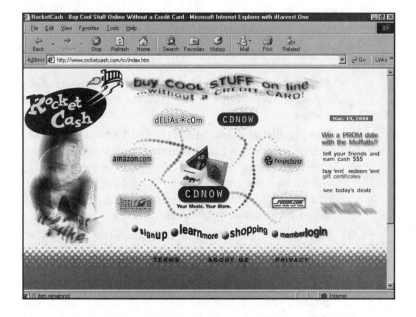

It's Best to Only Use Credit Cards to Start Kids' Accounts

When setting up and maintaining a kid's spending account, never use any method other than a credit card. That's because you get consumer protections with a credit card that you don't get when you use checks or some other method. If, for example, the kids' shopping site goes out of business and you've paid by credit card, you get the normal consumer protections that credit cards offer. But if you've paid by check or a similar method, you're out of luck—those protections don't hold.

After the money is in your kids' accounts, they can spend it at a variety of online stores—only those stores that have signed up with the specific buying site. Typically, the stores that sign up are well-known clothing, toys, music, entertainment, and similar sites. Often, you're able to determine from which of those stores your kids can shop. So if you want them buying clothing and books but not CDs, for example, you're able to limit their spending to clothing and book sites.

Your kids will never be able to overdraw their accounts. If the money isn't there, they can't buy. It's that simple. And as any parent knows, very few things are that simple when it comes to kids.

What to Ask Before Registering at Kids' Buying Sites

There are a number of kids' buying sites on the Internet, so be smart about which one you use. Before you sign up and hand over your credit card, here's what to ask.

➤ **What are the site's privacy rules?**   You've read this far in the chapter, so you know all the questions to ask.

➤ **What stores have signed up with the site?**   If the site sells only Geritol and garden fences, there's no point in signing up. Make sure there are stores from which your kids want to buy, and from which you want them to buy.

➤ **Does the site let you open savings accounts?**   You'd like to teach your kids to save, not just spend. Some of these sites let you open savings accounts for kids, as well as spending accounts.

➤ **Can your kids use the site to give to charity?**   It's never too early to teach your kids that everyone has a responsibility to give to the needy. So see if the site lets your kids use their money to give to charities.

113

Beware of Letting Your Kids Use Your Auction Account

Kids, just like adults, love to buy things at online auctions, such as www.ebay.com. But don't let your kids use your auction account to buy. If you give them your login information, they're able to bid as if they were you—and you could find yourself out big bucks. In fact, a teenager used his parents' credit card to run up a bill of more than a million dollars on eBay. eBay let the parents off the hook. But you don't want to find yourself bankrupted because your kids absolutely had to buy Elvis's solid gold Las Vegas jumpsuit.

➤ **Do you have veto power over what you kids buy?** At some sites, after your kids have decided what they want to buy, they have to first get your permission before the sale is made final. If you want to have veto power over what your kids can buy, make sure the site has this feature.

➤ **Is it easy to track how your kids are spending?** You want an account that shows you, in detail, how much your kids spend and how they spend it.

➤ **Can you change permissions whenever you want?** Maybe you've decided that your kids are spending too much money on CDs, and you'd like to limit their purchases in that area. Choose a site that makes it easy to change your permissions whenever you want.

The Best Kids' Buying Sites Online

There are a number of these sites that enable you to set up a buying account for your kids. Check these out and you won't go wrong.

DoughNET

http://www.doughnet.com

This is a good site. Not only are your kids able to buy at stores they like, but it also lets your kids save their money and donate money to charity as well. And if you want your kids to learn about investing, they can play online investing games. Don't worry, they won't have to pay a penny. It's all free funny money.

ICanBuy

http://www.icanbuy.com

This one's an excellent site. There's a nice selection of places where your kids can buy, you can open up a savings account here, your kids can give to charity, and there are even extra features, such as chat areas and the like. The policies are stated clearly, including excellent privacy rules. And it's easy to get started. The site is pictured in Figure 8.6.

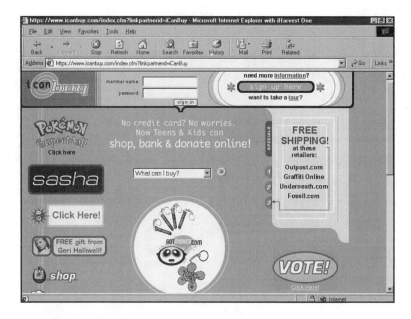

Figure 8.6

ICanBuy is one of the better sites that lets kids buy on the Internet.

RocketCash

http://www.rocketcash.com

Your kids will love this site. They can shop at great stores, such as Delia's, the Amazon bookseller, the excellent FogDog sports site, CD sites, game sites, and more. They're protected by good privacy guidelines—the kids' guidelines are put together by TRUSTe. The rules are easy to follow, and there are many specials. It's the most kid-centric site, as well. All in all, it's a great place for kids to go.

The Least You Need To Know

➤ Marketers target your children because they believe if they can get your kids to know about their brands, your kids will become life-long customers.

➤ Web sites gather information from your kids in many ways, including getting them to register, giving away things, and by automatically tracking their online activities.

➤ The Children's Online Privacy Protection Act (COPPA) requires that sites post their privacy policies about children, that you give your consent to your kids registering at the site, and offers other privacy protections, as well.

➤ If a site doesn't comply with the Children's Online Privacy Protection Act, you can make a complaint to the Federal Trade Commission.

➤ Before allowing your kid to register at a site, check the site's privacy policies, and look for a privacy seal from a group like TRUSTe.

➤ A safe way to let kids buy online is through a site where you can open an account for them, such as www.rocketcash.com.

Chapter 9

The Scoop on Newsgroups

In This Chapter

➤ Newsgroups finally defined and demonstrated (It's about time!)

➤ Learn how to decipher newsgroup names

➤ Find out what really goes on in newsgroups

➤ The lowdown on newsgroups for kids

Okay, okay—you've heard a lot of talk in this book about Internet newsgroups. But what are they, *really*? Do they have something to do with news events? Are they for news groupies? Is Dan Rather involved? Will your kids want anything to do with them? You're about to find out.

Newsgroups: What Are They?

Newsgroups are one of the Internet's oldest communication forums. They can best be described as online discussion groups. They're a cross between email, live chat, and an electronic bulletin board. The communication found on a newsgroup is based on posted messages that are read by everyone else who stops for a look. Posting a message is as simple as sending email to the newsgroup.

For example, someone might post a message in a computer-focused newsgroup about a problem he's having with his PC. Such a message might resemble the one shown in Figure 9.1. The next person who reads the message might respond with a suggestion, just like replying to an email. Another person might then view the message, as well as the response, and add a posting of her own. The next person might then add an entirely new topic to the discussion. It becomes a never-ending series of communication. Unlike chat, however, the postings do not occur in real-time; that is, a message posted on Monday might not see a response until Wednesday.

Name of newsgroup

Figure 9.1

Here's an example of a message from a newsgroup. Looks like regular old email, doesn't it?

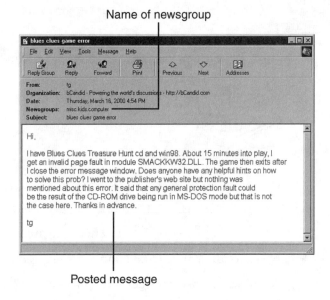

Posted message

Although newsgroups are not as flashy as Web pages—or as dynamic as live chat—they have served a purpose among the denizens of the Internet for many years. The heart of newsgroups is the exchange of information, thoughts, and ideas in written form. Newsgroups are focused on topics. For example, if gardening is a favorite hobby around your house, you and your family might enjoy the following newsgroups:

alt.garden.pond.chat   General talk about gardening, ponds, garden chat

aus.gardens   Gardening in Australia

ba.gardens   Gardening in the San Francisco bay area

rec.gardens   Generalized gardening discussions

rec.gardens.roses   Gardening discussion focused on roses

Newsgroups are great for sharing information about a particular hobby or interest. Check out Figure 9.2—it shows a list of newsgroups focused on parenting. You can find this list and others thanks to the Liszt Web site (www.liszt.com/news/), a site devoted to helping you look up newsgroups of interest.

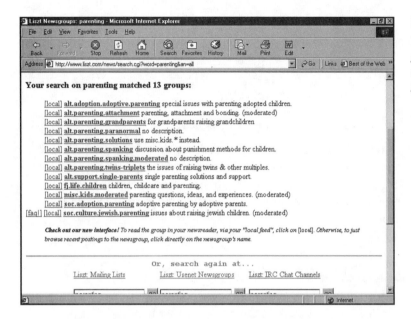

Figure 9.2

You can look up news-groups using a site such as Liszt's Usenet News-groups Directory.

There are thousands upon thousands of Usenet newsgroups on the Internet, covering every topic under the sun. If you can't find a news-group you like, you can, with a bit of effort, create your own newsgroup. But with more than 20,000 newsgroups out there, chances are your hobby or interest is covered somewhere.

For example, is your spouse interested in sky-diving? Visit the `rec.skydiving` newsgroup. Want to discuss a favorite Stephen King novel with other avid readers? Check out `alt.books.stephen-king`. Is *Ren and Stimpy* your kid's favorite cartoon? Look to the `alt.tv.ren-and-stimpy` newsgroup for other fans. Wondering what to make for dinner? Try `rec.food.recipes`.

Usenet

Short for *user network*, Usenet is a worldwide network of connected Unix systems that transmits postings to newsgroups. Usenet offers the largest collection of public news-groups on the Internet.

Some newsgroups are meant for kids, but most newsgroups are geared toward adults. Therein lie the danger and the reason for this chapter. Not all newsgroups are as innocent as a discussion on gardening or a favorite cartoon character. Among the many topical newsgroups are those that pose a danger to children. These include newsgroups for sex fetishes, hate groups, and other sordid interests. The people who utilize these groups often exchange explicit language and images that range from pornographic depictions to violent and morbid depictions. Naturally, this type of content is quite unsuitable for children, and as a parent, you need to know more about newsgroups before allowing your child access to them. To understand newsgroups, you must first learn how they work.

119

Where to Find Newsgroups?

When you check out newsgroups using your newsreader, your ISP downloads a list of available newsgroups—a pretty exhaustive list, at that. It might be easier to check out newsgroups with a little help from the Web. Yahoo's Newsgroup Listings can help, as can Deja News (www.deja.com) or the previously mentioned Liszt site. Tile.net is another place to start.

How Do Newsgroups Work?

In the past, users needed a newsreader program to access newsgroups. A newsreader program is a specific application that enables anyone to subscribe, read, and post newsgroup messages. Today's Web browsers have built-in newsreader programs. For example, if you're using Microsoft's Internet Explorer, you can use Outlook Express as your newsreader. America Online also has a built-in newsgroup reader.

Need a Newsreader?

If you prefer to use a stand-alone program to read newsgroup messages, there are many popular newsreaders to choose from, such as Free Agent, News Xpress, Trumpet Newsreader, and WinVN. Mac users can check out Nuntius and News-Watcher. You can find newsreaders on the Internet that you can download and install.

Newsgroup messages are presented much like regular email messages, in a list of recent postings. Figure 9.3 shows a list of messages posted to the rec.pets newsgroup, as viewed in Outlook Express. To view a message, select it (or double-click it to open a separate window) and read the posting.

Newsgroup
posting

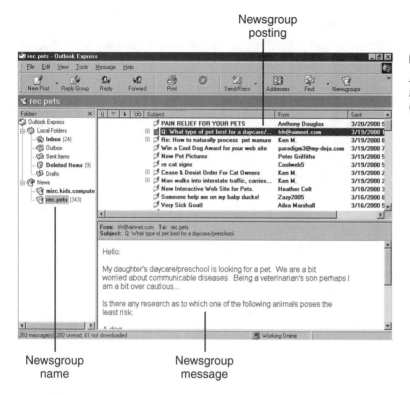

Figure 9.3

Here's an example of a newsgroup viewed through Outlook Express.

Newsgroup
name

Newsgroup
message

Each message includes the username of the person who posted it, as well as a subject heading describing the message. Because so many people post messages, it's not always easy to follow the topics discussed. Look for *threads*—that is, replies to an original post. You can follow threads from the original post to the most recent reply. You can reply to a message, post a new message, or just read the messages that are already posted.

You can also view newsgroup messages from the Web, which means you don't need a newsreader or a built-in application on your browser. Figure 9.4 shows a posting to the alt.tv.nickelodeon newsgroup, a group for kids. As you can tell from the figure, the messages aren't too lengthy in kid's newsgroups, so they're usually a quick read. Web sites like Liszt's Usenet Newsgroups Directory (www.liszt.com/news/) or Deja News (www.deja.com/usenet/) enable you to read and post newsgroup messages without a separate newsreader program or browser built-in.

Newsgroup messages are stored on news servers at universities, corporations, organizations, and Internet service providers around the globe. Most of these servers store only the most recent posts. If they saved every message, they'd have run out of storage space a long time ago.

Newsgroup name

Figure 9.4

You can also view news-group messages from the Web.

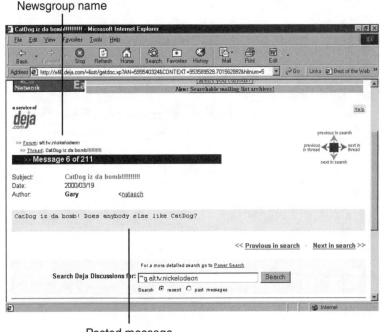

Posted message

Your access to newsgroups is dictated by the way you connect to the Internet. If you use an ISP to get to the Internet, the ISP might only subscribe to a certain number of newsgroups. Remember, there are thousands of newsgroups. ISPs try to provide the ones they think most of their users will enjoy. If you don't see the one you want, you can always ask the ISP to subscribe to that specific newsgroup.

If you use a commercial online service, you can find newsgroups in another way. Look among the program's menu system or buttons for an Internet portal. For example, if you're using AOL, you can open the Internet Connection window and click **Newsgroups**.

Because there are so many newsgroups, the first thing you, as a parent, need to do is figure out which ones to subscribe to, if any. Are there any your child might enjoy, such as a hobby- or sport-focused newsgroup? Or are there any that focus on topics your entire family would like, such as recreational activities? Don't worry, there's no fee for subscribing to newsgroups, and if it turns out you pick a few that aren't quite what you had in mind, you can always unsubscribe. The key is to check out the newsgroup thoroughly before allowing your child access.

After you subscribe to a newsgroup, you can view a current list of messages posted to that newsgroup each time you open your newsgroup view. The postings are usually frequent, so depending on the newsgroup, you might want to check for new postings every day, or you might want to check once a week. Even if you don't subscribe, though, you can visit a newsgroup any time.

Techno Talk

Newsgroups Versus Mailing Lists

Some people get mailing lists and newsgroups confused. Mailing lists are postings that are sent to your email address. With newsgroups, you can subscribe then view the postings whenever and as often as you want. With mailing lists, the messages arrive in your Internet account's Inbox as email, so you view them whenever you check your email. Mailing lists are more private than newsgroups.

Deciphering Newsgroup Names

Understanding newsgroup names is a bit of a science. They're broken down into categories, such as *comp* for computer or *rec* for recreational. Abbreviations are the norm, separated by periods (called *dots*), such as `alt.parenting.twins-triplets`. The prefix is an abbreviation for the newsgroup category. In the case of the example, *alt* means alternative Usenet newsgroup. Not a very descriptive category name is it? The second part of the name is the topic, such as *parenting*. Subsequent words tacked onto the name narrow the topic to a subtopic. In the case of our example, the group is about twins and triplets. Subtopics can use hyphens in the name.

To help you make heads or tails out of newsgroup names, here's a list of newsgroup categories:

Category	Description
alt	Alternative newsgroups
aus	Australian and Australasian newsgroups
biz	Business oriented newsgroups
clari	Clarinet News Service (commercial)
comp	Computer newsgroups
de	International German language newsgroups
fido	Newsgroups originating from the Fidonet network
finet	Finnish language newsgroups
fj	Japanese language newsgroups
fr	International French language newsgroups
it	Italian newsgroups
microsoft	This one's pretty obvious

continues

Category	Description CONTINUED
misc	Miscellaneous newsgroups
news	Usenet news
no	Norwegian newsgroups
rec	Recreational newsgroups
sci	Science newsgroups
soc	Social issues
shamash	Jewish newsgroups
talk	Talk newsgroups
tnn	Japanese newsgroups
tw	Taiwanese newsgroups
uk	United Kingdom newsgroups

You can usually figure out a newsgroup's focus by the name. For example, `rec.aviation` is for pilots and plane enthusiasts, `soc.adoption.parenting` is for adoptive parents, and `alt.gossip.celebrities` is for discussing (or debunking) rumors about the stars.

Newsgroups Everywhere

Many local and private newsgroups exist for your perusing pleasure. For example, your local ISP might offer a subscription to a local newsgroup. Many company intranets (internal Internets) have newsgroups for employees who can tap into them via their work computers.

Up until now, newsgroups might seem fairly innocent to you. As you're about to read, however, what goes on in some newsgroups isn't so innocent at all.

What Goes On in Newsgroups?

Newsgroups center around publicly posted discussions, which means anyone can read and post newsgroup messages. Some newsgroups are *moderated* by someone who manages the group by keeping the postings current and keeping the discussions on track, that sort of thing. Some newsgroups have strict rules of conduct (such as no bad language or no advertising); with others, it's anything goes. Some newsgroups are very technical in nature; others are quite silly. Unfortunately, with the onslaught of a growing Internet population, the early years of diplomacy and decorum in newsgroup correspondence are long gone.

It's not uncommon to see all kinds of foul language and flaming going on in newsgroups, as shown in Figure 9.5. *Flaming* is the action of attacking others, ranting and raving like a lunatic, and generally disrupting an otherwise civilized discussion. We're talking about language ranging from PG-13 rated expletives to X-rated obscenity. There's a lot of flaming among newsgroups, particularly those focused on hot topics (such as politics) or interests (such as sports teams). However, if you can get past the contributions of some users, newsgroups can be sources of inspiration, wisdom, and general amusement for adults. Unfortunately, not many newsgroup message postings offer much for children.

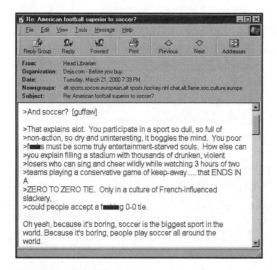

Figure 9.5

This is an example of people flaming in newsgroups. In the message shown, one user is debating another over the popularity of soccer. We had to edit out the bad words.

Time to talk about the darker side of newsgroups. Like all the other areas of the Internet, things are not exactly rosy when it comes to newsgroups. Hundreds of newsgroups focus on pornography and the obscene; porn can show up in just about any newsgroup, whether it's wanted or not. For this reason, parents need to be very aware of the dangers that lurk among newsgroups, even innocent-sounding newsgroups.

Users trade pictures and solicit other things (such as phone sex, physical visits, etc.) among adult newsgroups. Criminals exchange information on them as well, and hackers use newsgroups to pass around damaging viruses. Users exchange all manner of ideas, agendas, and information, including ideas that conflict with your family's values and beliefs.

For example, you can find passwords on Usenet newsgroups that will get you into pornographic Web sites. One father caught his two teenage sons sneaking into pay-per-view porn sites without paying and bypassing the age verification check. How?

They got passwords from newsgroup postings. The stolen passwords can easily be used for bypassing the checks that are meant to keep minors out of porn sites.

In some instances, flame wars that lead to users getting kicked off their Internet connection (ISP) develop between users. You and your children need to be very wary about online arguments in newsgroups. A user whom you insult graphically (using foul or threatening language), for example, can report you to your ISP who cancels your account. The ISP won't ask who started the fight, nor take time to listen to your side of the story.

On the other hand, some newsgroup users are finding their identities falsified. A hacker might use your name (or your child's name) in a newsgroup, and you might find your account canceled, or worse. Thankfully, ISPs are being more responsive to complaints, and now they have the technology to sort out fraudulent practices.

But what if your teenager logs on and wages a newsgroup flame war without your knowledge? It happens, and some parents have found themselves with a cancelled ISP account because of it. You and your family won't run into too many problems if you stick to the newsgroup's focus, mind your manners, and resist lashing out at others who abuse the system. If you do allow your children or teenagers access to newsgroups, it's imperative that you teach them how to conduct themselves online.

To give you some idea what to expect when browsing through newsgroup names, Figure 9.6 shows a sampling of what's available in the alt category.

Figure 9.6

The topic of sex fuels hundreds of newsgroup conversations...including some subjects you might not have known existed.

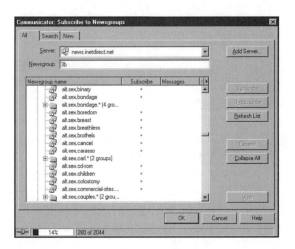

As you can clearly see, the topics are very adult in nature. Pedophilia is alive and well among newsgroups, and many pedophiles use these forums to exchange information and child pornography.

Do Children Participate in Newsgroups?

Kids can find some newsgroups of interest, but parents should be wary. As explained earlier in this chapter, what goes on among the message posts can be unsuitable for children. At best, you need to investigate newsgroups before allowing your child access. You might want to make newsgroup reading a family affair; this way your children aren't reading newsgroup material on their own. For example, Figure 9.7 shows what I found in a Pokémon newsgroup.

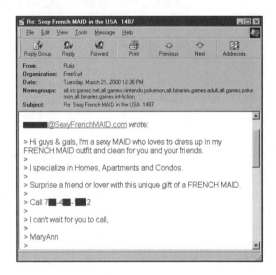

Figure 9.7

How did this post get into a newsgroup about Pokémon? And do you think she's only interested in cleaning?

Newsgroups for children are few and far between. There are some (such as `alt.tv.nickelodeon`) that grade-school children might find interesting. Other than that, the main appeal for kids is hobbies. Plenty of newsgroups that your kids might find interesting focus on pets and hobbies. A few newsgroups focus on pen pals (`alt.kids-talk.penpals`), but use caution. If there's anything you have learned thus far in this book it's that on the Internet not everyone is who they say they are. This includes people who post messages in newsgroups.

If your child is into computer and video games, the gaming newsgroups might offer hints and helps for getting through a game level. There are tons of game-focused newsgroups, as shown in Figure 9.8. Your child can post questions about a game and check back to see if anyone replies to the message.

As a parent, you might need to explore what newsgroups are available and how appropriate they are for your kid (or kids). For that matter, you might check with your kids to see what newsgroups they'd be interested in, such as hobbies or games. Be sure to instruct them on how to conduct themselves in the newsgroup. As a rule, newsgroups frown on spamming and advertising, and they expect participants to behave as they would elsewhere on the Internet. After all, hundreds of people read the messages posted in newsgroups.

Figure 9.8

This newsgroup features postings about the Jedi Knight game.

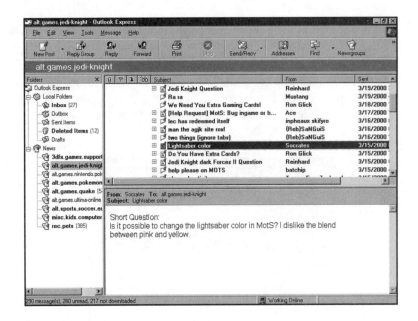

Teach your child to never share personal information with anyone on the Internet, including people they correspond with via newsgroup postings. They should never give out their real name, phone number, or address in any online venue, newsgroups included. Remember, newsgroups are public forums, so any information shared in postings can be read by everyone else.

If you prefer that your child not have access to newsgroups, you might want to install parental control software, like Net Nanny, to block newsgroup usage. Blocking and filtering software can block not only unsuitable Web sites and unauthorized searches, they can also block access to newsgroups. Check out Chapter 13, "All About Filters," to learn more about blocking software.

Newsgroups are a dynamic form of communication on the Internet, and the vast majority of newsgroups are adult-focused, so as a parent, newsgroup access is your call. Use caution and be aware of the dangers that lurk among message postings.

The Least You Need to Know

Now you know the scoop on newsgroups. Next time the topic comes up, you'll know what's going on.

➤ Newsgroups are like online bulletin boards where users post messages about a topic or interest.

➤ You can use a newsreader to read newsgroup messages, or you can use a built-in reader that comes with your browser.

➤ You can also read and post newsgroup messages from a special Web site.

➤ Newsgroup messages look a lot like regular email messages. They list the name of the person who posted the message, the message subject, and the message itself.

➤ The conduct within newsgroups can be very unsuitable for children. News-groups are notorious for flame wars (arguing back and forth, usually with name calling and bad language).

➤ Newsgroups are known for their obscene topics. You have only to check out some of the names to see what I mean.

➤ There are very few newsgroups suitable for children; the majority are targeted to adults. Be sure to check out any newsgroup before letting your child view its postings.

➤ Monitor the newsgroups in which your child is interested. If your kid is active in a newsgroup, spend some time watching his or her interaction with others in the newsgroup.

➤ Remind your children to never share any personal information such as real names, addresses, and phone numbers while participating in a newsgroup. You never know who is reading the message postings.

Chapter 10

Playing Games Online

In This Chapter

➤ A look at the various types of online games

➤ Learn what dangers exist with playing online games

➤ Sources where you and your child can find good games

Games? What could possibly be dangerous about games? Before you shrug off this chapter, there are a few things you, as a parent or guardian, need to know about Internet games. For example, if your child is playing online games, that means he or she is interacting online with other Internet users. As you've learned in previous chapters, not all online users are what they seem to be. Sure, there are plenty of innocent, ordinary games on the Internet, but there are also some types of games that are unsuitable for children. In this chapter, you find out what's what when it comes to gaming online.

Anyone Up for a Game?

Kids love games, no doubt about it. Kids, computers, and games go together like peanut butter, jelly, and bread. For that reason, computer gaming is a huge market these days. When you bought a computer for your home, the first thing your child probably asked was, "Does it come with any games?" And when you hooked up to the Internet, they probably said, "Let's download some games, can we, can we, pleeeaase?"

Techno Talk

Shareware

Shareware programs are those you can download and use free, then if you decide you like them, pay a small fee later. Freeware, on the other hand, is completely free.

The Internet offers a great wealth of games for players of all ages. There's something for everyone, from the classics—such as chess or checkers—to arcade games, sports games, word games, shoot-'em-up games, and much more. There are oodles of games on the Internet for downloading and playing on the home PC, and many of them are free or shareware programs. You and your child can find such games by conducting a search using the keyword "games."

Many of the Internet's downloadable games are meant to be played on the home computer with just one person. That's fine and dandy for some, but gaming enthusiasts want to challenge other players. That's where online gaming comes in. With online gaming, there's the thrill of testing skills against other players logged on at the same time, plus chatting with them while trouncing them in the game.

Most online games fit into a category of some type, and some fit into more than one:

➤ **Action games**   Included in this category are MechWarrior, Quake 2, and X-Wing versus TIE Fighter. These games typically involve fast-moving play, usually utilize weapons, and often require quick reflexes.

➤ **Business and economic games**   Included in this category are Eminent Domain and Zapitalism. These games teach financial and stock market principles.

➤ **Classic games**   This category includes computer versions of family favorites, such as Monopoly and chess.

➤ **Simulation games**   This category of games tests users in simulated environments, such as flying a plane or driving a tank. These can also include simulated civilizations or battles. Streets of SimCity, Armor Command, and FireTeam are some examples.

➤ **Racing games**   These games might involve cars, robots, or other types of vehicles. Monster Truck Madness and Pod are two examples.

➤ **Role-playing games**   These types of games allow users to explore an imaginary world and pretend to be a character within that world. Baldur's Gate and Ultima Online are examples of games that fall into this category.

➤ **Sports games**   This category revolves around sports, of course. Included in this category are Indy Car Racing and Football Pro, to name a few.

➤ **Strategy games**   This type of game tests users' strategizing skills. Examples include Age of Empires and StarCraft. These games aren't typically as fast-paced as other online games because they enable users to think through their next move.

➤ **Trivia games**   This game type tests users' endless knowledge of all things trivial. You Don't Know Jack is an example. Trivia games usually appeal to teens as well as adults.

➤ **Word games**   Strike A Match or Word Racer are included in this category. They test players' word skills.

Chances are, your child already knows about online games and perhaps has played a few. To help you, the grown-up, better understand what's out there, this section offers a look at several kinds of online games.

Age Matters!

The vast majority of online games—those meant to be played with other users—are not appropriate for younger children. To learn more about games for youngsters, check out Chapter 20, "Kid-Friendly Places on the Internet." You should decide whether a game is suitable for your child or not.

Role-Playing Games

Role-playing games are one of Internet's oldest activities. The very first role-playing games were MUDs. MUD stands for *multiuser dimension* (or *dungeon*). Variations on the MUD include MOO, MUSH, or MUCK, among other strange names. MUDs are real-time chat forums in which users can log on, assume a character, and wander about a predefined universe (a database of "locations" for the participants to move in and out of). The idea behind role-playing games is to give users the opportunity to tap into their imaginations, assume various characters, and set forth on various adventures. Akin to the Dungeons and Dragons genre, Internet role-playing games are very popular and there's quite a subculture that thrives on them.

Today's role-playing games come in a variety of setups. There are still numerous MUDs to be found on the Internet, plus other role-playing games to try. Some are commercialized and require software, others require a fee, and others are free. If you're using a commercial online service, you and your child can find them in the gaming area.

Role-playing games take a considerable amount of time as players develop characters, explore the game's universe, and just plain hang out with other users. There are several different genres among role-playing games on the Internet, including fantasy, science fiction, gothic, and so on. Do a search on the term "MUDs" to see what's out there (or just see Figure 10.1).

Role-playing games are ongoing; there's no stopping or restarting the game. Players assume characters and converse with other players as those characters—online acting, if you will. Some role-playing games involve fighting, which means characters can kill non-player characters (characters run by the game's system computer) or sometimes kill other players. If another player kills your character, you can just reinvent another character and start again. The idea behind many role-playing games is to amass weapons or money, find treasure, and advance a character's powers.

Figure 10.1

As demonstrated in these descriptions, Internet MUDs are all about the imagination.

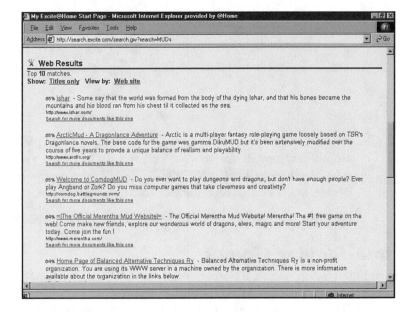

Will your kids want to play with MUDs? Older kids and teens might. Because role-playing games are text-based and chatty, they probably aren't the type of games most kids are interested in. There's a lot of reading and typing involved, plus a lot of time spent figuring out how the game works (which characters have what powers, how to make spells, how to enter commands without looking like an idiot). Check out Figure 10.2 to see an example of the Merentha MUD.

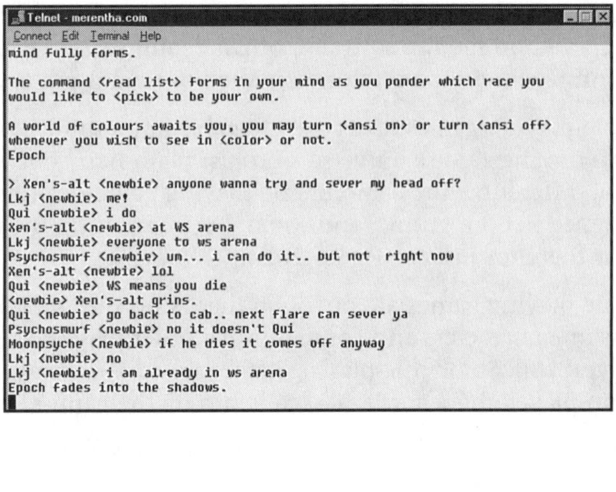

Figure 10.2

Here's an example of a MUD. Not too pretty to look at, is it?

Role-playing games can also be found among the commercial online services (see Figure 10.3). Such games are usually on a schedule and include anything from role-playing to SIMS (simulations) to free-form games.

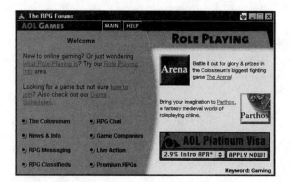

Figure 10.3

AOL has lots of role-playing games. Check the schedule to see what's available.

Not all role-playing games are typing and reading. Commercial role-playing games utilize dazzling graphics and multimedia effects. Baldur's Gate (by Interplay), for example, uses 3D technology. To play such games online, you must first purchase the software and install it on your PC. Buying special gaming software is an added expense to your family's Internet endeavors.

As a parent, you should check out any of the online role-playing games your child is interested in. Most require some form of registration and passwords, so be careful about giving out too much personal information (and don't lose the passwords). If the game seems to be too adult-oriented or violent, try to direct your child to a less violent game. There are truly hundreds to choose from, depending on where you look.

Multiuser Games

Multiuser games are just what the name implies, games played with one or more people online. Whether you're battling it out for supremacy of the universe or racing opponents to solve a word puzzle, multiuser games are fast-paced and fun. There are multiuser games for every kind of game category: action, strategy, SIMS, word games, arcade games, sports, game show games, and more. There are sites on the Internet dedicated to multiuser game playing, as well as areas of commercial online services that cater to the never-ending quest for a game. Some of these game sites require a fee, and others are free.

Figure 10.4 shows an example of a multiuser word game found on the Yahoo! game site (games.yahoo.com). Seven players are trying to spell words out of the puzzle in a race against time. Bonus points are awarded for using colored letters in the puzzle.

Figure 10.4

Kids might enjoy testing their spelling skills against other players.

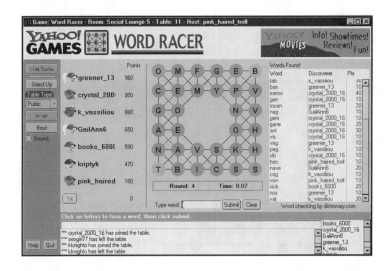

Older children, especially those that are really into games, will be very interested in playing multiuser games online. Just about every popular software action game has a multiuser game going on online. You must have a copy of the software to play, however. For example, if your teen loves to play Quake III, he can log on and play the game with others at a game site. On the downside, many of the most popular multiuser games are very violent.

If your child isn't interested in playing a certain game he or she already has, don't worry. There are plenty of other games online. With some, users must first download software to play. Others work using Java-applets (the game works onscreen while you're at the Web site), so there's no downloading of software involved. Most game sites require registration and passwords.

Caution

Parents Watch Out!

Some sites require some personal information before the user can enter and play. One of the sites visited when doing research for this book asked for a salary range in the registration form. That's a strange question if many of a gaming site's players are kids.

Online game services are really big on the Internet now. They combine the activity of playing games online with live chat, player rankings and tournaments, even prizes for tournament winners. Some of the top game services on the Internet include GameStorm (www.gamestorm.com), HEAT.NET (www.heat.net), MPLAYER (www.mplayer.com), Internet Gaming Zone (www.zone.com), and Total Entertainment Network (www.ten.net). These services offer access to scads of multiuser games, usually for a fee. Some of these services are free, but those that are free make heavy use of advertising while players are online. Figure 10.5 shows HEAT.NET's home page. Notice all the game channels available and the number of games in progress for each channel.

Figure 10.5

HEAT.NET offers over 150 games and has a free basic subscription, or you can opt for a premium membership for $4.95 a month.

Users can download various programs from these services, or purchase retail versions to play online. It's not uncommon to find demos available that you and your child can download and try before you buy. Most sites are pretty good about explaining how to get started, what you need regarding system requirements, how to download the software, and how to play the game. Figure 10.6 shows some instructions for playing Ants! on Microsoft's Gaming Zone site (www.zone.com).

Vendors that make game software, such as Westwood Studios and NovaLogic, also offer online gaming sites on the Internet. Mind you, users must use the software manufactured by the company to play.

Figure 10.6

Your kids might enjoy manipulating an ant colony in the Ants! game online. The ants are pretty cute, too.

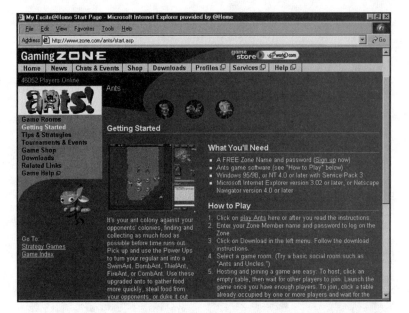

Dealing with IPX

When installing games for play online, IPX issues might arise. IPX stands for *Internet Packet Exchange*, a protocol that works like TCP/IP protocol that moves data around the Internet. IPX was created for local area networks, and game companies design their software to work with IPX protocols. With multiplayer games on the Internet, users might have to trick their software into thinking it's only using a local network and not the global network that is the Internet. This usually requires running another program that works around the problem. Be sure to check out the requirements for the online game that your child wants to play.

Fortunately, this problem occurs less and less frequently as time passes. Just about any new game will run over the Internet without requiring IPX. There's also a popular piece of software you can use to play an IPX game over the Internet. It's called Kali, and you can get it from `www.kali.net`.

Email Games

Another type of online game is email games (see Figure 10.7). In these games, users' email moves back and forth via messages. This is a popular playing method for strategy games such as chess and checkers, war strategy games, card games, trivia games, and more. For example, the Email Games site (www.emailgames.com) sponsored by Hasbro (the toy and game maker), features email games such as Battleship and Scrabble. Let's say your child wants to play Battleship with his cousin in Scranton, New Jersey. Purchase and download the Battleship software, open the game, make a move, then email the move to the other player. The other player, using the installed client software, makes a move and emails it back.

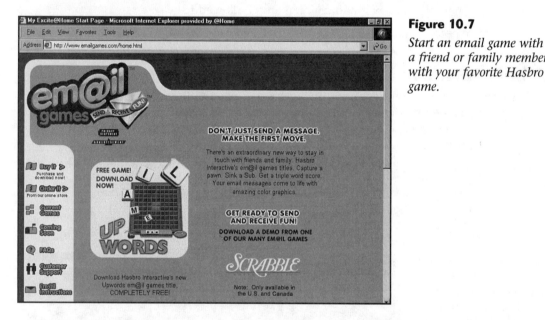

Figure 10.7

Start an email game with a friend or family member with your favorite Hasbro game.

Of course, you don't really need a sponsored site to carry on an email game. If both players have real game boards, they can email moves back and forth and keep track of the moves on their boards. Ah, but it's a bit more exciting to do this when computer software is involved instead.

Your child might enjoy playing a strategy game via email, such as chess. There are also a number of sophisticated strategy and conquest games, such as VGA Planets, designed around the play-by-email concept. You can conduct a search of the words "email games" to find links to numerous game sites that support this type of online gaming.

Gambling Online?

It's true, some of the adult-oriented games online focus on gambling games, including casino games, card games, cyberbingo, and dice games. Not all gambling games use money—some are just for fun. However, as a parent, you need to be aware that gambling games exist and children aren't allowed to play.

What Dangers Exist?

Anything online involves interacting with other people. That's one dangerous aspect of online games, particularly in games that also feature chat. Depending on the game and the players logged on, unsuitable language might be exchanged between the players. Sure, some of it's along the lines of, "I'm going to kick your butt" and so forth, but it can also get a bit obscene at times. Parents should always check out a game site or supervise online sessions to determine whether the site is worth visiting again. Although most sites have rules of conduct and render judgments when conduct is broken (such as revoking a player's account), others might not moderate the games or chat rooms. Mild flaming and taunting is often tolerated.

Figure 10.8

This trivia game lets users play and chat at the same time. It takes some coordination skills. Notice the flaming going on in the chat area.

Chat area

As with any aspect of the Internet, caution your child about exchanging personal information with other users. It can never be said enough: Don't give out your phone number or address to anyone you meet online. Teach your children this.

Whatever you do, don't give up supervising just because you don't understand what's going on in the game. Ask your child to explain how the game works, and allow him or her to teach you. (Chances are, he'd enjoy seeing you lose a game of Nascar racing anyway.) You should also make sure older kids realize that younger children are online in gaming areas, too, so don't let your own kids contribute vulgar language or actions.

If something occurs in a game that makes your child uncomfortable, assure him that he can always talk to you about the problem. Remember that kids will be kids when playing games. Sometimes fragile egos are involved; things are said between two players and feelings get out of whack. On the other hand, by now you shouldn't be surprised to learn that the Internet is a haven for bizarre characters and they like to play games, too. Some of these stranger netizens say and do scary things while playing online.

Violence is an area of online gaming that can be dangerous to children. Numerous studies have been conducted on the effects of violent video games, TV shows, and movies on children. Many of the most popular online games are quite violent. You and your child should discuss such matters and approach with caution. Constant exposure to violent acts, even in the arena of a computer game, can desensitize users to real violence offline.

Game addiction is another danger. Some people, including children, have a tendency to obsess over things such as games. Online addiction is a growing problem in our culture. Obsessed users feel compelled to be online, compulsive in the need to be playing and seeing what's going on. If your child shows such tendencies, you might need to step in.

Watch out for expenses, yet another gaming danger. Some sites charge by the hour to play games. Take time to understand the pricing method used by a site. There's nothing worse than getting an outrageous bill for something you didn't know was going on in your house.

Despite the negative sides of online gaming, there are quite a few positive aspects. There's a real sense of community among online gamers; most are very helpful to newer users and conduct themselves politely. Plus, there's always someone ready to play a game somewhere on the Internet. Besides, if online gaming doesn't work out, there's always the option of playing alone offline.

Where Can I Find Good Games for Kids?

Finding games is as easy as conducting a search or asking around. Lots of computer magazines feature game articles and recommendations (not to mention all the game advertisers found among the pages). Finding good games really depends on what's appropriate for your child. What games does your child prefer? What games would you prefer for him/her? You may need to sit down with your children and try a few to see what they like and what you like.

Check game reviews online and in magazines. Sites like FamilyPC (`www.familypc.com`), Gamespot (`www.gamespot.com`) or ZDNet (`www.zdnet.com`) can offer suggestions. You can also find game reviews of the more popular online games at the following Web sites:

Cybergames   `http://www.dvd-spin.com/cg/index.html`

Electric Games   `www.electricgames.com`

Gamezilla   `www.gamezilla.com` (see Figure 10.9)

GrrlGamer   `www.grrlgamer.com` (devoted especially to female gamers)

Internet Games   `internetgames.miningco.com`

Computer Games Online   `www.cdmag.com`

Your child will probably be influenced by what games the other kids are playing. Find out if the games your child's friends play are right for your child. Investigation is the key to finding good games.

Figure 10.9

Sites that review games, such as Gamezilla, can give you some idea as to what a game is about.

Perusing Games

To get you and your child started on the road to finding games, we've compiled a list of several popular game areas on the Internet (see Table 10.1). Visit these sites; use them to see what's available and what might be appropriate for your child. Many of these are geared toward older children, teens, and adults. Test a few games, download some demos, and get a feel for the site's sense of community and the attitude of the players. Some of these sites charge a fee when you do decide to join, others require that you purchase the retail software before joining.

More Sites

Check out Chapter 20, "Kid-Friendly Places on the Internet," for more sites that offer games for kids of all ages. The sites listed in Chapter 20 are all free. You might also like to check out *The Complete Idiot's Guide to Playing Games Online.*

Table 10.1   Popular Game Sites

Site	Web Address
Microsoft's Gaming Zone	www.zone.com
TEN (The Entertainment Network)	www.ten.net
World Opponent Network	www.won.net
GameStorm	www.gamestorm.com
Heat.net	www.heat.net
Mplayer.com	www.mplayer.com
Kali	www.kali.net
Kahn	http://kahn.descent4.org/
2am Club	www.2am.com
Gameshows.com	www.gameshows.com
Igames	www.igames.com
iMagic Online	www.imagiconline.com
Uproar	www.uproar.com
Playsite	www.playsite.com
Passport2	www.passport2.com
The Arena	www.thearena.com
Yahoo! Games	www.yahoo.com
Yahooligans!	games.yahoo.com/games/
(Kids section)	yahooligans.html
Multiplayer Matchup	www.ea.com
Game TV	www.gametv.com

Don't forget to check some of the more popular search engines. Many are starting to offer their own kid areas for safe searching as well as safe gaming. Figure 10.10 shows a list of games available on the Yahooligans! site for kids.

Figure 10.10

The games at Yahooligans! are safe for kids of all ages.

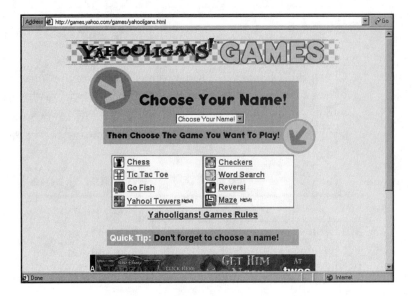

How's It Rated?

The software industry is trying to create a rating system to help parents determine whether a game is appropriate for their child. The next time you're out shopping for a commercial game, check the box for an ESRB code. Ratings include Early Childhood, Kids to Adults, Teen, Mature, and Adults Only. The code usually describes what, if anything, might make the game objectionable, such as extreme violence or sexual situations. You can check the ratings of popular commercial games at www.esrb.org.

For links to games around the Internet, try these Web pages:

Multiplayer.com www.multiplayer.com

Online Gaming Library www.oglibrary.com (see Figure 10.11)

Video Game Links   www.videogamelinks.com/networks/ign.shtml

Gamesmania www.gamesmania.com

Figure 10.11

Lots of sites on the Web list links to other gaming sites, as shown here at the Online Gaming Library Web site.

Online Service Games

If you and your family use a commercial online service such as AOL or CompuServe, you can locate plenty of games within the walls of the service without ever wandering out onto the Internet. Always start by checking out what's in the kids' areas of the service, as shown in Figure 10.12. There are usually enough games in the kids' area to keep your child busy for quite some time.

Check This Out

How Much Does It Cost?

Watch out for games that charge fees. Make sure you understand how the game pricing works before allowing your child to play. Some of the fee-based games let players try them free, but when the free-time is over, charges start racking up.

145

Figure 10.12

AOL's kids' area has lots of games to try, as shown in the list box on the left.

The AOL kids' area also features links to other popular kids' games on the Internet, such as MaMaMedia.com (www.mamamedia.com).

The table below lists some other free game areas older kids and teens can check out on AOL.

Game Area	Keyword
Strike a Match (word game)	STRIKE A MATCH (see Figure 10.13)
Slingo (combination bingo/slot machine)	SLINGO
Antagonist Online (role-play, strategy)	ANT
Amazing Trivia (live trivia games)	AMAZING
Gut Instinct (trivia)	GUT INSTINCT
NTN Trivia (trivia)	NTN
Free-Form Gaming (role-play)	FFGF
Puzzle Zone (word games)	PUZZLE
RabbitJack's Casino (bingo, card games)	RJCASINO

Figure 10.13

AOL's Strike A Match game lets players converse while playing the game.

Conversation area—

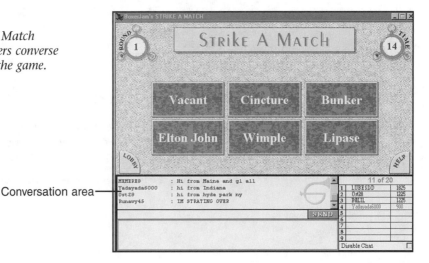

The Least You Need to Know

There's a game on the Internet for every man, woman, and child; for every personality type; and for every type of challenge. The trick is finding games appropriate for your child. You are not without resources, however, as gaming on the Internet is a thriving activity and there are plenty of games to investigate. Here's some last minute advice:

➤ Help your child to make good choices when selecting online games to play. The safest games are those your child plays by himself, but if he insists on trying out online games, offer your supervision and assistance to get him started.

➤ Remind children to never give out personal information to anyone they meet in a game's chat area.

➤ Teach kids how to conduct themselves while playing with other users.

➤ Some of the more popular games your child will want to play are going to cost money, either in subscription to the game service or by purchase of the game software required.

➤ Expect to encounter technical problems with online games from time to time. A game server's slowness (called *latency* or *lag*) depends on the number of players online or the slowness of the signal between the PC and the server.

➤ Avid gamers in your household should be made to take a break and get some fresh air on occasion.

Chapter 11

Other Ugly Stuff

In This Chapter

➤ Find out about hate groups on the Internet

➤ A look at the availability of drugs, alcohol, and tobacco online

➤ Learn how easy it is to access information that can lead to disaster

Let's see now—we've covered the dangers of chat, email, pornography, marketing, newsgroups, and online games. What could possibly be left? What other electronic dangers lurk out there ready to pounce on your children? Hmmm, perhaps a few you haven't thought about. How about hatred and bigotry? Pictures of mutilated corpses? Or drugs and alcohol? You might be surprised to know such things exist on the Internet. Cyberspace is populated with resourceful people who use it to advertise an agenda as well as a product. In this chapter, we take a look at some of the more subtle, but ugly, dangers your children might encounter while online.

Hatred and Bigotry for All

In case you haven't noticed, there is a lot of ugliness in the world, and most of it is brought on by fellow humans. Some of the ugliest can be found in the bizarre ideas people clasp onto, whether it is to justify their behavior or their warped thinking. We could spend several volumes discussing the philosophical and psychological possibilities of why some people insist on hating other people for no good reason, but I'd rather not. It would just depress us all. You do, however, need to be warned about the circulation of hatred and bigotry on the Internet. You also need to prepare your children for when they encounter such ideas.

The Internet is the ultimate in blindness when it comes to gender, age, skin color, nationality, or other physical qualities. That's because you can't see the people you meet online (unless you've both got one of those nifty video conferencing/camera devices, but let's not talk about those). You have no way of knowing whether the person to whom you're responding in a newsgroup is male or female. You don't know whether the person you're talking to in a chat room is white, black, purple, or green. (Yes, there have been reports of extraterrestrials on the Internet, so watch out.) You have no idea whether the person who hosts your favorite Web site is 15 or 50. Oh sure, you could ask. But who knows if the owner of the site will answer truthfully? The point is, you just don't know.

That's the real splendor of the Internet—it truly is a global community. Certain attributes that might bog us down offline are not to be found online. Here again, the anonymity factor comes into play, just as it does with issues of cybercrime. The anonymity that occurs when people connect to the Internet is practically complete—others can't see them. That's why people often go nuts and say things they wouldn't ordinarily say in person. People can pretend to be anybody on the Internet. There are no boundaries even between countries on the Internet. With all this global blending you would think there's no hatred or bigotry on the Net, right? Ha!

Unfortunately, hatred and bigotry have no boundaries either, and both are alive and kicking on the Internet. Why's that? It's the appeal of the global audience; it's the need to reach out and spread the agenda, as well as find others with the same agenda. The same freedom that enables us to be anything on the Internet also enables people to say and propagate some pretty ugly thoughts and opinions.

According to the Southern Poverty Law Center (an organization that tracks hate groups), there was a 20 percent increase in the number of hate groups in 1998, largely due to the Internet. At the time of the study, there were 474 hate groups around the country, many of which were related to the Ku Klux Klan. The study didn't include revisionist groups (those that deny the Holocaust).

The Internet has made it easier and more cost efficient for hate groups to publish their beliefs, and it gives members a larger sense of community. Like pedophiles who flock to the Web for justification of their practices, members of hate groups also find justification among others on the Internet.

On the plus side, the Internet has also shown an increase in the number of organizations speaking out against hatred and bigotry.

Check This Out

See It for Yourself

Visit the HateWatch Web site (www.hatewatch.org) and see for yourself the various types of hate groups out there on the Internet.

It's About to Get Ugly

Hate groups and other bigoted groups have found space on the Internet to shout their claims to anyone who might stop by and listen. This is especially true on the Web. Granted, much of what you find on these sites is pretty wacko (and full of typos and grammatical errors), but some do appear polished and professional. To better explain what's out there, it might be easier to just show you.

The first stop is the official Web site of the Ku Klux Klan, courtesy of the framework of `hatewatch.org`. Check out Figure 11.1.

Figure 11.1

This looks like a nice site. Patriotic music even plays in the background.

This site looks innocent enough, but when you start poking around the site, you run into stuff like what you see in Figure 11.2.

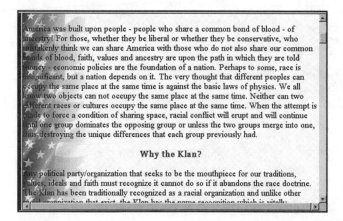

Figure 11.2

Check out the claims in this site's text!

According to the text in Figure 11.2, two or more races sharing the same space at the same time is against the laws of physics. In exactly which physics course was this covered? Apparently, I missed this class; perhaps you did too. The organization's true message here is buried in its Web site. After reading the various pages found on this site, it doesn't take a rocket scientist (or a physicist) to see some obvious biases and prejudices. Unfortunately, some readers may not be able to detect the biases and prejudices displayed at this site, particularly children.

How is this site different from any other group with an agenda? It depends on the agenda, doesn't it? A Web site devoted to promoting a certain brand of vitamin, for example, has an agenda to sell the product to the masses. The site might tout the vitamin as possessing unique qualities and ingredients for endowing the user with superhuman energy (as if your kid doesn't have enough of that already). Unlike hate sites, however, the agenda to sell vitamins or promote a company doesn't involve excluding or hurting anyone else (unless there's some really bad ingredient in the vitamin). The point here is to teach your children how to recognize and reason-through prejudices they encounter. You don't want them buying into a certain vitamin with purported powers anymore than you want them adapting a philosophy that ultimately results in hatred.

America doesn't have a monopoly on hate groups. There are hate groups all over the world, as you can see in Figure 11.3. This is an example of a site in Australia. Notice the list on the left of other countries with hate group Web sites. You can find a site speaking out against every type of religion, gender, social issue, or belief.

Figure 11.3

HateWatch tracks hate sites all over the world.

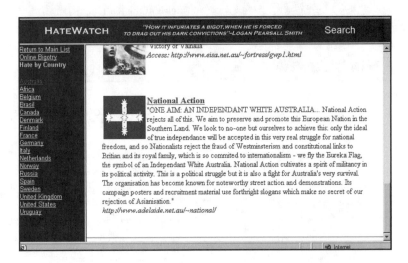

Hate groups also are alive and well on Usenet (newsgroups). Newsgroups such as `alt.skinheads` (see Figure 11.4), `alt.flame.jews`, `alt.revisionism`, and `alt.politics.nationalism.black`, are forums in which people say all kinds of things concerning the group's focus (typically some form of hatred or bigotry), share links to hate sites, share pictures depicting their hatred, and so on.

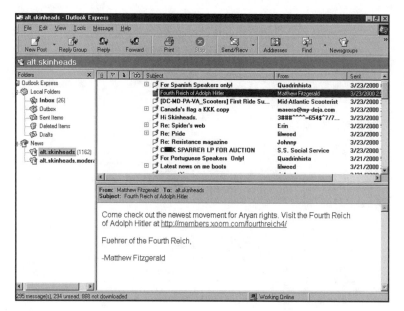

Cults, Too

In case you were wondering, cults are alive and flourishing on the Internet too. Without doubt you heard about the Heaven's Gate cult and the members' mass suicide in 1997. Its Web site offered many clues concerning the mass suicide by some of its cult members. Yep, there's yet another online danger to watch out for!

Hate groups are also targeting new members on the Web, and that means youth and kids. After all, you've got to recruit children or your hate group will die out, and you wouldn't want that to happen, now would you? Take a look at the World Church of the Creator (WCOTC), a known hate group that advocates racial separatism, shown in Figure 11.5. Their Web site sponsors a kids' creativity site that features games and puzzles. If you look closely at the crossword puzzle in Figure 11.6, it focuses on the WCOTC agenda. What a great tool for teaching the kids! (Yes, you did detect some sarcasm in that last sentence.)

Figure 11.5

This kids' site looks innocent enough....

Figure 11.6

Hey kids, have fun while learning about endorsing and practicing racism. Yee-hee!

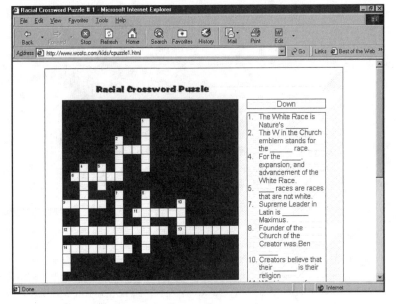

It's easy to find these hate sites by using search engines or links found in newsgroups and other online venues.

What You Can Do About It

Many of the filtering programs can help block access to hate sites (see Chapter 13, "All About Filters," for more information) such as those described in this chapter. You can never rely on filtering software to catch everything, though.

The practical thing to do is sit down and talk to your child about your values, the prejudices of others, and how to deal with such things when they are encountered on the Internet. If that doesn't work, why don't you make a crossword puzzle that teaches your children about tolerance?

Seriously, the Internet is a global community, so your children will encounter people from all walks of life. They will also encounter all kinds of ideas online, from the bizarre to the brilliant. It's up to you to instruct your kids on how to discern hatred and bigotry. A filtering program can't help you battle such things, but your influence can. The reality is that hate sites will never disappear from the Internet. But the example you set for your kids is the most powerful protection you can provide.

Yes, You Can Find Drugs, Alcohol, and Tobacco on the Internet

Do you know you can buy drugs, alcohol, and tobacco online? There's a market for every kind of vice on the Internet. Plus, there are plenty of sites that promote all of these products. Why tell you about them? Because your children are the future market for such products, so naturally such sites are appealing to them.

Let's start with drugs. Take a gander at Figure 11.7. It shows the search results for the word "drugs" on a typical search engine. Notice that there's even a link for a site that can help you pass a drug test. That'll come in handy for your kid's first job.

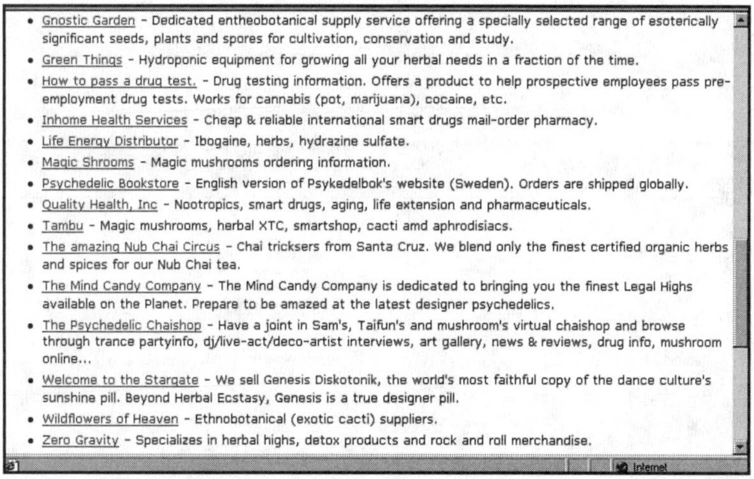

- Gnostic Garden – Dedicated entheobotanical supply service offering a specially selected range of esoterically significant seeds, plants and spores for cultivation, conservation and study.
- Green Things – Hydroponic equipment for growing all your herbal needs in a fraction of the time.
- How to pass a drug test. – Drug testing information. Offers a product to help prospective employees pass pre-employment drug tests. Works for cannabis (pot, marijuana), cocaine, etc.
- Inhome Health Services – Cheap & reliable international smart drugs mail-order pharmacy.
- Life Energy Distributor – Ibogaine, herbs, hydrazine sulfate.
- Magic Shrooms – Magic mushrooms ordering information.
- Psychedelic Bookstore – English version of Psykedelbok's website (Sweden). Orders are shipped globally.
- Quality Health, Inc – Nootropics, smart drugs, aging, life extension and pharmaceuticals.
- Tambu – Magic mushrooms, herbal XTC, smartshop, cacti amd aphrodisiacs.
- The amazing Nub Chai Circus – Chai tricksers from Santa Cruz. We blend only the finest certified organic herbs and spices for our Nub Chai tea.
- The Mind Candy Company – The Mind Candy Company is dedicated to bringing you the finest Legal Highs available on the Planet. Prepare to be amazed at the latest designer psychedelics.
- The Psychedelic Chaishop – Have a joint in Sam's, Taifun's and mushroom's virtual chaishop and browse through trance partyinfo, dj/live-act/deco-artist interviews, art gallery, news & reviews, drug info, mushroom online...
- Welcome to the Stargate – We sell Genesis Diskotonik, the world's most faithful copy of the dance culture's sunshine pill. Beyond Herbal Ecstasy, Genesis is a true designer pill.
- Wildflowers of Heaven – Ethnobotanical (exotic cacti) suppliers.
- Zero Gravity – Specializes in herbal highs, detox products and rock and roll merchandise.

Figure 11.7

Drugs are available on the Internet if you know where to look.

Alcohol is heavily promoted on the Web as well. Figure 11.8 shows a site that lets you send a "free drink" (actually just a photo) to someone on the Internet. That's not so bad, really. There are all kinds of sites that let you send email visuals to other Netizens (such as sending a taco from the Taco Bell site). Among the Internet's many shopping venues are sites where you can purchase alcohol with a credit card and have it shipped to your address, as shown in Figure 11.9.

Figure 11.8

Hey kids, send your friends "free drinks" on the Internet!

Figure 11.9

Anybody with a credit card can buy alcohol online.

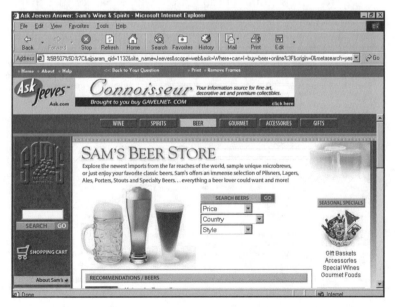

You can also buy tobacco online. With the rise in cigarette prices due to taxes, we'll probably see more sites like the one shown in Figure 11.10.

An alarming trend has popped up recently among teens, the smoking of *bidis* (or beedies). Bidis are trendy little sweet-smelling cigarettes made in India of shredded tobacco hand-rolled in herbal leaves, called *tendu*. Cheaply priced ($2 for 20), bidis are affordable to teenagers.

The bidis trend started on the West Coast and has spread rapidly over the past year. They are very addictive and pose greater risks for cigarette-related cancers. Called the "poor man's cigarette" in India, bidis come in different-

Darn Those Pornography Sites!

I did a search on the word "beer" with Lycos, clicked a search result link advertising free beer only to end up at a porn site in Amsterdam. Consider yourself warned.

ent flavors and are available in stores in the United States. Sadly, bidis are often manufactured in India by children who have been bonded to moneylenders and forced to work in bidis factories. Ironic, eh—manufactured by children there and smoked by children here.

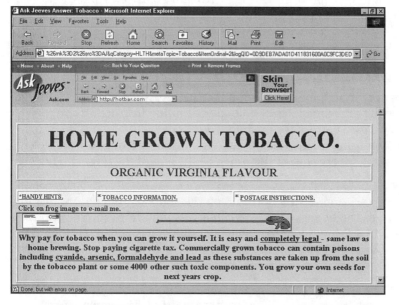

Figure 11.10

This site offers you a kit to grow your own tobacco.

Many experts say smoking bidis is a gateway to smoking other cigarettes and drugs. Bidis Web sites (see Figure 11.11) say the products contain no tobacco. Many teens have been duped into thinking bidis are safer than real cigarettes. Sadly, they are worse, having 3 to 7 times as much nicotine and carbon monoxide and 5 times as much tar. Users must also puff about 28 times more than on regular cigarettes just to keep the product lit.

Figure 11.11

Bidis are advertised on the Internet.

The only way to protect your child from online dangers such as drugs, alcohol, and tobacco is to sit down and talk about these things. Explain your views and the health risks, and discuss the problems of peer pressure. There's plenty of information on the Internet to back up your views, particularly on the health front.

Dangerous Information at Your Fingertips

You can find information about anything on the Internet—including recipes for disaster. You've probably heard several tales of youngsters finding instructions on the Internet for making bombs. There's a well-publicized case of two 13-year-old boys who built a smoke bomb using instructions they found online via one boy's home computer (under no adult supervision at the time). Sadly, one of the boys was burned very, very badly.

Of course, you can find the same instructions in your local library, but who wants to drive all the way down to the library when you can access it all from the comfort of your home PC? Figure 11.12 shows you the table of contents from the infamous *The Big Book of Mischief*. This online book teaches readers how to create and set off bombs. Not exactly the kind of information you want your rebellious child to find, is it?

Such explicit instructions are easy to find on the Net. Just type the word "bomb" into a search engine and see what you get. Making bombs isn't the only dangerous info you might find online. There are dozens of sites that teach users how to hack computers, read other people's email, and set things on fire. (Figures 11.13 and 11.14 show what I mean.)

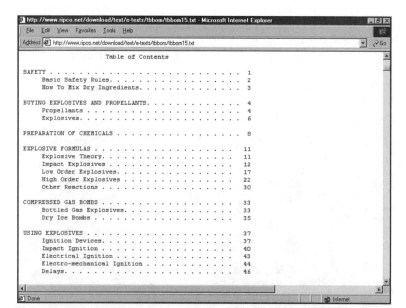

Figure 11.12

Believe it or not, you can find instructions for building your own bomb on the Internet.

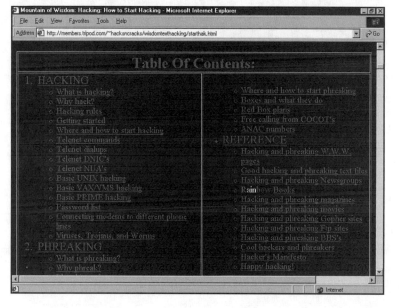

Figure 11.13

You can even find hacking instructions for beginners. What a nice hobby for the entire family!

The Internet is home to many frustrated anarchists, and if you know where to look, you can find all kinds of instructions for creating all kinds of dangerous things and making all manner of mayhem. The same goes for your child. Filtering software can help block some of it, but it can't block all of it. Be sure to check out Chapter 13, "All About Filters," to learn the pros and cons of filtering software. Truth is, even if you install filtering software on the home PC, your child may still have access to the dangers described in this chapter via an Internet-connected computer at school or at a friend's house. So the best way to combat these online dangers is to educate your children and be involved with their Internet access. Give your children the knowledge and values they need to stand up to peer pressure and stay out of trouble.

Figure 11.14

None of these links worked, but the Web page sure looked anarchistic.

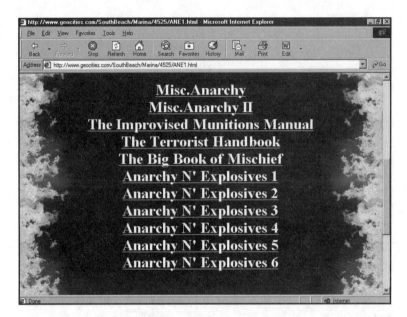

The Least You Need to Know

Your child is bound to run into some ugly stuff on the Internet from time to time. Prepare him or her to handle such material and to make the right decisions regarding the more subtle aspects of online dangers.

➤ Hate groups are proliferating on the Internet, and many of them are targeting younger people.

➤ Thankfully, for every hate group, there's another organization that tracks the hate group's agenda.

➤ Make sure your child is ready to handle online marketing for vices such as drugs, alcohol, and tobacco.

➤ Just because you read it on the Internet doesn't make it true. Much of the information you see on noncommercial sites is on the same level as the National Enquirer.

➤ Yes, you and your kids can find tips for making bombs online, but many of the instructions are inaccurate.

Part 3
Preparing Your Computer

Now it's time to get down to the nitty-gritty. It's time to start taking steps to make sure your kids are safe and secure whenever they go online.

In this section of the book, we show you all the ways to keep your kids safe online. We teach you how to do things like make sure your kids haven't mucked around in your computer's innards, letting hackers in to have a field day. We show you how to protect your computer against viruses, and to make sure that your kids don't get into trouble downloading files. We give you the inside scoop on how to make sure your kids are safe whenever they search the Web. We tell you everything you need to know about filters—software that can protect your kids against pornography, hate sites, and more. And we show you how to keep your kids safe whenever they go onto America Online.

After you're done with this section, you'll see all the ways that you can prepare your computer so you needn't worry about how safe your kids are when they head online, and you needn't worry what they'll find when they get there.

Making Your Computer Safe

One of your first lines of Internet defense as a parent is to make sure you know how to set up and use your kids' (or your) computer so they are safe and secure online. I know, this sounds scary—after all, you're a parent, not a computer geek. How will you know what to do?

In fact, as I show you in this chapter, it's pretty easy to do. I teach you how to handle what are called Web "cookies" that are placed in your kids' computer. (No, they're not Oreos, as much as your kids wish they were.) I show you how to use browsers so that no one can snoop on your kids or steal their email addresses. And I talk about things like "personal firewalls" and how to watch out for dangers posed by cable modems. So don't worry if you're not a computer geek. In this chapter you get enough information to be able to set up a computer so it's safe for your kids.

Are Cookies Really Sweet?

What's your kids' favorite cookies? Oreos? Double chocolate chip? 'Nilla Wafers? Or maybe all of the above?

Well, a cookie in the kitchen is one thing; when it comes to the Web, a cookie might not be so sweet. In fact, these kinds of cookies leave a bad taste in some people's mouths. Cookies are little bits of information that Web sites put on your computer's hard disk when you visit them. They use those cookies to track what you or your kids do on the site, and also offer extra services, such as customized Web pages. Cookies are also used to deliver ads pitched to you or your kids' interests.

If you don't like the idea of Web sites putting cookies (or anything at all) on your kids' hard disk, there's something you can do about it—and I'll show you how. Even if cookies don't bother you, read on; this way you learn everything there is to know about cookies, except for perhaps how to bake the macadamia chocolate chip ones.

Just What Are Web Cookies?

Few people know this, but when you or your kids visit many Web sites, these sites put information on your hard disk that you don't know about. Those bits of information are cookies.

Each cookie a site leaves on your hard disk is a very small text file that looks like it's made up of meaningless garble—kind of like your kids' homework on a night when they're rushing through it.

Cookies have become ubiquitous on the Web. Just about every Web site you visit uses them, and many Web sites use more than one. If you were to look at your hard disk to see them all, you'd be amazed at just how many there are. Figure 12.1 shows some of the cookies from sites I've visited. Busy, busy, busy!

Figure 12.1

Here's a list of just some of the cookies on a hard disk—all put there by Web sites.

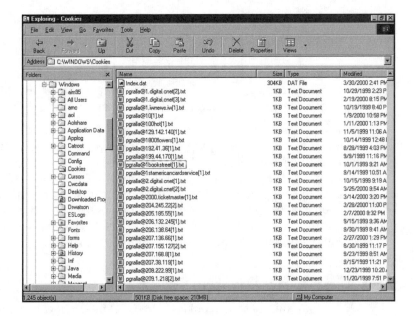

Why Are Web Sites Serving Cookies?

So why should Web sites serve up cookies like this? Because it gives them an easy way to track what you or your kids do when you visit their site. It uniquely identifies you, so the Web server knows what you're doing whenever you visit. So from visit to visit, it can easily build a profile about you. That profile is worth a lot of money to Web sites, because after they have it they can sell advertising targeted at people's specific interests. Do your kids spend a lot of time on a site looking at the sports scores for a particular team or listening to a certain kind of music? Web sites would like to know, so they can sell advertising targeted at your kids.

What Ingredients Are in Cookies?

Cookies are data files placed on your hard disk. Each cookie is made up of two elements—the cookie's "name" and the "value." The value is the actual data in the cookie itself, and each Web site can put all kinds of different data into the "value." There will often be an expiration date (the date the cookie expires—kind of like a "sell by" date on real cookies); the domain (the address of the server that delivered the cookie to you); and often things such as usernames and passwords. Often, much of the data is scrambled, so that only the Web server can understand it, not you.

At one time, only the Web site that placed a cookie on your hard disk could read that cookie. So when your kids went to the Nickelodeon Web site, the Yahooligans site couldn't read the information on that cookie. The idea was that doing things that way would preserve a little bit of privacy, because if every Web site could read everything your kids ever did on the Internet, the amount of information available about them would be mind-boggling.

These days, though, the Internet advertising agency DoubleClick.com has built up a network of Internet sites that in essence can read each other's cookie information. All that information is combined, and profiles are put together about everyone who reads DoubleClick ads.

This doesn't bother some people, because they figure that the information isn't dangerous. But it does make some people uncomfortable, especially when information like this is gathered about kids. After all, kids are amazingly susceptible to advertising pitches. (If you don't think this is the case, think of how many times a week you hear your kids singing commercial jingles, or watch their behavior in a grocery store near the cereal aisle.) So you might not want an advertising giant like DoubleClick gathering all this information about your kids in order to allow advertisers to pitch them double-fudge brownie morning cereal. (As Ralph Nader used to say, the cardboard box is more nutritious than what's inside it.)

Here's a great, little-known fact: You can stop DoubleClick dead in its tracks. All you have to do is what's called "opt-out" of DoubleClick on your kids' (and your own) computer. When you opt out, DoubleClick stops putting cookies on that computer, and it isn't able to build a profile about your kids or you.

Opting out is easy. Go to a special area of the DoubleClick site at http://www.doubleclick.com:8080/privacy_policy/privacy.htm. Read about cookies and the opt-out policy. Click **Opt Out Click Here**. That's all there is to it. When you do that, you'll see a screen like the one in Figure 12.2.

Figure 12.2

Much sweeter than cookies: This message tells you that you've opted out of the DoubleClick advertising network.

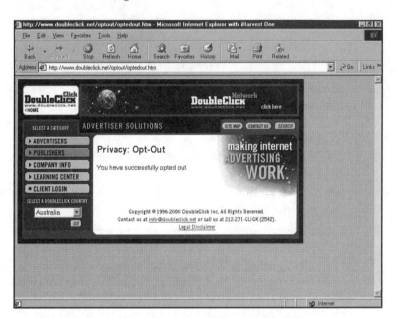

Where Are Cookies Stored? (Hint—It's Not in Your Cupboard)

When a Web server puts a cookie on a computer, it puts it into a specific location on the hard disk. Where that cookie is put depends on whether you use Microsoft Internet Explorer or Netscape Navigator, and even on what version of those browsers you use. (Thanks again, technology companies, for making all our lives so much easier. Do you think maybe these folks had a hand in designing the tax code?)

166

Microsoft Internet Explorer and Netscape Navigator each handle cookies a bit differently. Here's what you need to know about each.

Where Microsoft Internet Explorer Stores Its Cookies

If you're using Microsoft Internet Explorer, look in either the Windows\Cookies or Windows\Profiles*UserName*\Cookies directory, where *UserName* is your name. That's where you'll find cookies...and more cookies...and more cookies. If you spend much time on the Web, that folder will be chock full of the little goodies.

Check This Out

Cookies Can Also Be Sweet

By the way, I don't want to give the impression that cookies are the Great Satan. In fact, cookies can provide some very cool things for your kids on the Web. For example, they can log them automatically into Web sites so your kids don't have to remember their passwords. (And kids are notorious for losing passwords.) They can let your kids customize what they see on a Web page, or give them information they might be interested in without your kids having to ask for it.

Believe it or not, you can tell a good deal about a cookie just by looking in a directory that holds them. In Internet Explorer, each cookie is a separate text file and ends with the extension .txt. The cookie starts with your abbreviated name, is followed by the @ sign, and is then followed by the name of the Web site that put the cookie on your hard disk—and it ends in the extension .txt.

So, for example, if your abbreviated name was joejoe, and you visited www.homeruns.com, it would put a cookie on your hard disk with the name of joejoe@homeruns.txt. That means you can learn which Web sites have put cookies on your hard disk just by looking in the Cookies folder.

You can also see the date and time it was put there or modified. Just look at the date and time for the file in the directory—that's the last time the Web site touched the cookie.

Sometimes you can find out more about the cookie. For example, you might be able to see whether it's used to put in your name, password, and other information. Of course, usually, you find garbled and incomprehensible characters, but it can't hurt to take a look.

To look inside a cookie, double-click it. You see something that looks like Figure 12.3.

Figure 12.3

What ingredients are inside this cookie? Garble, as usual.

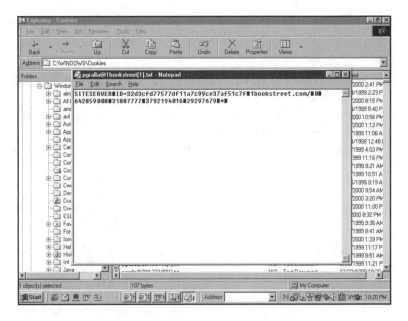

Sometimes you see English words in there that might give you a clue as to what the cookie is doing, and you might even see your username and password.

Where Netscape Navigator Stores Its Cookies

Netscape handles cookies differently from Internet Explorer. Instead of creating separate text files for each, it stores all your cookies in a single text file called—yes, what else—cookies.txt. (How surprisingly logical. That'll never happen again.) Look for the file in the folder, C:\Program Files\Netscape\Users*Username*, where *Username* is, of course, your username.

Check This Out

Some Cookies Can Reveal Your Kids' Web Passwords to Snoopers.

If you look through your kids' cookie files, you might be surprised to notice that some cookies list their usernames and passwords for Web sites. Usually cookies encrypt those usernames and passwords on cookies, but not all do. If it's not encrypted on the cookie, anyone with access to your kids' computer can open the cookie files and steal passwords. So if you're worried that someone other than your kids has access to your computer, delete the cookies that show usernames and passwords. See the section later in this chapter for information on how to kill cookies.

168

Figure 12.4 shows a typical `cookies.txt` file. You're able to see the name of the Web site that put the cookie on the hard disk, and the usual incomprehensible information along with the occasional English word. You don't see the date and time the cookie was put there, though.

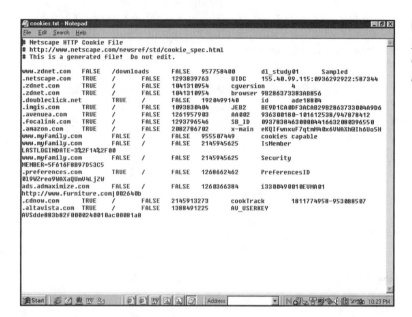

Figure 12.4

Here's how to look at cookies in the `cookies.txt` *file of Netscape Navigator.*

You Can Use Cookies to See Where Your Kids Surf

I hesitate to mention this because it can be abused, but you should realize that you can use cookies to see where your kids have been surfing. Remember earlier in the chapter that I mentioned the first part of a cookie was made up of the name of a site? If you're worried that your kids are visiting sites that you don't want them to, you can look at their cookies files, as previously explained. That way, you're able to know where they're surfing online. If you do this, though, be very careful, because the truth is, the best way for your kids to stay safe online is if they trust you and talk to you. And if they feel you've been snooping behind their back, they're less likely to trust you.

How You Can Make Cookies Crumble

You don't have to allow Web sites to put cookies on your kids hard disk—after all, whose computer is it anyway? And you can also clean cookies off their hard disk. In fact, there's a good deal you can do to ensure your privacy and make cookies crumble.

How To Delete Cookies from Your Hard Disk

It's quite easy to delete cookies from your hard disk. You can do it yourself, but often a much better way is to use a "cookie-killer" program—a program that enables you to

169

delete and manage cookies. If you're worried at all about cookies, I strongly recommend that you get one of these programs. There are many out there. All-in-one family privacy, security, and filtering software, such as Norton Internet Security 2000 or McAfee Internet Guard Dog, include cookie-killer programs. There are also programs that are made to kill and manage cookies, such as CookiePal, available at www. kburra.com. I recommend Norton Internet Security 2000 or McAfee Internet Guard Dog, though, because they do a whole lot more than protect your kids' privacy and security. (I explain more about them later in the chapter.)

If you're not using a cookie-killer program, you can still delete cookies from your hard disk. In Microsoft Internet Explorer, go to the Windows\Cookies or Windows\ Profiles*UserName*\Cookies directory, where your cookies are stored. Then, to delete a cookie, simply delete it as you would any other file. That's it. It's over. The cookie is history. Delete as many or as few as you'd like.

Why Are Deleted Cookies Showing Up in My \Windows\Temporary Internet Files Directory?

If you've deleted Internet Explorer cookies, you might be surprised to see them in the directory that temporarily stores Internet files. Well, believe it or not, you see the cookies in that directory, but they don't really exist! Because of the peculiar way that Internet Explorer handles cookies, the names of those cookies show up, even though they've been deleted. Don't worry, the cookies are really gone. Web sites won't be able to use them, because they don't exist, even if it looks like they do. Very Zen–like and mystical, these cookies.

In Netscape Navigator, you aren't able to delete cookies one by one. Instead, you have to either delete every Netscape cookie or none at all. To delete all the cookies, go to \Program Files\Netscape\Users*Username*, and delete the cookies.txt file. There. All gone. To leave them, don't do a thing.

By the way, a word of warning here: Don't try to edit your cookies.txt file. Bad things could happen. Netscape didn't design the file to allow it to be edited.

How to Keep Cookies Off of Your Hard Disk

If you're a real hard-core cookie hater and don't want them on your kids' hard disk, you can stop them from being put there in the first place. To do so, you can use a program such as Norton Internet Security 2000 or McAfee Guard Dog, or you can customize Microsoft Internet Explorer and Netscape Navigator to do it.

To do this in Internet Explorer, click the **Tool** menu, and choose **Internet Options**. Then click the **Advanced** tab. Scroll down until you see the Cookies section. To stop all cookies from being put onto the hard disk, choose **Disable all cookie use**. When you do this, every cookie is automatically rejected. I don't suggest going this far— after all, many cookies have their uses. Instead, I recommend choosing the **Prompt Before Accepting Cookies** option. That way, before a cookie is put on your hard disk, you're asked first, so you have the option of whether to accept it.

To do this in Netscape Navigator, choose the **Edit** menu and then choose **Preferences**. Click **Advanced**. As in Internet Explorer, you're able to reject all cookies, or instead first be asked whether to reject individual cookies.

Does the "Content Adviser" in Your Browser Do Any Good?

Handling cookies is just one of the things you can do to make a computer safer for your kids. Another thing you can do is determine what kinds of content your kids can be allowed to see when they surf the Web. The safest way to do this is to use filtering software. (See Chapter 13, "All About Filters," for details on how to do that.)

But what if you don't have filtering software? Built into Microsoft Internet Explorer is something called the Content Adviser. In Netscape Navigator, it's called NetWatch. In theory, when you use this, you're able to block your kids from viewing Web pages with content you don't think is suitable for them.

I used the words "in theory" on purpose; in practice, this feature is somewhat problematic. When I turned it on to test it out, it in fact did block me from visiting pornographic Web sites. But it also blocked me from visiting almost every single other site on the Web, as well.

That's because it blocks access to sites without an RSACi rating. This is a rating that takes into account vulgarity, violence, nudity, and sexual content. Sounds good, yes? The only problem is this: The sites rate themselves. So you're trusting that the sites will police themselves, and in some cases that's like having the foxes guard the henhouse.

A bigger problem is that very few sites bother to use an RSACi rating. And if a site doesn't have that rating, it's blocked. That means much of the Internet is blocked when this feature is fully turned on in a browser.

Still, the companies say that one day this thing will work. Who knows? Maybe it will. If you're interested, here's how to use it:

In Internet Explorer, choose **Internet Options** from the **Tools** menu. Click **Content**. You see a screen like the one pictured in Figure 12.5.

Figure 12.5

Here's how you can control what kinds of Web pages your kids can see while they use Microsoft Internet Explorer.

To use it, click **Enable** in the **Content Adviser** area. To control the different settings, click **Settings**. The screen pictured in Figure 12.6 shows onscreen settings.

Figure 12.6

Use this screen to change the settings in the Content Adviser.

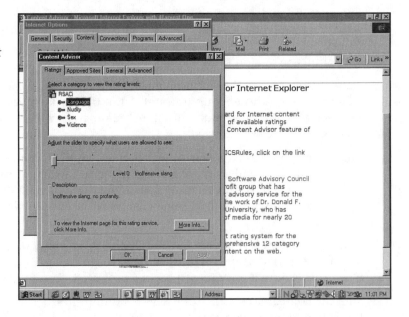

You're able to determine what kinds of content your kids can see based on offensive language, nudity, sex, and violence. There are five settings for each. For example, for language, you can allow them to view Web pages only with inoffensive slang and

172

nothing worse, or you can allow them to view Web pages with explicit or crude language. Simply move the sliders to the level of content that you're comfortable with to block offensive content

When you do this, you also set up a "supervisor password." Only someone with a supervisor password can change the settings and turn the Content Adviser on and off. If you use this feature, keep your password in a safe place.

To use this feature in Netscape Navigator, choose **NetWatch** from the **Help** menu. You're sent to a page on the Internet. Click **Click to set up NetWatch**. Then click **New User** and choose the settings and rating system you want to use, or both. Next, choose a NetWatch password. Keep it in a safe place, because you need it to change the settings. Then, turn it on, and it works just like the Internet Explorer version.

Using a "Personal Firewall"

One of the most effective ways to set up your computer so your kids are safe online is to use what's called a "personal firewall." A personal firewall protects your kids in many different ways. The best-known personal firewalls are Norton Internet Security 2000 and McAfee Internet Guard Dog. Although they have somewhat different features, here are the ways they protect your kids:

➤ **They block access to offensive Web pages.** They have filtering software built right in. For more information about filtering software, turn to Chapter 13, "All About Filters."

➤ **They stop hackers from getting inside your kids computer.** Hackers have all kinds of nefarious ways to worm their way into computers. Install one of these personal firewalls, and your kids and their computers are safe.

➤ **They stop your kids from sending out personal information.** You're able to set these firewalls so that if you kids try to send someone information you think shouldn't be sent, that information doesn't make it out of the computer.

➤ **They let you determine how long your kids can be on the computer.** You can set time limits and have the computer enforce them.

The good news about these programs is that you can try them free. Go to www.symantec.com for Norton Internet Security 2000 and www.mcafee.com for McAfee Internet Guard Dog. Search for products; there you can find free tryout software you can test for 30 days. Another good personal firewall is ZoneAlarm, available at www.zonealarm.com. You can also find tryout software at download sites such as www.zddownloads.com.

Evil TV? What About Cable Modems?

A great way to get onto the Internet is to use a cable modem. It offers very high-speed access, and it's on all the time—you don't have to dial in. As soon as you turn on your computer, you're connected.

Cable modems enable you to get onto the Internet at very high speeds. You get online using the same cable that comes into your home for cable TV—and you can browse the Internet and watch cable TV at the same time.

Techno Talk

A Cable Modem Isn't Really a Modem

When is a modem not a modem? When it's a cable modem. When you get onto the Internet via a cable modem, you're not really using modem technology. Instead, you install something called a *network card* into your computer, as well as a special device that is attached to the network card to let you browse the Internet using the same cable that comes into your house for cable TV.

But there are potential dangers with cable modems. Cable modems are different than regular modems; when you have a cable modem and you turn your computer on, it automatically connects to the Internet without you having to do anything, and you stay connected for as long as your computer is on. This means that your computer or your kids' computer can be connected for a dozen or more uninterrupted hours a day.

When a computer is connected like this at high speeds for many hours, it becomes a sitting target for hackers. Call your cable modem service and ask if they have any special security features you can turn on to stop hackers from getting at your kids' computer.

There's another potential problem. When you're using a cable modem, you're really part of a computer network, and the people in your neighborhood or town are part of that computer network. If your cable modem service is configured a certain way, and if your Windows 95 or Windows 98 computer has certain settings turned on, anyone in your town or neighborhood can see every single file on your computer—and can copy them to their own computer. This isn't a theoretical danger. I know someone who was able to look inside many people's computers connected by cable modem.

Luckily, there's a way to combat this problem. People can only look inside your computer if you have something called *file sharing* turned on. It's easy to see if you do—and it's easy to turn it off. To turn off file sharing, open Windows Explorer. Scroll down until you see an icon called Network Neighborhood. Right-click **Network Neighborhood** and choose **Properties**. Next, click **File and Printer Sharing**. You should see the dialog box shown in Figure 12.7. Make sure both boxes are unchecked. If they're unchecked, no one can look at the files on your computer.

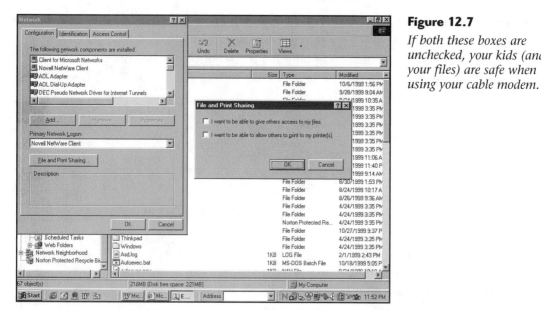

Figure 12.7

If both these boxes are unchecked, your kids (and your files) are safe when using your cable modem.

Your Kids' Browser Is a Snitch—What You Can Do About It

When your kids (or you) head onto the Web with their browser, they're announcing all kinds of personal information about themselves—things like email addresses, recent Web sites they've visited...and more. Here are just some of the things Web sites can find out:

➤ **Their user ID**   When you install Internet Explorer and Netscape Navigator for your kids, they get a user ID. Web sites can look inside the browser and find out what it is.

➤ **Their email address**   Yes, the browser can reveal that, as well.

➤ **Recent Internet sites they've visited**   It's easy for a Web site to find out which sites you've visited. Your browser keeps this kind of information in several places. It keeps it in the URL windows itself at the top of the browser; click on the drop-down arrow to the right, and you see the history of sites you've visited. And it keeps even more detailed information in a special area of your computer called a *browser cache*. That cache contains not only a record of where you've visited, but graphics, text, and other pieces of the Web pages themselves.

Luckily, there are things you can do to your computer to keep this kind of stuff secret. In the next sections I show you how.

175

Get Rid of a Cache Without Spending Any Cash

When your kids visit Web sites, entire Web pages and all their elements are kept in a special browser cache on their computer in a special directory. Potentially, a Web site could get its hands on this information and see where your kids have been surfing.

Where Is All That Cache Stored?

Exactly where cache files are kept depends on the browser and its version number. However, Internet Explorer usually puts them in the c:\Windows\Temporary Internet Files folder, and Netscape Navigator puts them in c:\Program Files\ Netscape\Users*username*\Cache, where *username* is the Netscape username.

Luckily, it's pretty easy to clean out browser caches. Both Internet Explorer and Netscape Navigator have ways to let you do that. In Internet Explorer, first choose **Internet Options** from the **Tools** menu. Then, in the section under Temporary Internet Files, click **Delete Files** (see Figure 12.8). That cleans out all the files in your Internet Explorer browser cache.

Figure 12.8

Cleaning house in the Internet Explorer cache.

Internet Explorer also has a neat feature that cleans out your browser's cache every time you shut down the program. That means you don't have to do it yourself—your browser does your housecleaning for you. To get there, choose **Internet Options**

from the **Tools** menu. Then click the **Advanced** tab. Scroll down until you see the Security section. Then check the box next to **Empty Temporary Internet Files when browser is closed**. Now, every time you close down your browser, your cache is cleaned with no muss and no fuss.

To clean out your Netscape Navigator 4.0 cache, choose **Preferences** from the **Edit** menu. Click the + sign next to Advanced, and choose **Cache**. Click **Clear Disk Cache**. That action deletes all the files from your browser cache. You can also click **Clear Memory Cache**. Doing so deletes all the files currently in your computer's memory. If you use a browser other than Navigator 4.0, the procedure might be slightly different.

The personal firewall products I mentioned earlier in this chapter automatically do all this for you, so if you have one of those programs, you don't need to worry about doing this.

How To Hide Your Kids' Email Addresses

When your kids surf the Web, your browser can reveal their email addresses to the world. It's not that hard for sites to find it out.

However, if you do a little bit of work, you can hide their email addresses—or you can even put in false email addresses if you like. You only need to change the browser settings or the settings in their email program.

In Netscape Navigator, it's a straightforward process. If you use Netscape 4.0 or above, choose **Preferences** from the **Edit** menu. Then click **Identity**. You should see three fields, for your child's name, email address, and organization. Delete the text from any of those that you wish to keep secret. (Write down the information somewhere, though, so you can put it back in if you wish.) Your children's email addresses and names are now hidden when they visit a Web page.

In Microsoft Internet Explorer, click the **Mail** button, and then choose **Read Mail**. Doing so launches the email program. You now have to delete their names and email addresses from the email program. Every program handles this differently, so check your manual on how to do it. In Outlook, first choose **Accounts** from the **Tools** menu. Then click **Mail**, and click your child's email account (or accounts). Click on **Properties**. Fields for your child's name, email address, and organization appear. Delete the text from any of those that you want to keep secret. (Write down the information somewhere, though, so you can put it back in if you wish.) Your children's email addresses and names are now hidden when they visit a Web page. Be aware that this makes it more difficult for your kids when they want to send email—they'll want to put all that information back in so people know who's sending the mail. Security and privacy have their price at times.

The Least You Need to Know

➤ Cookies are bits of data that Web sites put on computers so they can track what people do online.

➤ You can use your browser to delete cookies from your kids' hard disk.

➤ "Personal firewalls" protect your kids against many different kinds of online dangers.

➤ The Internet Explorer "Content Adviser" sounds like a useful feature, but it doesn't really work.

➤ You can use your browser to make sure people can't find out your kids' email addresses without them knowing about it.

Chapter 13

All About Filters

In This Chapter

➤ Find out about the content-filtering debate

➤ Different types of parental control software explained

➤ A look at how one popular filtering program works

➤ Lists of parental control software and kid browsers you can check into

Parental control software—What is it, and why use it? Quite simply, parental control software is a tool parents can use to help keep children safe online. There are actually several different kinds of filtering software, and in this chapter you find out what they are, where to find them, and how to put them to work on your computer. Let's jump right in, shall we?

To Filter or Not to Filter, That Is the Question

It seems as if everyone is in an uproar over Internet content. After working your way through some of the chapters in Part 2 of this book, you can certainly see why. Parents, child advocates, legislators, and law enforcement officials are demanding ways to keep children safe from unsuitable content and other online dangers.

One way of controlling the content children see on the Internet is to filter or block it. Filtering and blocking software is designed to keep "bad" sites off the computer while providing access to "good" sites. But who decides what's bad and what's good? And what if some of the good is blocked along with the bad? We get to that later in the chapter.

The controversy over filtering is particularly acute when it comes to Internet access at local and school libraries. Some folks believe in over-filtering, and others think libraries and schools don't need any filters at all. A big part of the problem is that efforts to block access to pornography can also block legitimate information, such as sexually transmitted disease prevention and maternity information. There are issues of free speech and the need to offer the widest range of information to the general public. A library must meet the needs of a diverse population. On the other hand, children are part of a community's diverse population, and no one in their right mind would want children to see harmful material on the Internet. So how do school and public libraries go about making everyone happy?

Libraries are adopting different methods for protecting kids online, depending on the community. Some use filtering software only in the kids' area of the library, and others use a combination of rules throughout the facility. Some libraries follow a "tap on the shoulder" policy. If a librarian sees someone using a computer and its Internet connection in an inappropriate way, he gently reminds the patron of the rules.

Other libraries follow the "anything goes" policy. There are numerous stories from librarians about patrons they've never seen before coming in and using the library's Internet terminal for hours on end to view pornography. In one such story, a man viewing porn even lured some little boys to come over and have a look. The librarians, because of their particular library's open Internet policy, did nothing to stop it. Let's all collectively shake our heads in bewilderment and shame. (And for cryin' out loud, where were the boys' parents?)

As a parent, you need to be aware of the policies that govern online use at your public and school libraries, and you need to realize that your kids will have different experiences using computers outside your own home. Some statistics state that more than 70 percent of Internet access by children occurs away from the home. Hopefully, this doesn't mean little Johnny is over at the neighbor's house downloading porn, but rather that he's using the Internet for educational purposes at school. Another study found that users are accessing pornography and obscene material through library and school computers hooked up to the Internet at a rate of 4 times a minute. Aha! And you thought little Johnny was in the school library researching 20th century inventions. Well, I guess you can call it that if you want.

The point is, find out what your school library or local library policies are, and if needed, get involved with helping them form good policies for the community and the children. One more thing—somebody needs to have a talk with little Johnny.

Controversies are raging over the filtering process itself. Some groups say the filtering is too severe and is blocking sites that shouldn't be blocked. Organizations such as the Electronic Privacy Information Center have performed their own tests (based on information they think children might want to look up online) on various filtering software and concluded that the software is blocking too much useful information. What falls under the category of "useful information" these days? And with the vastness of information available on the Internet, just how much information does a child really need to access anyway? The filtering debate will continue, but when it concerns your own child, you are the only true filter.

Is Filtering Censorship?

You filter when you shop for groceries or when you look for something to watch on TV. Filtering is merely being selective about what you bring into your home. There's nothing wrong with being selective when it comes to what your children are exposed to. The grocer is selective about what items are stocked in his store, and the librarian is selective about what books and magazines appear on her shelves. Filtering doesn't mean the rest of the items that weren't chosen aren't available elsewhere—they are. If you want to call filtering censorship, you can, but in this connotation (the safety of your children), it's not a bad thing.

Keep a Real Perspective

Thankfully, our focus in this book is on the home computer, not Internet access at the library. Nobody can really dictate how you control your own child's access on the old PC in the family room but you. Your decisions regarding whether to use filtering software depends on you and your children.

First and foremost, you need to realize the following:

➤ Parental control software is only a *tool* to help parents keep kids safe online.

➤ No software can ever fully protect your child. That duty still falls on your shoulders. Depending on your expectations, software can sometimes let you down (and make you crash, too).

➤ There's no way to rid the Internet of all its dangers; no software ever written can do that for us.

➤ Despite all your best intentions and safeguards, sooner or later (hopefully later) your children are likely to encounter something yucky online. It's up to you to prepare them for future yuckiness.

➤ The government will never be able to fully protect us from the evil that lurks online. Nope, it's all up to you.

Feeling a little pressure?

Deciding to Filter or Not

To help you decide whether to try to control what your child sees or doesn't see on the Internet, ask yourself a few questions:

➤ **Is your child too young to worry about Internet controls just yet?**
If your child is a toddler or a younger child who doesn't surf the Internet (especially without your help), you probably don't need to worry about setting up controls or filters just yet. You effectively become the filter with younger kids.

➤ **Do you let your children surf the Internet without your supervision?**
If so, a monitoring program can keep track of where they go online, or a filtering program can help keep them out of unsuitable areas.

➤ **Are you worried your child might try to find unsuitable information or materials on the Net?**   Has your child done so in the past? If the answer is "yes," parental control software might help prevent access to bad Internet content.

➤ **Have you or other family members received email of questionable nature?**   If yes, filtering software can help prevent future encounters.

➤ **Does your child send email, participate in chats, or fill out online forms?**   If yes, you can use a filtering program to prevent disclosure of personal information.

➤ **Is your child interested in surfing the Net?**   If not, you don't need to worry about installing filtering software. Those times your child does go online, you can supervise his activities.

Granted, there's a lot of bad content on the Internet you don't want your children exposed to—you probably don't want to be exposed to it yourself—but don't jump off the deep end and entertain extreme paranoia. There's no reason to install every piece of parental control software you can get your hands on. Use good judgment and common sense. This might be difficult because there's not a lot of common sense to go around these days, or so it seems. If you need help controlling what content is accessed by your child on the Internet, there are tools out there you can utilize. For those of you who do decide to use a filter of some type, read on. The remainder of this chapter educates you about what's available.

What's Available in Parental Control Software?

Software companies are churning out numerous products to help parents control what Internet content comes into the home, as well as what personal information goes out. There are different types of software, all of which have different uses. Needless to say, sorting out all that's available can be very confusing for parents. To help you make sense of it all, let's take a look at the types of parental controls first. Later in this chapter we go into some detail about how a typical program works.

Types of Parental Controls

Time-limiting software is designed to set limits on how much time your child spends online. It also lets you control when your child can go online. That's pretty much all it does, so the control aspect is in your hands. When the child is allowed online, they need your supervision or proximity. Time-limiting software can be a useful tool if your pre-teen or teenager is spending too much time online. It allows you to set a limit and stick with it. Once your child hits the limit, the online connection is terminated.

Monitoring software works behind the scenes to track the way the computer is used, keeping a log of sites visited, email, and even chat sessions. Some monitoring programs even store snapshots of what your children are viewing online. Unlike filtering software, monitoring programs don't restrict access; instead they alert you to what your child is doing online. If your child knows monitoring software is installed, it might deter him or her from using the computer in a way of which you don't approve.

Blocking and filtering software identifies inappropriate Web sites and denies access. There are lots of variations of filtering software. With some, parents can pick from pre-set categories of what's inappropriate and what's not, leaving the parent in charge of content. With others, the software maker decides what's filtered, and parents have no input.

Filtering software uses several components when blocking sites. Depending on the program, one or all of the following might be used: keywords that trigger a block (such as sexually explicit terminology or lingo for sexual organs), a predetermined list of unsuitable Web addresses (URLs that are known to deposit the user at a porn site or a hate site), or the PICS rating service (more on this in a minute).

Keyword-based filters work on the premise of keywords found on Web sites. Many are designed to look at the words in the context of the site before determining whether the site is objectionable. For example, if the program encounters the word "breast," it looks at the context in which the word is used (such as "breast cancer" as opposed to "breast ogling"), before deciding to block the site or not. Context-sensitive filters are less likely to block access to educational sites that offer information about health-related issues.

Predetermined lists of unsuitable sites are compiled by software companies. Many of the software companies have employees and other experts examine Web pages and assign categories (such as graphic violence or sexually explicit material). Human-maintained lists are usually more precise because they're based on a person's judgment rather than a computer program's determination. Parents can log onto the software maker's Web site and download updated lists every few weeks. Some filtering software allows parents to add and subtract sites from the lists, and others do not offer this flexibility.

Another type of filtering might rely on PICS (Platform for Internet Content Selection), a standard that governs the format for rating codes that can be applied to Web sites. In a voluntary effort at self-policing, Web site operators can have their sites labeled and rated by third parties, then incorporate the rating label on the Web page. Browsers that feature parental control options can then read the rating label and block the site, if needed. (You won't ever see the rating label because it's embedded in the site's HTML code.) Newer versions of Microsoft's Internet Explorer and Netscape's Navigator support PICS. PICS is a good idea—a lot like rating movies, for example—but with so much content on the Internet, not many sites are rated thus far.

Where Did PICS Come From?

The PICS standard was developed by the World Wide Web Consortium (WWWC or W3C) in 1995. The WWWC is charged with developing standards for the Web and includes members from all kinds of Internet companies and organizations. The idea behind PICS was to create a standard that would enable rating services and filtering products to screen sites based on content ratings. PICS doesn't actually rate any sites; that's handled by rating services such as SafeSurf and RSACi (Recreational Software Advisory Council on the Internet).

Speaking of browsers, yet another parental control option to consider is browsers made specifically for kids. Kids' browsers work just like regular browsers, but tap into filtering schemes and lists to direct kids to safe content. Depending on the browser, different options can be set by parents. Regular browsers also offer content controls, or at least the newer versions do. For example, with Internet Explorer 5.0 (shown in Figure 13.1), users can set levels based on RSACi ratings. RSACi stands for Recreational Software Advisory Council on the Internet, the industry leader in rating services for the Internet.

Kids' search engines is another route you might choose to take. Search sites such as Yahoo! offer safe search tools families can use to browse for the good stuff while avoiding the objectionable stuff (see Figure 13.2). These specialized search engines rely on filtering schemes or preselected lists of safe content users can search through. On the down side, users don't have much control over how the search tools work or what is filtered.

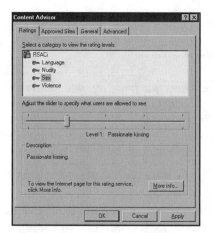

Figure 13.1

Using Internet Explorer, parents can set rating levels for sites and specify approved sites.

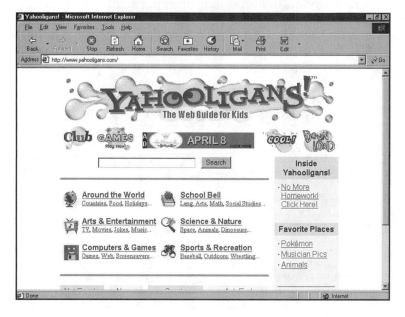

Figure 13.2

Your child can conduct a safe search from the Yahooligans! search site.

Most commercial online services offer their own versions of parental controls, as shown in Figure 13.3. With AOL, you can have up to seven different account names so that everyone in the family can log on under his/her own name. Parents can set controls for each account name. You can turn off chat access for younger children, for example. Turn to Chapter 16, "Playing It Safe on America Online," to learn all about setting the parental controls for AOL.

Figure 13.3

Parents can control which AOL features are accessed by other account users.

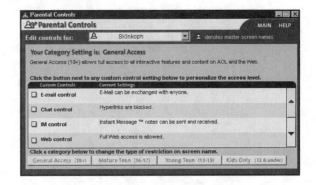

Utility programs have also jumped into the act, and newer programs have added parental control features that help block Internet content. For example, Norton Internet Security (from the famous Norton AntiVirus people) has a utility that not only includes Internet security options for the home PC, but also provides parental control options that enable you to specify which site categories to block while surfing the Internet (see Figure 13.4). Like other filtering software, the lists can be updated regularly. The same holds true for Internet Guard Dog, from utility company McAfee.

Figure 13.4

Parents can also look to utility programs, such as Norton Internet Security, for filtering capabilities.

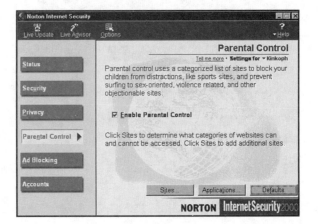

Is your head spinning yet? All of the parental control software types mentioned so far are those parents can install and use on the home PC. Another route to look into is server control software. These programs are installed by your ISP on their server to help control Internet content. Unlike PC software, users don't have many options for turning features on or off with this type of control because it's installed on the server at the ISP's location. On the other hand, your kids can't figure out how to turn the filtering off. If this type of filtering option appeals to you, check with your ISP to see whether they offer this feature and how you can subscribe. The nice thing about server-based filters is that you, as the end user, don't have to worry about updating the content lists.

There are also ISPs that are strictly family-oriented. When you set up an account with them, your Internet access is automatically filtered through the ISP's installed parental control programs. So in essence, you get prefiltered service.

Corporate Filtering

Filtering software isn't just for kids. Software makers are also meeting demands made by companies who are having difficulty keeping employees focused on work instead of porn sites. Frivolous Web surfing, such as online shopping and stock watching, as well as perusing pornographic pictures, is a growing problem for companies around the globe. For example, Xerox Corporation fired 40 employees in October of 1999 for viewing pornography during working hours on company PCs. Some people just can't wait till after hours to view their porn.

The Net Nanny Example

To help you better understand how parental control software works, let's take a look at a popular filtering software: Net Nanny. Net Nanny was the first filtering program to hit the market, back in 1995. Net Nanny works on the home PC to help parents filter out unwanted Internet materials. It's one of the most versatile filtering programs on the market and includes customizable lists (so you—the parent—can add or remove sites as you deem necessary), free update lists from the Net Nanny Web site, as well as a filtering of Web sites, email, newsgroups, and chat rooms.

Net Nanny also allows parents to set different profiles for different users in the household. This means you can set options for your youngest Internet surfer without making the options apply to an older child as well. Net Nanny, shown in Figure 13.5, also lets parents monitor online and offline activity by keeping logs. The software even lets parents set options for the sending of personal information (called *screening*), which is helpful if you're worried about your child disclosing a phone number or address to someone they meet online.

More About Net Nanny

Visit the Net Nanny Web site (www.netnanny.com) to learn more about this product and find a trial version of the software you can download.

Can Grownups Still Surf?

Parents can turn off NetNanny using the password, and surf without filtering. The on/off feature varies by filtering programs. A filtering software assigns parents passwords to give them the opportunity to set options and turn the program on or off. Just remember to keep your passwords in a safe place where the kids won't find them.

Figure 13.5

Net Nanny is a popular Internet filtering program with an interface that's surprisingly easy to use.

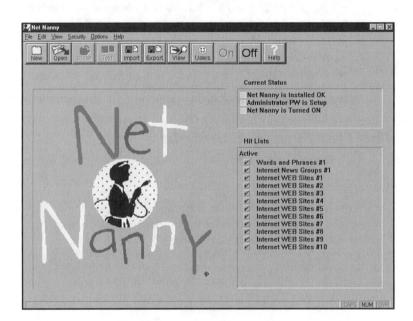

Net Nanny's current version, 3.1, is being updated. The next version, 4.0, due for release in the summer of 2000, promises even more options for greater flexibility. New features will include timing settings to control how long a child is allowed online, audit trail features to track entire chat conversations, and profiles for up to 12 users (if you have that many kids in the house).

To see how filtering software works, look at Figure 13.6. It shows one of Net Nanny's preset lists of unsuitable Web sites. You can tell just from the names why these sites aren't good for children. The options on the right allow parents to control what happens if a child tries to access a site on the list. The visit can be logged, a warning message can appear onscreen, a message box appears saying the site is completely blocked, or the entire computer system can be shut down.

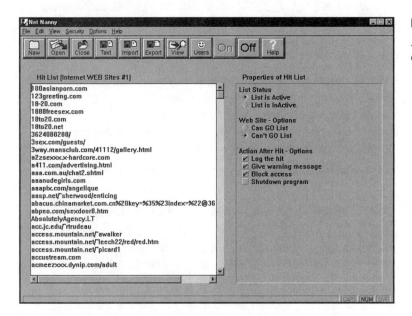

Figure 13.6

Parents can set various options for unsuitable Web sites.

Figure 13.7 shows what kids will see when they try to access a site from Net Nanny's lists, whether by accident or on purpose.

Figure 13.7

Your child will see this warning prompt if he tries to access a site deemed unsuitable for children.

Net Nanny, like other filtering programs, is very customizable; parents can set it up to work with the way they use the Internet. Net Nanny also works with AOL. It has options for protecting files on your computer, which prevents accidental deletions.

Every filtering program works differently, but this gives you some idea how the programs typically work.

189

Installation Issues

Every software program installs differently. Be sure to check out the instructions for installing a filtering program safely onto your computer. Some programs require that you set filtering options during the installation setup rather than after the program is installed. Pay attention to the requirements. Also, take time to learn how to uninstall the program in case it's not what you need.

A Huge List of Software to Choose From

With the escalating awareness of Internet dangers, software makers are combining many of the features and types described earlier in this chapter. Newer versions of many parental control applications offer a variety of features and flexibility. For example, you can find parental control software that includes timing limits and monitoring features as well as filtering and blocking features.

It doesn't do much good to compare parental control software side by side because each program has different features; depending on what you need, one program might be better suited for your family than others. Many filtering software makers offer free trial versions you can try out to help you decide whether the software is what you're looking for. Most filtering software is affordable, so shop around for the program that's right for your household. You can also search the Internet for shareware and freeware versions of filtering software.

Table 13.1 lists a variety of parental control software makers and their Web sites you can investigate. This list is not exhaustive by any means, but it's a start.

Table 13.1 Parental Control Software

Software	Web site
Net Nanny	www.netnanny.com
CYBERsitter	www.cybersitter.com
Cyber Snoop	www. pearlsw.com
SurfWatch	www.surfwatch.com
X-Stop	www.xstop.com
Cyber Sentinel	securitysoft.com

Software	Web site
Cyber Patrol	www.cyberpatrol.com
SOS KidProof	www.soskidproof.com
ClickChoice	www.clickchoice.com
We-Blocker	www.we-blocker.com
SpectorSoft	www.spectorsoft.com
Internet Detection	www.protectyourfamily.net
CrossingGuard	www.crosswalk.com/crossingguard
Internet Guard Dog	www.mcafee.com
Norton Internet Security 2000	www.norton.com
Email for Kids	www.email-connection.com/EMKFINAL.html
Momma Bear	www.mommabear.com
WinGuardian	www.webroot.com
Enuff	www.akrontech.com
FamilyConnect	www.familyconnect.com
MoM	www.avsweb.com/mom
Restrictor	www.guardone.com

How Do I Choose?

For help in evaluating which type of parental software to use, stop by the GetNetWise Web site at www.getnetwise.com. Follow the Tools link to an evaluation page where you can select what features you're looking for, as well as which computer platform you're using. After you've entered you're selections, the site lists software makers and links that evaluate the software's features and details about each program. This is an excellent tool that can help you investigate parental control software.

When choosing parental control software, spend some time thinking about what kind of features you're looking for. As mentioned, many of the popular programs offer dozens of features, but perhaps you are only interested in a few. Here's a checklist of typical filtering features and system-related features to think about:

- ❏ Blocks foul language/words
- ❏ Blocks porn, cult, hate speech, dangerous speech (like how to build bombs) sites
- ❏ Filters incoming email
- ❏ Filters outgoing email
- ❏ Filters email attachments
- ❏ Uses predetermined lists of good sites
- ❏ Offers updated site lists online
- ❏ Lists can be customized by parents
- ❏ Monitors online activities
- ❏ Monitors offline computer activities
- ❏ Sets time limits for online use
- ❏ Blocks chat rooms
- ❏ Blocks instant/private messages
- ❏ Blocks newsgroups
- ❏ Screens outgoing information for personal disclosure (such as phone numbers or addresses)
- ❏ Is the software very tamper resistant? (Can your 4-year-old figure out how to turn it off?)
- ❏ Does it work with your Web browser?
- ❏ Does it work with your commercial online service software?
- ❏ Does it come in a version that's compatible with your operating system?

Depending on the age of your child and the amount of protection you want, the features you check off will help you determine what sort of parental control software will work best for your family. When you check out the software, look for the features you selected in that list.

Use Plug-Ins

You can also find browser plug-ins that filter content as children browse the Internet, such as Surfin' Annette (www.spycatcher.com/details.htm) or Prowler (www.webkeys.com/parents.htm). Don't forget, Internet Explorer and Netscape Navigator also offer filtering features you can employ.

The other alternative is to use server-based filtering programs, such as NetFilter, CleanScreen, and I-Gear. Check with your ISP to see whether they offer such software. Your ISP might have several programs to choose from, or you might have to ask them to install a program.

In addition, some ISPs cater specifically to parents and schools that want protected Internet access. These ISPs offer prefiltered access to the Internet. Table 13.2 lists a few family-friendly ISPs you can contact. Check your area to see what's available.

Table 13.2   Family-Friendly ISPs

ISP	Web site
Beacon Filtered Internet Access	www.bkon.net
Flash Net	www.flash.net
Mayberry USA	www.mayberryusa.net
this.com	www.this.com
CleanSurf	www.cleansurf.com
Family.Net	www.family.net
Family Online Network	www.fam.net
Dotsafe	www.dotsafe.net
ClearSail Communications	www.clearsail.net
Clean Family Internet	www.cleanfamily.com
Integrity Online	www.integrityonline.com
Veracom	www.veracom.net
SafeBrowse.com	www.safebrowse.com
JuniorNet	www.juniornet.com
Power OnLine	www.polnow.net
iSelect Internet	www.iselect.net
KwykNet	www.kwyknet.net
SmutStopper	www.smutstopper.com

Don't forget, utility programs also feature filtering options these days. Check out programs such as Norton Internet Security or McAfee's Internet Guard Dog.

The bottom line is there are many great products on the market today that can help you control the Internet content that comes into (or leaves) your home PC. If you're looking for some help with guarding what your child encounters on the Internet, the tools described in this chapter can definitely offer some much-needed protection. Although they are in no way substitutes for parental supervision, these tools can be an asset in any parent's protection arsenal.

Table 13.3 lists a few kid browsers, browser software that lets kids surf safely from a predetermined list of safe sites.

Table 13.3   Kid Browsers

Browser	Web site
The Childrens Browser	www.chibrow.com
KiddoNet	www.kiddonet.com
Kidnet Explorer	www.members.tripod.com/~rescom/kidnetex.htm
Surf Monkey	www.surfmonkey.com
Prowler	www.webkeys.com/parents.htm
Crayon Crawler	www.crayoncrawler.com
KidDesk Internet Safe	www.edmark.com

The Least You Need to Know

Regardless of which type of filtering software you choose, the end result will be peace of mind, knowing that your child has some degree of protection when using the Internet. Here's what you learned in this chapter:

➤ Parental control software gives parents options for controlling how children use the Internet.

➤ There are a variety of types of parent control software; some might be more suitable for your child than others.

➤ Filtering software blocks access to unsuitable Web sites. Depending on the software, options might include monitoring, time limits, and screening features.

➤ Today's Web browsers offer filtering options. You can also find browsers made just for kids.

➤ Utility programs, such as Norton Internet Security, also offer filtering features.

➤ Many ISPs use filtering software on their end. Check with your ISP to see what's available.

➤ Your decision to add filtering software to your home PC depends on your children and the type of protection they need.

➤ Plenty of good filtering programs are available; some offer free trial versions you can download. You can also search for freeware or shareware programs on the Internet.

Chapter 14

How to Search the Web Safely

In This Chapter

➤ What are search engines, and how do they work?

➤ What dangers do search engines pose to kids?

➤ How to keep your kids safe when they use search engines

➤ A list of the best kid search engines on the Internet

➤ How to use built-in family filters on popular Internet search engines such as Lycos and AltaVista

As anyone who's spent any time on the Internet can tell you, it's almost impossible to find exactly what you want online. With zillions of Web sites covering everything from teen idols 'N Sync to dwarf rabbits to political news to the weather in Bali, there are far too many places to go. It's a wilderness out there.

Search engines can help your kids find what they want on the Internet, but they can also lead them to pornographic sites, hate sites, and other inappropriate areas—even if their search has nothing to do with any of the previously listed dangers. In this chapter, you learn how to make sure your kids are safe when they use search engines. This way they can get the most out of the Web, and you can have peace of mind.

What Do I Need to Know About Search Engines?

Search engines such as Yahoo (www.yahoo.com), Lycos (www.lycos.com), AltaVista (www.altavista.com), Excite (www.excite.com), and others help you through the thickets on the Web. Instead of having to jump from site to site, you can go to one place, type in words that describe what you're looking for, and let the search engines do your work for you. They search their databases for Web pages and report back to you with sites that match the words you typed in.

When it comes to your kids, your big worry is that these search engines can lead them to places you'd rather they didn't go, such as pornographic or hate sites.

Before you learn how to make sure your kids search safely, let's take a minute or two to see how search engines work. After you understand that, it's easier to make sure your kids' experiences with search engines are rewarding ones.

What's a Portal?

Portal is a fancy name for a search engine, such as Lycos, Alta Vista, or any other site that hopes to be your entry point to the Web. These search engines serve as portals that give you a view onto the Internet. But I think maybe the real reason they're called portals is that *portal* sounds a lot more important than *search engine*. Investors might be happier spending money on a stock that sounds as important as a portal.

How Search Engines Work

When you use a search engine to search for something—let's say the holiday Kwanzaa—the search engine doesn't really search the entire Internet. It searches a database of Internet Web sites that it maintains. It looks inside that database to see if any of those sites are related to Kwanzaa. When it finds sites related to Kwanzaa, it provides you with a list of those sites, along with a brief description of each site. Figure 14.1 shows what happens when you search for Kwanzaa on AltaVista (`www.altavista.com`).

After you see a list of the sites, read the brief descriptions. Click the ones in which you're interested, and go take a look at them. After you click a site in the list, you are sent straight to the Web site. Search engines provide the fastest way to get information from the Internet. Kids use them all the time.

So far, so good. Now comes the tricky part. Remember, when you go to a search engine, it just searches its database of sites, not the entire Internet. So how do search engines put together that database?

Most do it by sending out what are called—believe it or not—spiders that "crawl" over the Web, gathering information about sites as they go. (Get it? Spiders on the Web? Cute, not?) These spiders are pieces of software that gather information about the sites automatically and send it back to the search engine, where it's put into the database.

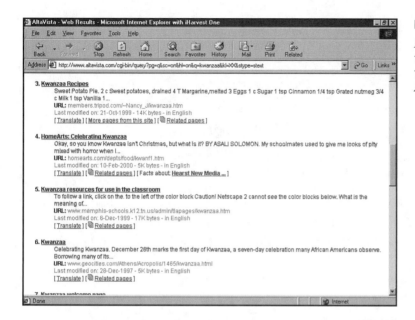

Figure 14.1

Here's what you see when you search for the word Kwanzaa on the AltaVista search engine.

Not all search engines work this way. Yahoo, for example, doesn't use spiders. Instead, it uses real-life human beings (what a concept!) to look at sites and categorize them.

No matter how they work, though, information about the sites is put into a giant database. And when you use a search engine, you search that database.

I know what you're probably thinking right now. Big deal—so what if that's how they work. What does that have to do with protecting your kids?

Plenty, it turns out. These search engines follow rules when gathering information about Web sites and putting them into the database, and they follow certain rules when you type in a search term. There are tons of sites that mention the word *Kwanzaa*, for example. Why do some sites come up first on the list and others come up 279th on the list? This happens because the search engines weigh different factors about each site when deciding which to show first, which to show last, and which to show at all. They look at the words on the page and other factors. They even look at words that are *hidden* in the page—words that you can't see, but that are in the page. These words are called *meta tags*.

What all this means is that sites can fool search engines, and they can fool you and your kids as well. They can put words in their meta tags that fool the search engine into thinking they're about one thing, when in fact they're about something else. For example, a racist site might put words such as NAACP or Martin Luther King in its meta tags, even though the site itself has racist content. And those meta tags might fool the search engine, so that when your kids search for information about the NAACP, they come across a racist site instead.

What Are Meta Tags?

The Web is put together with a language called Hypertext Markup Language (HTML). The instructions in the language are called *tags*. Most tags are used to do things like tell a browser how to display text, such as making it big or bold. But meta tags aren't used to tell the browser to display things. Instead, they often contain information about the page. For example, many sites use words in meta tags to describe the content of the site so that search engines can better understand what the site is about.

What Dangers Are There in Search Engines?

Now that you understand how search engines work, let's get down to the nitty-gritty. What kinds of problems might your kids run across when they're using a search engine? Here's what you need to be concerned about:

➤ **Your kids might accidentally come across pornographic sites, hate sites, or other inappropriate sites.** It's not always easy, when they're using a search engine, for your kids to know ahead of time when they'll come across an inappropriate site. The brief description that the search engine provides might not really explain what the site is about. Then, when your kid clicks, he's sent to the bad site.

➤ **Your kids might purposely look for pornographic sites, hate sites, or other inappropriate sites.** When using a search engine, it's easy to find these kinds of sites. Face it, at some point, your children might *want* to find sites that you don't want them to find.

➤ **Your kids might come across other kinds of inappropriate Internet content, such as inappropriate chat rooms or discussion areas.** Search engines don't only search the Web, they also search other areas of the Internet, enabling you and your kids to look for chat rooms, discussion areas, and similar places.

Beware of "Pagejacking"

There's a new term on the Internet: *pagejacking*. It refers to a technique in which a site copies a legitimate site exactly, so that it looks to search engines like the legitimate site. But then, when people try to visit, instead of being sent to the legitimate site, they're redirected to a pornographic site. Pagejacking is rare, but if you come across it, report it to the search engine and to the site being copied. If possible, the search engine tracks down the perpetrators. At worst, the site is taken off the search engine list.

That's Pretty Scary Stuff! What Can I Do About It?

Luckily, there's a lot you can do as a parent to make sure your kids don't find inappropriate sites when they use search engines. The answer, by the way, isn't to keep them away from search engines. These sites are great educational tools, and kids love them. The more they learn how to use them, the better they'll be at research and using the Internet.

So here's what you can do to keep your kids safe at search engines:

➤ **Teach them how to recognize inappropriate sites and how to stay away from them.** When your kids do a search and receive the results, they see a brief description of the site. Usually, if your kids read closely enough, the description is a giveaway. They should look for telltale words having to do with sex, hate, or pornography, for example. Make sure they always read the description of the site; site names can often be deceptive.

➤ **Have them use kid-friendly search engines.** A number of search engines, including Yahooligans! (www.yahooligans.com), pictured in Figure 14.2, filter out pornographic sites, hate sites, or other inappropriate sites. Point your kids to these sites, and you know that they're safe when they search and surf. A list of kid-friendly search engines is provided later in this chapter.

➤ **Use the family filters in search engines.** Some search engines, such as AltaVista (www.altavista.com), allow you to use family filters on them. When your kids search at sites like this, they see only content suitable for kids. You can turn these filters on and off when you want, using a password. The next section shows you how to use family filters, and it also provides a list of search engines that include family filters.

Figure 14.2

The Yahooligans site is a great place for kids to start their searches on the Internet—all the sites there have been checked and are okay for kids.

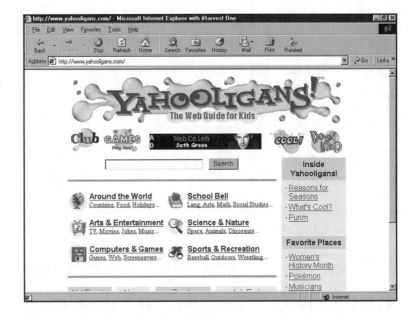

➤ **Install filtering software on their computer.** Filtering software blocks kids' access to objectionable sites, whether it's found via search engines or some other way. For more information on how to install and use these filters, turn to Chapter 13, "All About Filters."

How to Use Family Filters on Search Engines

Some of the big search engines, such as Lycos (www.lycos.com) and AltaVista (www.altavista.com), allow you to use family filters. These filters ensure that your kids don't see inappropriate content when they use the search engines.

Each of these filters works somewhat differently, but the idea on all of them is the same. You control whether to turn the filters on or off by using a password.

You usually get a variety of options on how to use the filters—and again, these options vary from site to site. With the SearchGuard feature of Lycos (see Figure 14.3), for example, you can enable or disable access to message boards, chat, racist content, violent content, sexual content, and content about weapons. You choose which to allow and which to filter out.

Check each search site individually, because they vary so much. And if you decide to use filters, make sure to use the filters on all the computers in your house, not just your kids' computer. If your house is anything like the Gralla household, kids use every computer within easy reach—and even those that are hard to get to!

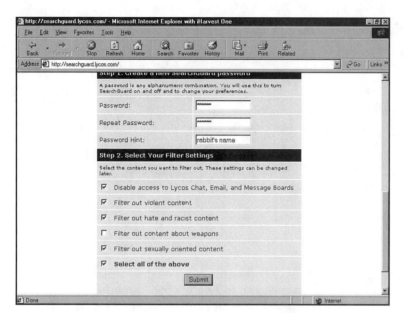

Figure 14.3
Here's how to turn on the SearchGuard family filter on the Lycos search engine.

Occasionally Monitor Search Sites to Make Sure the Family Filters Are Working

Family filters are great helps at search sites. But you should check every once in a while to make sure yours are turned on and working. For example, several years ago the Excite search engine (www.excite.com) made a mistake with its filtering, and allowed ads for pornographic sites to appear while the filter was in use.

Safe Places Where Your Kids Can Search the Internet

Searching the Internet is one of the great pleasures of the vast superhighway, and you don't want to deny that to your kids. So if you're worried that they might come across inappropriate content, here's where to have them go to search. There are two types of search engines listed here: kid-friendly search engines (such as Yahooligans) and regular search engines that allow family filtering (such as AltaVista).

The Best Kid-Friendly Search Engines on the Internet

So to which kid-friendly search engines should you point your kids? Head them to these sites and they can't go wrong.

AOL Kids-Only Search

`www.aol.com/netfind/kids/`

Here's a nice, simple search engine. It's made up of a search box where kids can search, and some links to very good kids' sites. When your kids search here, they are sure to get kid-friendly sites.

Ask Jeeves for Kids!

`www.ajkids.com/`

This is a kid-friendly version of the great Ask Jeeves! search engine. Unlike at other search engines, your kids can type in a question in English here, and the engine understands what they type in (well, sort of, anyway) and gives them kid-friendly, matching sites. What your kids will love about this site is that they can see what other kids are searching for. You can see Ask Jeeves for Kids! in action in Figure 14.4.

Figure 14.4

Unlike other search engines, Ask Jeeves for Kids! answers questions your kids type in.

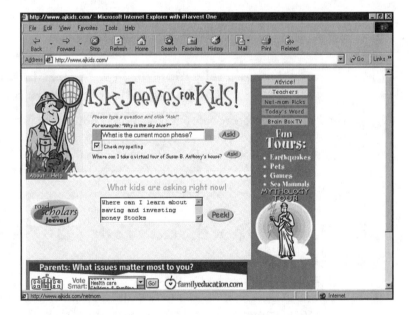

KidsNook

www.kidsnook.com

A very nice search engine for kids, KidsNook lets kids browse through categories of sites, such as Family Matters and School Zone. There are also good links to favorite places for kids.

Yahooligans!

www.yahooligans.com

This search engine, brought to you by the same people who created Yahoo!, is great not only for kid-friendly searches, but for browsing as well. Your kids can find many categories of kid-friendly sites to browse through, such as School Bell and Sports & Recreation. It also includes links to great kids' activities and all other kinds of stuff kids like.

Search Engines with Family Filters

Sometimes kids want to use search engines that are more comprehensive than the ones designed only for kids. If they're looking for regular search engines with family filters, point them to these sites.

AltaVista

www.altavista.com

To turn on the family filter for this powerful search engine, either click **Family Filter** on the front page or go to http://doc.altavista.com/cgi-bin/globalff. You can filter out unsuitable content from all searches, and can also disable access to images, video, and audio. You can see the filters being set in Figure 14.5.

Go Network

www.go.com

This popular search engine lets you filter out objectionable material whenever your kids do searches here. Click **Go Guardian** to turn the filter on and off.

Lycos

www.lycos.com

This excellent search site has very good family filters—they're the most flexible of any search site on the Internet. To set the family filter, go to http://searchguard. lycos.com/. You can filter out racist content, violent content, sexual content, and content having to do with weapons, as well as access to Lycos chat, email, and message boards. And you can turn each option on and off individually.

Figure 14.5

Here's how to turn on the AltaVista Family Filter.

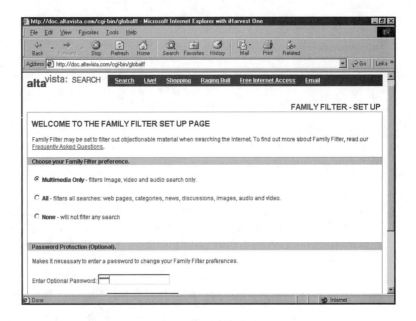

The Least You Need to Know

The Web is a great place for your kids to do research and find out anything they might ever want to know. To do that, they'll use search engines. But search engines can lead them to unsuitable content. To make sure they don't come across inappropriate sites, here's what you should know.

➤ Sites can fool search engines by using false meta tags that trick the engine into believing an inappropriate site is a legitimate one.

➤ Your kids might accidentally come across pornographic sites, hate sites, violent sites, or other inappropriate sites when using search engines.

➤ Teach your kids to recognize inappropriate sites when using search engines—it's one of the best ways to keep them safe.

➤ Point your kids to kid-oriented search engines, such as Yahooligans! (www.yahooligans.com) and Ask Jeeves for Kids! (www.ajkids.com/).

➤ If your kids want to use a more comprehensive search engine, have them use one that includes a family filter that you can turn on or off, such as Lycos (www.lycos.com) and AltaVista (www.altavista.com).

Chapter 15

Downloading Do's and Don'ts

In This Chapter

➤ What kinds of dangers are there in downloading?

➤ The damage computer viruses do

➤ How to run antivirus software

➤ Top tips for making sure your kids don't get hit by a virus

➤ What you need to know about MP3 music files

➤ Learning about other download dangers

Near the top of every kid's list of fun things to do online is to download programs and files—in other words, transfer them from the Internet to their computer. There are all kinds of files they can download, from games to music to animations and more.

But there are dangers in downloading. The biggest danger is that your kids might download a program that has a virus on it. But there are other dangers as well, such as downloading illegal software or illegal music. In this chapter, you'll find out about the dangers in downloading and how you can avoid them.

What's a Computer Virus?

One day, your child comes to you and complains that something funny is going on with her computer. The files (on their own) have started growing in size. Then they start vanishing. Maybe weird messages pop up on the screen. Or suddenly the computer just won't start any more.

Bad news, buddy! Your child's computer might well have been hit by a computer virus.

Computer viruses can do all kinds of damage to your child's computer. They can be as harmless as just displaying a silly message on the screen, and they can be as destructive as wiping out an entire hard disk.

Why Do People Create Computer Viruses?

No one really knows. Usually, it's just plain maliciousness—someone just wants to harm other people. Other times, it's an attempt to get fame as a virus creator. And rarely, someone is out for revenge or wants to attack a company or group and writes the virus to put it directly onto someone's computer or network.

There are many different kinds of computer viruses, but they all have one thing in common—they do something you don't want them to do, and they do it stealthily, hiding their action, possibly until it's too late for you to do anything about it. Usually, they're destructive, but they don't have to be—sometimes, they just display a message on your screen. And other times, they're just plain eccentric. Take the Smiley virus (please!). When it infects a computer, smiley faces suddenly appear and start bouncing around the screen—kind of like a 1970s flashback. You almost expect the entire family from *The Brady Bunch* to appear, all sunny, bright-eyed, and dressed in horrifying fashions.

How Do Computer Viruses Work?

Computer viruses are sneaky critters. (I know, you probably think your kids can be sneaky, but these things are even sneakier, believe me.) They work by burrowing their way into a file on your hard disk—usually a program file that ends in the extension .exe or .com, such as WORD.EXE. But they can infect other kinds of files as well, such as Word documents and files needed to start your computer.

After the virus infects a file, that file needs to be run for the virus to do its dirty deeds. It can't run by itself. When you run the infected file, it gets to work. One kind of virus looks for another program file to infect, and after it infects that one, looks for another file to infect, and so on. No matter how the virus works, though, after you run an infected program, it does whatever damage the virus programmer instructed it to do.

How Do You Get a Computer Virus?

There are many ways your kids can get a computer virus. It might come from a program or file that your kids download from the Internet. But they can be acquired in other ways as well, such as from a disk your child was given, or even from an attachment to an email message.

What Kinds of Viruses Are There?

There's an astounding number of nasty viruses out there. Here's your brief field guide to the most common types of viruses and what they do:

➤ **Time bombs** These viruses are programmed to do their damage on a certain date or after a certain amount of time has elapsed. For example, the infamous Michelangelo virus was programmed to lie dormant until March 6, when it was supposed to spring into action.

➤ **Trojan horses** Remember the story of the Trojan horse? (If you don't, ask your kids—they'll know it appeared to be a gift, but in fact harbored the Greek army within, which sacked the city of Troy.) In the same way, a Trojan horse virus appears to be an innocuous or helpful program, such as a game, but when your kids run the program, it damages your computer. The most infamous Trojan horse virus of all time is a program called Back Orifice. It enables someone to completely take over your computer—they can delete files, copy files, and even remotely control the computer by issuing it commands.

➤ **Self-replicating viruses** This is the kind most like a biological virus. When your kids run an infected file, it looks for other files to infect, and when those are run, it looks for files to infect, and so on. Sometimes, these viruses make each file they infect larger—which can result in a clogged hard disk. Other times, they lie dormant until a critical mass of them is reached, and then they spring into action.

➤ **Boot viruses** These viruses infect the boot sector of a PC—the files that start up your PC. These can be deadly because they can make the computer unable to start; because they start before other programs, they can also easily infect other programs.

Is There Such a Thing as a Mail Bomb?

I've found that kids sometimes threaten each other with something they call a *mail bomb*. A mail bomb sounds like a virus, but it isn't—in fact, it isn't even a file. Instead, a mail bomb is an attempt to clog up someone's email box by sending hundreds of phony pieces of email.

➤ **Memory resident viruses**   These are viruses that, when run, stay in a computer's memory. While there, they can infect other programs.

➤ **Document viruses**   Viruses can infect Word and Excel documents. That's because Word and Excel can run things called *macros* that are like little programs embedded in the documents. So, viruses can run in macros and, in that way, infect document files. The infamous Melissa virus was a document virus.

➤ **Dangerous Java applets and ActiveX controls**   Java applets and ActiveX controls are technologies used to make World Wide Web pages more interactive and useful. In essence, they're programs. Although the Java applets and ActiveX controls can't actually be infected by viruses, the applets and controls can be programmed to do damage to a computer when a page is visited and the files are run.

Keep Your Kids Safe with Antivirus Software

The best way to make sure your kid's computer is never damaged by a virus is to install antivirus software and always have it running on their computer. When used properly, antivirus software detects infected files before they're run, and can then kill the virus before it does any damage. You should also regularly scan the hard disk for infected files with antivirus software. In Figure 15.1, you can see Norton AntiVirus, my favorite virus killer, checking my computer for viruses. Luckily, it found none.

Antivirus software does more than just find, as well as kill, viruses. It can kill them as well. Sometimes it kills the virus and repairs the file the virus infected, which makes life easy. Other times, it cannot repair the file, and you have to delete whatever file was infected.

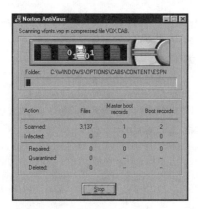

How Does Antivirus Software Work?

Antivirus software detects viruses in several ways. It looks for tell-tale signatures—information embedded in virus files or information that viruses leave behind that is a sure sign a virus is present. It can also check your kids' computer for odd behavior that indicates a virus is present. (On the other hand, it can't check your kids for odd behavior; for that, you have to rely on your pediatrician.)

Antivirus software can help protect your kids' system in these ways:

➤ **It checks the files to see if they've been infected.**   Just run the software, and it does the rest. It reports any infected files it finds.

What Does Zip Mean?

When your kids download a file from the Internet, it's usually been compressed—that is, shrunk in size. It's been shrunk so it can be downloaded faster. After it's on your kids' computer, they have to uncompress it to run the program. The most common way that files are compressed is by using a compression standard called Zip. Uncompressing a file that has been zipped is called unzipping it. There are many programs that unzip programs that you download. The most popular is called WinZip, and it's available at many download sites on the Internet, including ZDNet Downloads at www.zddownloads.com and the WinZip site at www.winzip.com.

➤ **It can check files before they are opened to see if they're infected.**
You can tell antivirus software to automatically scan files before they're run.

➤ **It can check system files to make sure they haven't been infected.**
The software can keep a constant vigil, watching system files to make sure
nothing nasty is happening to them.

➤ **It can remove viruses from a system.**   After it finds a virus, it can kill it.

➤ **It can repair files that viruses have damaged.**   When viruses do their
dirty work, they typically damage the files they infect. Antivirus software can
not only kill viruses, it can also repair the damaged files so you can still use
them. Keep in mind, however, that this isn't always the case. Sometimes antivirus software cannot repair the damaged file, and you have to delete it entirely.

How to Run Antivirus Software

There's a simple first step you need to take before running antivirus software—get a
copy of one. Any one. Any antivirus software is better than none. You can buy the
software in a retail store or on the Web. And if you want, you can try out a copy free—
you can download and use all major antivirus software free for a certain amount of
time. Head to any of the major download sites, such as the ZDNet Software Library at
www.zddownloads.com.

I have to be clear about my prejudices here, though. From my point of view, the best
antivirus software is Norton AntiVirus from Symantec Corp. It's the most comprehensive, the easiest to use, has the best features, and, I believe, is the most reliable. I've
tried them all, and it's the one I use. Another popular antivirus software is VirusScan
from McAfee.

Using antivirus software is fairly simple. Start off by reading the manual. (That is, if
you can—most manuals are as inscrutable as hieroglyphics.)

When you're familiar with how your antivirus software works, follow this advice:

➤ **Set the virus scanner to Auto-Protect.**   Most antivirus software lets you
keep it running permanently on your system, scanning files for viruses before
they're run, or while they're copied or moved. Always use the Auto-Protect option.
It's the best way to make sure the computer will never get infected. This is especially important because you're talking about a kids' computer. After all, if you
can't count on your kids to clean up their rooms, can you trust them to run
antivirus software? You might also be given various options on how to use
Auto-Protect—in other words, whether to use the feature only when you run
files, only when you copy them, or only when you download them from the
Web. Use Auto-Protect all the time. In Figure 15.2 you can see how to set the
Auto-Protect options in Norton AntiVirus.

210

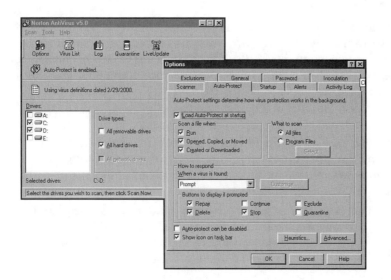

Figure 15.2

Make sure you always set antivirus software to Auto-Protect mode on your kids' computers.

Check This Out

Your Kids Might Have to Disable a Virus Scanner Before They Download and Install Certain Programs

Some programs require that the virus scanner be disabled before the programs can be downloaded and installed. The most notable example is Microsoft Internet Explorer. It's fine to disable your kids' virus scanner temporarily when downloading Explorer. But only have them do this for a file from a well-known source that you know does virus scanning. And as soon as the file has been installed, turn the virus scanner back on. In fact, if you're worried that your kids might not turn the scanner back on, don't show them how to turn it off, and make sure you're present whenever they install software.

➤ **Inoculate the system.** Many antivirus programs include an inoculation feature. It basically takes a snapshot of your system files and then regularly compares that snapshot to the current state of your files. If it notices a difference, this could mean you've been hit with a virus, and it alerts you.

➤ **Set the virus scanner to automatically check files as they're downloaded from the Web.** Virus scanners can check files for viruses before they're saved to a computer. Make sure your kids set it up this way for maximum safety.

➤ **Even if you virus-scan a file downloaded from the Web, virus-scan it again after you install it.** Often, when you download a program from the Web, it comes as a single, compressed file. Your virus scanner checks that file for viruses. But after you install the program, it expands into many files, and the scanner might not have been able to check them all for viruses during the download. So whenever you install a new program from the Web, do a virus check.

➤ **Scan regularly for viruses, even if you use Auto-Protect.** Yes, Auto-Protect scans all the time for viruses, so in theory, you don't need to tell your virus scanner to look for viruses. On the other hand, it can't hurt. I do it all the time, just for safety's sake.

➤ **Regularly visit the Web site of the company that makes your anti-virus software.** Companies continually release new versions of antivirus software; and to be safe, you should always have the newest version. To make sure you have the newest version and to get any other news about viruses, regularly visit the Web site of the company that makes your antivirus software.

➤ **Download new virus definitions every month.** New viruses are coming out all the time. If your antivirus software doesn't know about them—and their unique signatures—it might not be able to protect you against them. Make it a habit to download new virus definitions every month. You can get them from the Web site of the company that makes your antivirus software. Most antivirus software has a built-in feature that lets you download and install these virus definitions easily. Figure 15.3 shows the LiveUpdate feature that Norton AntiVirus uses for getting new definitions.

Figure 15.3

To be absolutely safe, get new virus definitions every month.

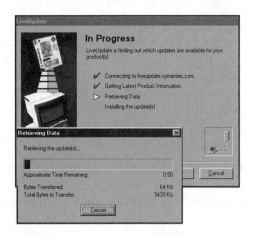

Can Antivirus Software Report a False Virus Reading?

Yes. It's possible to get a report that you have a virus when in fact you don't. There can be a number of causes for this, including an error in the program's virus definition file. Still, though, it's a good idea to listen to your program's advice when it tells you that you have a virus.

Top Tips for Avoiding Viruses

Using antivirus software is important, but it's not the only thing you can do to make sure your kids' computer is never attacked by viruses. There's a lot more you can do. Here's the rundown:

➤ **Tell your kids to download files only from Internet sites that virus check their software.** There are a lot of sites on the Internet where your kids can download software—hundreds, if not thousands, of them. But the vast majority of those sites don't check their files to see if they've been infected with a virus. That means your kids stand more of a chance getting a virus on that site than on one that does virus checking. To be safe, allow them to download only from sites that virus check the files on their site. Check the Help or FAQ area of a site to see if they do virus checking. ZDNet Downloads at www.zddownloads.com, for example, virus checks all the software it carries.

➤ **If someone gives your kids a floppy disk with files on it, have them virus scan the files on it before copying them to the computer.** Kids often exchange files on floppy disks. Make sure your kids virus-check any file on any disk given to them. Keep in mind that even document files such as Word files (that end in a .doc extension) and Excel files (that end in an .xls extension) can carry viruses, so make sure they check them as well.

Check to See Whether a Site Uses Multiple Virus Scanners

When it comes to virus scanners, two are better than one, and three are better than two. Ideally, you'd like a download site to check its files with more than one virus scanner to make it even less likely that a file it carries has a virus.

213

➤ **Your kids should never open a file sent to them via email from someone they don't know.**   This is a common way of spreading viruses. The stranger might tell your kids it's a screen saver or some other program, but it might in fact be a virus. This is also a way some hackers steal passwords. They send out a file that appears to be a useful program, but in fact, behind the scenes it's stealing passwords and sending them off to the hacker, who greedily waits for access to them. Even when your kids know who is sending them a file, they should virus scan it before opening it. To do that, tell them to save the file to their hard disk, but don't open it. Then run the virus scanner on it to see if it's infected. If you want to be completely safe, tell your kids never to open files sent via email, even if they're from friends.

➤ **Keep up to date about virus news.**   New viruses come out all the time. To find the latest information, go to a well-known Web site that tracks virus alerts, such as www.zdnet.com, www.anchordesk.com, or www.wired.com.

➤ **Disable macros in Word and Excel.**   The reason Word and Excel files can be infected with viruses is that they contain macros, which are like little programs inside the files that can automate certain tasks and give you extra features. To be safe, show your kids how to disable the macros in any Word or Excel file. Viruses can be spread only if the macro is run, so a virus inside a file cannot spread, because you disabled the macro. When they open a Word or Excel file that has a macro in it, they'll get a note asking if they want to disable the macros in the file. Tell them to choose **Yes**. If for some reason, they cannot use the file because the macro has been disabled, have them close the file and check it with a virus scanner to see if it contains a virus. If it's clean, have them open it back up and enable the macros.

How to Enable Word's Built-In Macro Guards

It's easy to have Word warn you every time it opens a file with macros in it—this gives you the option to disable the macros and protect yourself against viruses. In Word 97, choose **Options** from the **Tools** menu, and click the **General** tab. Click **Macro Virus Protection**, and things are set. In Word 2000, choose **Options** from the **Tools** menu, then click **Macro and Security**, and make sure the Security Level is set to **Medium** or **High**. A dialog box explains what each setting means.

Uh Oh! Your Kids Have a Virus. Now What Do You Do?

Your kids have a virus. What to do? Keep them home from school, get them chicken soup, and make sure they stay in bed? Come on, get serious. Computer viruses, after all, are a serious matter.

If they get a virus, there's only one thing to do: Follow the directions that the virus scanner offers. If it detects a virus, it usually asks whether it should try to get rid of the virus—and yes, that's certainly a good idea. It kills the virus and tries to repair the file. If it can't repair the file, it deletes it instead. Bite the bullet and go ahead. It's good for your kids, even though they might not know it.

Backup, Backup, and Backup. Oh, and Did I Mention Backup?

Your kids might get a virus that kills their hard disk. That deletes all their homework. That destroys all their games. That wipes out all their friends' email addresses. And if they don't back up their hard disk, there's nothing you can do about it.

Backing up your hard disk means making a copy of the programs and files on it. You can back up to a zip disk, to another hard disk, to a tape drive, to floppy disks, and even, these days, to a backup service on the Internet. I can't stress how important it is to do this. Yes, it's annoying to do. Yes, it can be time-consuming—although only the first backup takes a long time. And yes, you don't want to do it.

But do it. Believe me, your kids will be much happier for it. Just tell them it hurts you more than it hurts them to do it—they've certainly heard *that* before, haven't they?

What You Need to Know About MP3 Music Files

If you have kids over the age of 10, they're most likely downloading and collecting what are called MP3 files from the Internet. MP3 files are high-quality music files that can be played with a piece of software called, not surprisingly, an MP3 player. A popular MP3 player called WinAmp is pictured in Figure 15.4.

Your kids can't get viruses from MP3 files, so you don't need to worry about that. But you should know that the vast majority of MP3 files violate copyright laws. Most of them are popular songs that are downloaded or traded on the Internet without the author's permission.

215

Figure 15.4

Let the music begin: When kids download MP3 music files, they have to use an MP3 player, such as WinAmp pictured here, to listen to the music.

Don't expect Eliot Ness and the Feds to come knocking on your kids' doors so they can send your loved ones up the river to Sing Sing. Your kids won't get into legal trouble for using MP3 files. But they should at least know that they're doing something illegal when they download those files. By the way, you should know that it's perfectly legal for your kids to record their own MP3 files from CDs they own. Some of the MP3 sites your kids go to might not be the best places for them to hang out, either, because you might find ads for pornographic sites there. You won't have any problems if they go to a site like www.mp3.com that carries only legal MP3 files, but sites that specialize in illegal MP3 files can be problematic.

Another issue with MP3 files is that they can eat up hard disk space and lots of it. Each MP3 file usually takes up 2MB or more. And kids can easily download over a hundred songs—so that means hundreds of megabytes of hard disk space can be chewed up by the files. Soon, the entire hard disk can be full.

MP3 files end in .mp3, so you can easily search through their hard disk to see how many MP3 files your kids have.

Use the Windows Find Feature to See How Many MP3 Files Your Kids Have

Want an easy way to see how many MP3 files your kids have? Use the Windows Find feature. To use it, choose **Find** from the **Start** menu, and then choose **Files or Folders**. In the top box in the menu that pops up, type ***.mp3** and then press **Enter**. When you do that, your entire hard disk is searched for MP3 files, and you are presented with the entire list of every MP3 file your kids have. Be patient—if they're music lovers, it could take a while.

Other Potential Problems with Downloads

When it comes to kids, there are some other potential problems you should know about downloads. Here's the rundown:

➤ **They might download pornographic or other inappropriate pictures or videos.** Sad, but true: A lot of pornographic and inappropriate pictures and videos are available on the Internet. The best way to make sure your kids don't download this material is to use filtering software, so check Chapter 13, "All About Filters," for details. Also, spend time browsing through your kids' hard disks to see what material they've downloaded. And make sure your kids know they shouldn't be downloading that type of material.

Check This Out

Use the Windows Find Feature to Look for Graphic Files

A moment ago, we showed you how to use the Windows Find feature to locate MP3 files. You can use a similar technique to see how many graphics files reside on your computer. To do so, choose **Find** from the **Start** menu, and then choose **Files or Folders**. In the top box in the menu that pops up, type ***.jpg** and then press **Enter**. When you do that, your entire hard disk is searched for a popular graphic file format, and you see the entire list of every such file on your computer. JPG files aren't necessarily pornographic, but if you see a stash of them you aren't familiar with, you can double-click one or two of them to check them out. A bonus of this technique is that Web browsers save temporary copies of graphics they display, so you can sometimes tell if your child visited an adult site even if he or she didn't download anything. You can also search for other picture files in this way as well, such as those that end in .pic and .tif.

➤ **They might download pirated software.** There are sites on the Internet known as *warez* sites that allow people to download illegally pirated software—in other words, regular commercial software that should be paid for. Tell your kids it's illegal to download that kind of software and delete any you find on the hard disk. To find this kind of software, check the Windows desktop and the Programs section of the Start menu for any commercial software that you haven't paid for.

What Are Shareware and Freeware?

There are thousands of programs that can be downloaded free from the Internet, so most software your kids download is legal. *Shareware* is software that can be downloaded free, but that is expected to be paid for after a certain amount of time. And *freeware* is software that never needs to be paid for.

The Least You Need to Know

➤ Make sure your kids always run antivirus software and have it set to Auto-Protect.

➤ Your kids should always virus-scan any file or disk that someone gives to them.

➤ Tell your kids to never open a file attachment sent via email by someone they don't know.

➤ Make sure they get new virus definitions once a month from the antivirus maker's Web site.

➤ Check your children's computer for illegal MP3 music files.

➤ To make sure your kids don't download pornographic or inappropriate material, use filtering software.

➤ The best protection you can provide your children with is time with them to ensure they know the rules of the road. Always make time to spend time with your children to review what they are doing when they are online.

SAFE!!

AOL

SCRAAAACK

Chapter 16

Playing It Safe on America Online

In This Chapter

➤ The dangers your kids might face on America Online

➤ How parental controls can help you keep your kids safe

➤ Using the basic parental controls

➤ How to customize parental controls

➤ What to do if your children have been harassed on America Online

➤ Tips for kids and parents on how to stay safe on America Online

---

Any parent who subscribes to America Online (AOL, for short) knows that the service is heaven on earth to kids far and wide. After all, what's not to like? Every hour of the day and night there are thousands of kids chatting and ready to talk. There are tons of cool areas for kids to visit. There's easy email. There's instant access to the Internet. There are ways for kids to easily create their own home pages. What else could a kid want? (Aside from free Christina Aguilera tickets, every Pokémon card ever created, and a lifetime supply of M&Ms, that is.)

I can attest from long personal experience that both of my kids, Gabe and Mia (this is Preston talking), spend tons of time on the service. Trying to take AOL away from them would like trying to take away MTV, the *Harry Potter* books, or their CD players. It's just not going to happen.

But although America Online has just about everything kids want, it also has some things parents *don't* want: potential dangers. There are a host of dangers America Online poses for kids. Because it allows kids easy access to the Internet, it lets them easily get into trouble. And because it's so easy for people to disguise their identities on the service, it's easy for adults to target kids while posing as youngsters.

In this chapter, I teach you all about the kinds of dangers your kids face on America Online. More importantly, I show you how you can make sure your kids stay safe when using the service.

What Kinds of Dangers Do Kids Face on America Online?

America Online has gotten so big in large part because of how family-friendly it is and because kids spend so much time on the service. But its very size means that there are potential dangers lurking. After all, with more than 10 million subscribers, it's the size of a world-class city—and any city of that size has some bad neighborhoods and bad characters. It's your job as a parent to keep your kids away from the bad neighborhoods and make sure they know how to handle any bad characters they might come across.

Here's the rundown of the dangers on America Online you need to be worried about:

➤ **Your kids could be targeted in chat areas.** As you already know, your kids love to chat...and chat...and chat...and chat. They might not talk to you, but they'll gab for hours online with their friends and strangers. Unfortunately, adults can hang out in chat areas, posing as kids, looking for vulnerable, gullible kids to target. In fact, this is one of the biggest concerns parents have about kids' use of the Internet. According to a study by National Public Radio, 85 percent of people surveyed worried that dangerous strangers might make contact with their children.

Check to See Which Chat Areas Are Monitored on America Online

Some chat areas on America Online are monitored by adults to make sure no kids are targeted and that no inappropriate language is being used. Mostly these chat areas are found in the Kids Only area of the service. To get there, use the keywords "Kids Only."

➤ **Your kids could be targeted via instant messaging.** High on the kids' popularity list on America Online is instant messaging, the ability to hold private one-on-one conversations with others. There's a special danger in instant messaging—these conversations can't be monitored by anyone else, so they're a perfect way for strangers to target your kids. Making them even more dangerous is AOL Instant Messenger. This is a free program that anyone on the Internet can use to send instant messages to anyone on America Online. So it's not just America Online users you have to worry about—it's literally anyone with access to the Internet. Figure 16.1 shows AOL Instant Messenger in action.

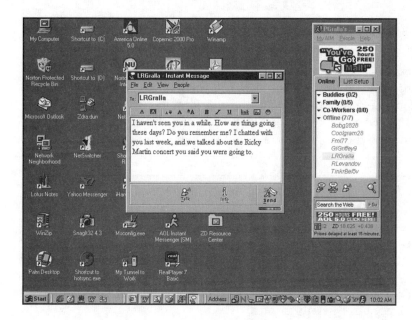

Figure 16.1

Anyone on the Internet can chat with your kid using AOL Instant Messenger—and the conversation can't be monitored by anyone.

➤ **Your kids can be targeted or harassed via email.** Just as adults can disguise themselves while chatting, they can disguise themselves via email. Your kids can also be sent harassing messages from other kids as well as from adults.

➤ **Your kids can receive inappropriate material via email.** Sending and receiving pictures on America Online is a breeze. It's great for sharing family photos. But it also means that your kids can be sent pornographic or other inappropriate pictures. Making things worse is that there's no way for your kids to know before looking at a picture whether it's pornographic. And making things even *worse* is that you can count on your kids being sent junk email asking them to visit pornographic or other inappropriate sites.

➤ **Your kids' passwords can be stolen.** Possibly the most common scam on America Online are people posing as America Online employees, asking users for their passwords via email or instant messaging. The requests are *always* false. America Online employees will never ask for a password.

➤ **Your kids can get viruses.** It's easy to download things on America Online. That means it's easy for kids to download virus-ridden files.

Computer Viruses Can Be Spread Via America Online Email

Kids don't have to download software to catch viruses on America Online. They can also get computer viruses via email. If your kids open a file attachment and that attachment has a virus in it, then your kids will get a computer virus. So make sure they know never to open file attachments from strangers. And even if they know the person who sent them the file, they should always virus-check it. For information on virus-checking software, turn to Chapter 15, "Downloading Do's and Don'ts."

➤ **Your kids can visit Internet sites and areas that are inappropriate.** America Online makes it very easy for kids to use the Internet. That means they might come across areas you consider inappropriate, such as pornographic or hate sites.

➤ **Your kids can have their privacy invaded.** It's amazingly easy to gather information about people on the Internet. That means whenever your kids are online, their privacy can be easily invaded.

Pretty scary sounding, we know. But we didn't tell you all this just to scare you. It's to make you aware of what you're up against. And there's good news here. America Online gives you tons of tools you can use to make sure your kids stay safe when they log on. So read on to see what those tools are and to learn how to use them.

Protect Your Kids with Parental Controls

There are a number of ways you can protect your kids on America Online, but the best and most comprehensive way is with a service called Parental Controls. From this single area on America Online, you can control just about every aspect of the way your kids use the Internet and America Online. For example, you can block them from viewing pornographic or inappropriate Web sites, and you can limit the way they can use chat or email. There's a lot more you can do as well, and I show you how to do it all in this section. What's great about this area is that you set all the rules for how your kids use the service, and you can change the rules whenever you want. For example, you can have more stringent rules for a young child, but when the child gets older and you're more confident the child can explore areas on his own, you can set less restrictive rules.

Getting Started with Parental Controls

First things first. To get started you have to go to the Parental Control area of America Online. To get there—surprise!—use the keywords, "Parental Controls." Figure 16.2 shows the screen that is displayed.

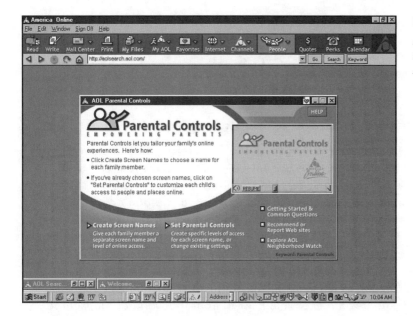

Figure 16.2

Here's the area where you set parental controls on America Online.

Before you set the controls, you need to create a separate screen name for each of your children. A *screen name* is the identity each kid uses to get onto America Online. It gives them each a separate account, including a separate email address, and enables you to set different levels of control for each. If you've already done this, you don't need to do it again; if your kids already have screen names, you're ahead of the game.

It's simple to create a screen name from the Parental Control area. Click **Create Screen Names**. Then, just follow the directions. Believe me, it really is that easy. If only raising kids were this simple!

What's great about parental controls is that you can set different rules for each of your kids. So if you have a brood of kids, you can have one set of rules for your five-year-old son, another for your eight-year-old daughter, another for your 12-year-old-son, and yet a different set for your 14-year-old daughter. (Four kids under the age of 15! Are you ready yet for a rest home?)

When you set parental controls, you block kids from going to certain parts of the Internet and America Online, and you restrict their access to certain services that could lead to problems, such as chat and downloading software. Internet sites are blocked by special site-blocking software built into America Online that's much like the site-blocking software people buy to block kids from visiting certain Internet sites. (For more information about this kind of software, turn to Chapter 13, "All About Filters.") On America Online, because the software is built into the service, this service is free.

Don't Share One Screen Name Among Your Children

Perhaps you don't want to go through the trouble of creating a separate screen name for each of your children. Take our advice—create separate screen names for each. Unless you do, you won't be able to control what your kids can and can't see and do on America Online. Just as important, if you don't create separate screen names for them, they'll have access to your email, and can even send out email under your name. (Just try explaining to your boss why you included him on a chain email letter warning that he'll die within the next three days unless he sends the letter on to 15 friends.) And if you don't create separate screen names, you'll get your kids' email, which generally means many of the aforementioned chain letters, silly jokes, incomprehensible missives from the world of Kid Culture, and general all-around goofiness.

How to Set Basic Parental Controls

When you use Parental Controls, you have two main choices: You can use a set of prefabricated built-in controls, or you can mix and match to create customized controls based on what you want each of your kids to be able to do online. It's much simpler to use the built-in ones, but they're also less flexible.

To use the basic, built-in controls, click **Set Parental Controls** when you get to the Parental Controls area. A screen like the one in Figure 16.3 should appear. It lists all of the screen names in your account and lets you set the Parental Controls for each one individually.

For each screen name, click the controls you want to set. The choices are Kids Only, Young Teen, and Mature Teen. (If you don't want any controls set for a screen name, leave it at General Access, which is the default.) America Online recommends that Kids Only be set for kids 12 and under, Young Teen be set for kids 13 through 15, and Mature Teen be set for kids 16 to 17.

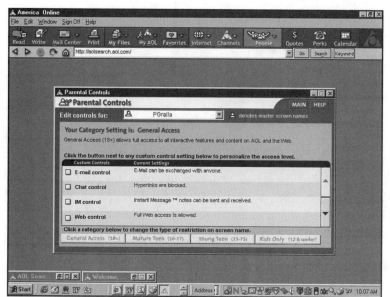

Figure 16.3

Now you're in control: Here's how to set parental controls on America Online.

When you do this, you might notice it's not all that clear what these controls actually do. You only get a very brief description, as you can see in Figure 16.3. That brief description helps a little bit, but not a whole lot. So here's the rundown on exactly what each of the settings mean:

➤ **Kids Only**   This lets kids visit only one area of America Online: the Kids Only channel. And it only allows kids to visit Web sites that are selected for age-appropriate content for kids up to 12 years old. Everything else is blocked. So kids can't send or receive Instant Messages. They can't join member-created or private chat rooms—although they can visit public chat rooms in the Kids Only area. They can't send or receive file attachments or pictures in their email. They're also blocked from Internet newsgroups that allow file attachments. (That's because objectionable pictures and other material can sometimes be found in newsgroups that allow file attachments, regardless of the newsgroup's subject.)

➤ **Young Teen**   This lets teens visit some chat rooms—but they can't visit member-created chat rooms or private chat rooms. They can only visit Web sites that have been judged appropriate for kids under 15. They're also blocked from Internet newsgroups that allow file attachments.

➤ **Mature Teen**   This restricts teens' access to certain Web sites—they can only visit sites that have been judged appropriate for kids under 17. They're also blocked from Internet newsgroups that allow file attachments.

What's a Newsgroup File Attachment?

Newsgroups are public Internet discussion areas that anyone can join. (For more information about newsgroups and their potential dangers, turn to Chapter 9, "The Scoop on Newsgroups.") But these groups aren't used only for public discussions. They're also used to trade and download pictures and other file attachments. Newsgroup reading software lets you download and view file attachments to messages in newsgroups. (America Online includes this software built into the service.) There are many newsgroups that are used to post pornography, which is why it's a good idea to block kids from newsgroups.

Here's the bad news: even newsgroups that have nothing to do with pornography aren't always safe. Because it's just as easy to send a message to one hundred newsgroups as it is to send a message to one, people often post pornographic pictures to every newsgroup they can think of.

Parental Controls Also Block Access to Premium Services

Parts of America Online charge money in addition to your normal monthly fee. For example, some online gaming areas charge a per-hour fee. Some kids can run up big bills playing online games or visiting other premium areas. Parental Controls blocks access to these premium services, which is a good idea for anyone worried about financial health.

Have It Your Way: Customizing Parental Controls

Basic Parental Controls are great. They're easy to set up, and they do the job. But they treat all kids the same, and you might want to allow your kids freedoms in certain areas, but want to restrict them in others. For example, maybe you trust your kids to visit only appropriate Web sites, but you're worried about their use of chat or email. Or maybe you're not worried about chat, but don't want them to visit certain newsgroups. In that case, you're in luck, because America Online offers a way to mix and match controls in any way that you'd like.

To customize controls, after you've gone to the area where you can set controls, click the screen name for which you want to set controls. Now you can customize how your kids can use chat, Instant Messages, email, the Web, and newsgroups, as well as how they can download files. For example, you can allow them full access to Instant Messages, but restrict their use of newsgroups.

To set controls for any of these services, click the control and then click the button at the bottom of the screen. For example, click **Chat control** to set controls for chat. (For once—logic on America Online!) When you do that, you see a screen like the one in Figure 16.4. You can set controls for each screen name just by clicking on the control you want to set.

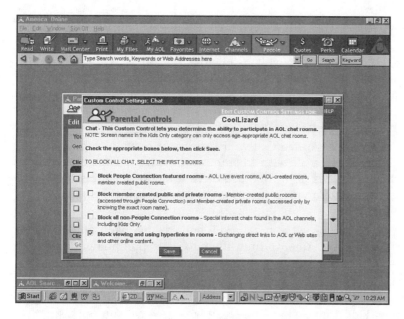

Figure 16.4

Customizing Parental Controls on America Online.

As you can see, there's a whole lot of choices, and not a lot of explanation of what they all mean. So here's the rundown on each:

➤ **Chat control** You get several ways to block different parts of chat. You can block chat hyperlinks—that way, if someone sends your kid a link to a Web site, inappropriate or not, he cannot click the link and go there. You can also block kids' access to chat in the People Connection, which is aimed at an older audience than kids and includes a number of adult topics. You also can block access to member-created chat rooms in the People Connection and to access to conference rooms—large chat rooms on America Online. You get to choose which of these to block and which to enable.

You Have to Close America Online Software for Parental Controls to Take Effect

Here's something annoying about Parental Controls: When you set them, they don't go into immediate effect. You have to sign off the service and then close down the America Online software. Until you do both those things, they don't go into effect. So, if one of your children uses America Online after you've set the controls, but you didn't close down the America Online software, the controls aren't in effect and won't be until the software is closed down and then started up again.

➤ **Instant Message control**   As I explained before, Instant Messages are private, live, one-on-one conversations. You can choose to block your kids from using Instant Messages. Whether someone is trying to send them a message from directly within America Online or from the Internet using AOL Instant Messenger, the messages will be blocked.

➤ **Downloading control**   Worried that your kids might download inappropriate pictures, programs, or a file with a computer virus in it? Then block their ability to download files. You can block them from downloading files directly on America Online or via an Internet service called FTP, a popular way to download files.

➤ **Web control**   If you're worried that your kids are viewing inappropriate sites on the Web, use this control. You can limit them to sites appropriate for kids 12 and under, ages up to 16, or ages up to 17.

➤ **Email control**   This one offers a mind-boggling number of choices. You have an incredible amount of control over how your kids can send and receive email. You can block your kids from exchanging email with anyone. You can also allow them to get email only from America Online members or only from specific Internet email addresses. And you can block them from getting email from specific America Online members and addresses. You can also block them from getting pictures or attachments in any email messages.

➤ **Newsgroup**   As with email, you have a whole lot of control over how your kids access newsgroups. You can block all access to newsgroups. You can instead block their access to specific newsgroups. Alternately, you can only allow them to go to certain newsgroups. You can even block your kids' access to newsgroups that contain specific words in their description. And you can block them from getting any of the graphics, sounds, animations, and photographs found on newsgroups by not allowing them to download files from newsgroups.

What Can You Do if You Find That America Online Didn't Block Your Kids from Visiting an Inappropriate Site?

The software that America Online uses isn't perfect—there's no way it can know about every site on the Internet that might not be good for your kids to visit. If you come across a site that you think should be blocked, go to the Parental Controls area, and click **Recommend or Report Web Sites.** Then fill out a form that lets you put the site location in as well as a description of the site and why it should be blocked. You can also ask that a certain site *not* be blocked—for example, a site about breast cancer that the software might have inadvertently blocked. In both cases, your request goes to the company that does the site blocking, and they make the final determination about what should be blocked and what shouldn't.

What to Do if Your Child Has Been Harassed on America Online

No matter how good a job you do as a parent protecting your kids on America Online, your child could possibly be harassed. They could get harassing email or Instant Messages, or they could be harassed in a chat room. If that happens, immediately report the harassment to America Online at keyword TOS.

Keep detailed information about the harassment. Make sure your child has the screen name of the person doing the harassing. Note the time and date that the harassment occurred. Most importantly, print out a copy of the harassment and send that along as well. If you don't, America Online might not take any action at all. One of my daughter's friends (this is Preston talking), received a death threat on America Online via an Instant Message. Her parents contacted America Online and had the screen name of the person who sent the threat. But because they had no actual record of the threat, America Online refused to take action.

Part 3 ➤ *Preparing Your Computer*

You Can Block Harassing or Annoying Email Sent from an Individual

What can you do if your child receives harassing or annoying email from an individual? You don't want to block your kids' use of email altogether, but on the other hand, you want to solve the problem. It's simple—you can block your kids from getting email from individual addresses. To do that, customize Parental Controls and choose **Email control**. Then follow the directions for blocking an individual address. I can vouch from personal experience that this works. Someone was harassing my daughter via email (this is Preston speaking; I blocked the address, and my daughter was never bothered again).

Kids' Safety Tips on America Online

Technology can help keep your kids safe on America Online—but technology can go only so far. Teaching your kids how to stay safe works even better than depending on technology to do it for you.

America Online has put together a good set of simple safety tips. Give it to your kids and have them read it and follow it:

1. Don't give your AOL password to anyone, even your best friend.
2. Never tell someone your home address, telephone number, or school name without your parent's permission first.
3. If someone says something that makes you feel unsafe or funny, don't respond. Take charge—keyword: Kid Help.
4. Never say you'll meet someone in person without asking your parent's permission first, and your parent should accompany you to the first meeting, which should be in public.
5. Always tell a parent about any threatening or bad language you see online.
6. Don't accept things from strangers (for example, email, files, or Web page addresses).

A Few Final Words to Parents

Remember, the best way to keep your kids safe anywhere online, including America Online, is to be a good parent and follow safety tips. For more information on general safety tips, see Part 4, "Preparing Your Kids."

To protect your kids' privacy, make sure they don't create an America Online member profile or, if they do, that they don't give out any personal information in it. To do that, have them use the keyword Profile and click **Create or Modify My Profile**. Check the profile they create so you can be sure they're not giving out personal information.

And for an excellent central place to go for advice of all kinds on safety on America Online, go to the Neighborhood Watch area by using the keywords "Neighborhood Watch."

Have Your Kids—and Yourself—Take a Safety Test

How much do you and your kids really know about online safety? You can find out in a special America Online area. Head to the Safe Surfin' Challenge area (at keyword, "Safe Surfin'") to find a site full of safety information, tips, and quizzes to make learning about online safety fun.

The Least You Need to Know

➤ Adults can disguise their identities in America Online chat areas, bulletin boards, and email when communicating with your kids.

➤ Basic Parental Controls let you make sure your kids don't do things or access areas that could be harmful. To get there, use the keywords "Parental Controls."

➤ If you want more control over how your kids use America Online, customize the Parental Controls.

➤ If your child has been harassed, keep a record of all the relevant information about the harasser and report him or her to America Online.

➤ Have your kids read and agree to follow America Online's safety tips for kids.

➤ Go to the Neighborhood Watch with the keyword "Safety" to get advice and help on how to keep your kids safe on America Online.

Part 4
Preparing Your Kids

Learning the ins and outs of your computer and the Internet, and using filtering software, are great ways to make sure your kids are safe when they go online.

But the truth is, the greatest protection they'll ever have has nothing to do with hardware, software, or even technology. The greatest protection they have is you, and the advice you give them about how to keep themselves safe when they venture online.

Ah, you're probably thinking, but what advice should I give them?

We're glad you asked. That's what you learn in this section of the book. Here's where you find out how to set guidelines for your kids and enforce rules about Internet use at home. You learn how to teach "Netiquette" to your kids—in other words, how they should behave when they're online. You find out about what you can do if things go really bad and you need to contact law enforcement about online problems. And finally, we give you a great list of kid-friendly places your kids can go on the Internet.

So dive right in. This last part of the book might be the most important part of all, because in it you give your kids the knowledge they need so they can keep themselves safe online without any help from others.

Chapter 17

Setting Guidelines for Your Kids

> ## In This Chapter
>
> ➤ Basic parenting tips for keeping your kids safe online
>
> ➤ What advice you can give your kids that will make sure they stay safe and secure on the Internet
>
> ➤ Basic guidelines your kids should agree to before they go online
>
> ➤ How using the Parenting Pledge makes you a better parent when it comes to your kids' Internet use
>
> ➤ Deciding how much time your kids should spend online

As you've seen throughout this book, technology can do a lot to help you keep your kids safe and secure when they're online. But the truth is, when it comes to keeping your kids safe on the Internet, there's something that's a whole lot more important than technology—you and your relationship with your children. The best way to keep them safe is to develop guidelines for how they use the Internet, making sure they're comfortable with the guidelines, and that they come to you whenever they have problems online. Nothing can keep them safer and more secure than that.

In this chapter, you take a look at how to set guidelines with your kids, and how to make sure the Internet brings you closer together as a family, and doesn't drive you further apart.

Your Best Line of Defense: Good Parenting

All kinds of advice, tips, software, and Web sites are available to help you keep your kids safe and protect their privacy when they go online. They're all necessary, and they're all useful. But the truth is, being a good parent is more important than all of that put together. It sounds trite, I know. After all, we all think we're good parents.

But I've noticed that when it comes to the Internet, parents can get strange. They act as if the Internet is separate from the rest of their and their children's lives. They can start to trust their children less, or feel unsure that the things they've taught their children about the real world carry over into the online world.

More important than everything else in this chapter is the need to apply the same common-sense rules of parenting to the Internet that you apply in the real world. Go back to the basics: teach your kids right from wrong; show them what's appropriate for them to do and view online and what isn't. Recognize that the online world is like the real world; you want to know who your children's friends are and where they're visiting, but try not to be overbearing or intrusive about it. Most of all, you want your children to trust you—enough that they come to you if they need advice, want to know whether visiting certain Web sites is suitable, or are made uncomfortable by things that have been said to them in chat rooms or via email.

And, as many of us have learned the hard way, often the best way to get your kids to trust you is to show that *you* trust *them*. That means that although you want to know what your kids are doing online, you should be careful about not being intrusive, and you shouldn't try to find out what your kids are doing online without them knowing about it.

Check This Out

Get a Helpful, Free Pamphlet on How to Protect Your Children

An excellent resource for any parent concerned about how to keep their children safe online is "Child Safety on the Information Highway" or "Teen Safety on the Information Highway" by the National Center for Missing and Exploited Children and the Interactive Services Association (8403 Colesville Road, Suite 865, Silver Spring, MD 20910). Much of the information in this section of the book is inspired by that pamphlet. You can read the entire pamphlet and get more information at the National Center for Missing and Exploited Children Web site at www. missingkids.org.

I can tell you from personal experience that this works (this is Preston talking). I've given my kids pretty free rein in what they do online, and it's paid off. They regularly ask me before they download files from the Internet, whether they can register at certain sites, and when they come across something online that makes them uncomfortable. Again, just make sure that however you handle your kids' online use, it brings you together instead of pushes you apart.

First Things First: Talk with Your Kids

As many parents know from instinct and experience, the most important thing you can do with your kids is talk to them. That isn't any less true online than it is in the real world. Here's a gentle reminder: Don't do all the talking—listen to what they have to say as well. You'll find that you learn as much as they do, and you'll develop a closer relationship with your kids.

When you talk, you should teach them rules about how to stay safe—in essence, teach them to be what's known in the "real" world as "street smart," but that's called "CyberSmart" online.

Teenagers Are the Most at Risk

The children most at risk online tend to be teenagers. One reason is that you're more likely to leave them unsupervised than you would younger children. Teenagers go online largely to meet other kids, send and receive email, participate in bulletin boards, and chat...and chat...and chat. Now not only do teens tie up your phone line by talking on the telephone, but they also tie it up by dialing in to the Internet to chat. In fact, Preston's teenage daughter, Mia, can often be found talking into the phone, while chatting online at the same time—often to the same friends! Mia, get off the phone already! Mom needs to use it!

But what should you be talking with them about? These are the kinds of things you should explain when having a talk with them about the Internet:

➤ **Warn them about the kinds of sites they should stay away from.**
Using site-blocking software just isn't enough. You kids will use the Internet at places other than your home computer. And kids being kids, they might find ways around site-blocking software. So make clear that you don't want them viewing pornographic sites, hate sites, or other kinds of sites you don't want them to visit. Don't merely issue a command—explain why you don't want them visiting those sites, and listen to what they say in response.

➤ **Explain to them that sites might not be what they seem.** The many hate groups that create Web sites have become increasingly sophisticated about disguising their ulterior motives and who they really are. Often, a hate site doesn't appear to be one at first blush. In fact, one racist site even has photos that apparently extol Martin Luther King—until you read more closely. Teach your kids how to recognize the real thing from the phony.

➤ **Let them know that if they're in doubt about whether they should visit a specific site, they should come to you.** Make sure your kids trust you, and tell them that if they have any doubt, they should come to you to see whether a site is suitable for them to visit. They should also let you know if something or someone online makes them uncomfortable. If they come to you, you might see something that angers you, but don't lash out at your kids or blame them—they might be less likely to tell you next time.

➤ **Make sure they don't give out personal information.** Personal data (such as home address, school name, or telephone number) should never be revealed in public or private message areas such as bulletin boards, chat rooms, via Instant Messages, or via email. When your kids give out this information, it's easy for a stalker or predator to learn everything about them, and ease their way into kids' lives. There was even a case near where I live in Massachusetts in which a predator learned where a child lived via the Internet and then broke into her house to try to abduct her.

➤ **Don't allow your child to meet someone person-to-person that they've met online without getting your approval.** If you agree with such a meeting, you should go along, and the meeting should be held in a public place.

➤ **Tell them not to respond to messages that are suggestive, obscene, threatening, or that make them feel uncomfortable.** If your children come across any messages like that, they should tell you about it. The next course of action is to contact your online service or service provider, send them the message, and ask for their help. If the message is truly threatening, contact the police.

Child Pornography Is Illegal

Laws regarding adult content on the Internet are currently being tested in the courts, but child pornography is illegal on or off the Internet. If you become aware of any use or transmission of child pornography online, contact the National Center for Missing and Exploited Children at 1–800–843–5678 and notify your online service.

➤ **Make sure your children know that people might not be who they say they are.** They should always keep in mind that it's easy for someone online to pose as someone else. It's easy for a 45-year-old man to pose as a 10-year-old girl. Even having a scanned picture should not be taken for proof.

Have Your Kids Agree to These Rules Before They Go Online

Talking with your kids is good. But these discussions needs to be reinforced, preferably with guidelines. And just so they don't forget the guidelines, consider typing them out and having your kids sign them.

What guidelines to use? The National Center for Missing and Exploited Children and the Interactive Services Association have come up with a set of rules that kids should agree to before going online, to protect their safety. Every parent should visit www. missingkids.org (see Figure 17.1).

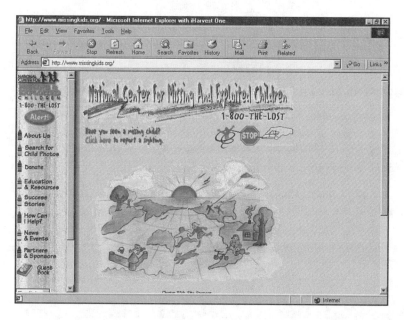

Figure 17.1

For information on missing kids and help with online safety, go to the National Center for Missing and Exploited Children site at www. missingkids.org.

Here are their rules. They're good ones. Have your kids agree to them before they go online. Consider posting them next to their computer so they can refer to the rules whenever they are online.

➤ I will not give out personal information such as my address, telephone number, parents' work address or telephone number, or the name and location of my school without my parents' permission.

➤ I will tell my parents right away if I come across any information that makes me feel uncomfortable.

➤ I will never agree to get together with someone I "meet" online without first checking with my parents. If my parents agree to the meeting, I will make sure that it is in a public place and bring my mother or father along.

➤ I will never send a person my picture or anything else without first checking with my parents.

➤ I will not respond to any messages that are mean or in any way make me feel uncomfortable. It is not my fault if I get a message like that. If I do, I will tell my parents right away so they can contact the online service.

➤ I will talk with my parents so we can set up rules for going online. We will decide upon the time of day I can be online, the length of time I can be online, and appropriate areas for me to visit. I will not access other areas or break these rules without their permission.

Check This Out

Teach Your Kids Not to Harass Others or Pose as Someone Else

It's not enough to teach your kids how to be safe online—you should teach them to respect the rights of others as well. Some kids bully, harass, and demean other kids in chat rooms—teach your children never to do that. Most of this kind of online behavior probably comes from children, not adults.

Tell your kids they shouldn't pose as someone else. Too often, posing as someone else is a license to exhibit the kind of harassing or unfriendly behavior they'd never do if they were using their real name. For more information about how your kids should—and shouldn't—behave online, turn to Chapter 18, "Teaching Netiquette to Your Kids."

Make Sure Your Kids Don't List Private Information in Their Member Profiles

Your kids might think they're following all the rules you give for online safety, but might be breaking one of the most important ones—giving out private information—without realizing it. America Online, as well as many Web sites and message boards, allow kids to create online profiles. This is where kids can list their hobbies, names, addresses, birth dates, and much more identifying information that you don't want made public. When they list that information, it is available to anyone who wants to see it.

Make sure to tell them they should not list any of that information in their member profiles. If you use America Online, there's a way to check your kids' profiles. First, click the **People** link at the top of the screen, and then choose **Get AOL Member Profile**. (If you want, you can just use the shortcut **Control-G**). Next, type in the screen name of your child and click **OK**. Your child's profile comes onscreen. Make sure it doesn't contain any identifying information. If it does, get your kid to change it.

Take the Parents' Pledge

Having your kids agree to those rules helps a great deal in making sure they stay safe online. But those rules alone don't let you off the hook. You have some responsibilities as well.

Yes, you get a set of rules as well—rules that govern how you treat your kids when they go online. These were developed by a *Los Angeles Times* columnist named Larry Magid and are posted at his excellent Web site www.safekids.com (see Figure 17.2).

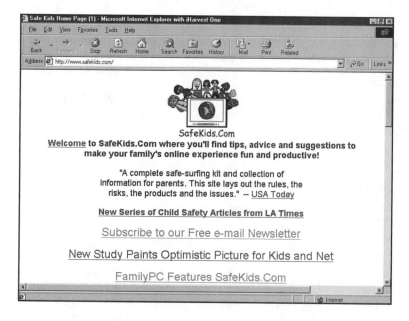

Figure 17.2

SafeKids.Com is another good site for parents who want information on how to keep their kids safe online.

Here's your Parents' Pledge. Read it, sign it, and live by it.

➤ I will get to know the services and Web sites my child uses. If I don't know how to use them, I'll get my child to show me how.

➤ I will set reasonable rules and guidelines for computer use by my children and will discuss these rules and post them near the computer as a reminder. I'll

241

remember to monitor their compliance with these rules, especially when it comes to the amount of time they spend on the computer.

➤ I will not overreact if my child tells me about a problem he or she is having on the Internet. Instead, we'll work together to try to solve the problem and prevent it from happening again.

➤ I promise not to use the Internet or computers as an electronic babysitter.

➤ I will help make the Internet a family activity and ask my child to help plan family events using the Internet.

➤ I will try to get to know my child's "online friends" just as I try to get to know his or her other friends.

Spend Time Surfing with Your Kids

You can do more than sign the Parents' Pledge. If you spend time browsing the Web with your kids, they soon learn what's an appropriate site and what isn't. So guide them—but make sure to look for sites they're interested in or it won't be of much use.

I've found that when you're planning a family vacation, or if you're in the market for buying a car or other goods, are perfect times for going on the Web with your kids. We've planned many vacations together and had great fun.

Leading your kids to kid-friendly search sites is a great idea as well. For more information about those sites, turn to Chapter 14, "How to Search the Web Safely."

The Time Crunch: How Much Time Should Your Kids Spend Online?

Now we come to probably the most contentious of all family computing issues—how much time should your kids spend online, or even spend using the computer? (And these days, using the computer almost always means spending time online.)

If you're a kid, the answer is "all the time." If you're a parent, you sometimes think the answer should be "never."

The answer, obviously, is somewhere between the two, although that's a whole lot of territory to cover.

The first rule of thumb should be this: If computer use interferes with your children's normal life instead of enhances it, then they're using the computer too much. How much time that is varies from family to family. But if they're no longer as physically active as they once were, or if they're spending less time with friends or on homework, you've got a problem. If their conversation is more about the Internet and computers than about other things, you've got a problem. If you can tell that they're constantly only going through the motions of doing other things so they can get time on the computer, you've got a problem.

Check This Out

Some Products Can Control the Amount of Time Kids Spend on the Computer

If you want to be absolutely sure that your children use the computer only for certain hours during the day and the week, several pieces of software can lock them out except when you specify it. The most well-known is Guard Dog, which is also a "personal firewall" and site-blocking software.

All parents, though, should agree to rules with their children about computer use, particularly how much time can be spent on the computer, and during what hours they can be on the computer. Make the rules detailed and explicit. If they're not, kids will inevitably find ways around them. They find ways around every other rule that's squishy, so why not this one?

Some parents I know have come up with a no-weekday computer rule. During Monday through Thursday, the computer is only to be used for schoolwork. All other use of it is *verboten*. During the weekends, however, kids can use the computer. In fact, at the Gralla household, we currently have a modified version of that rule: During the week, our kids have to ask permission to use the computer, and then it's only for a limited time.

By the way, notice I said that we *currently* have the rule. That's because we often experiment with the best way to handle computer use. After you come up with a plan, make sure it works. If it doesn't, come up with a better one.

Above All, Have Fun

By the way, here's one last word about setting guidelines for Internet use. Above all, have fun with your kids online. Making sure your kids are safe shouldn't be about confrontation. It should be about making sure you can all have a great time together online and as a family.

The Least You Need To Know

➤ Apply the same common-sense rules of parenting to Internet use that you apply to your kids' normal life.

➤ Don't allow your child to meet someone person-to-person that they've meet online without getting your approval; plan to be there with the child and meet in a public place.

➤ Your kids shouldn't give out information—such as home address, school name, or telephone number—that can be used to identify them.

➤ Make sure your children know that people they meet on the Internet might not be who they say they are.

➤ Have your kids agree to rules for online safety—and you should sign the Parents' Pledge as well.

➤ If your kids don't spend as much time as they used to with friends, home-work, or on physical activity, they're spending too much time online.

AND DON'T SPIT!!

GOTCHA!!

Chapter 18

Teaching Netiquette to Your Kids

In This Chapter

➤ Why your kids should be concerned about Netiquette

➤ The basic rules of Netiquette to teach your kids

➤ How to make sure your kids don't become hackers

➤ What your kids should know about chat room Netiquette

➤ What they should know about message board Netiquette

You teach your kids to say "please" and "thank you," in the real world. You teach them to respect their elders. You teach them not to eat their peas with their butter knives. (Or at least I *hope* you teach them not to do that.)

Well, when they head off into cyberspace, they need to learn the proper way to behave as well. And that proper way to behave while online is called *Netiquette*.

In this chapter, you find out what you should teach your kids about Netiquette so they have the best experience possible online. As to eating peas off their butter knives—that's something you have to deal with by yourself.

Why Bother to Teach Your Kids Netiquette?

"What's the big deal about Netiquette?" you might wonder. Does anyone really care how people act in cyberspace? What consequences are there if kids don't behave properly?

What Does "TOS" Mean?

On America Online, TOS stands for Terms of Service. They're the conditions you agree to when you sign on to the service. If you or your kids break them, you can be kicked off the service. For details, use the keyword "TOS" on America Online.

In fact, there are a lot of consequences. Here are the main ones:

➤ **Your child will lose friends.** If your child antagonizes others, he'll lose out on one of the best things about the Internet—the chance to make friends and communicate with others.

➤ **Your child could be kicked off message boards and out of chat areas.** If he breaks the rules often enough, he won't even be allowed in areas to talk to others.

➤ **Your America Online or other account could be terminated.** For example, America Online has what are called Terms of Service. If your kid breaks those, you could be kicked off of America Online.

➤ **Your child could get into legal troubles.** A child might think that it's a lark to do hacking or harass someone online. But there are serious consequences for those actions—legal ones.

➤ **Your child will help contribute to the deterioration of the Internet.** Perhaps the best thing about the Internet is the way that it connects people to one another. But when courtesy and rules break down, so do the connections. And the Internet loses one of the main things that makes it special.

One final thing to keep in mind here: When your children observe proper Netiquette, that means that they'll be happier online as well. People will like them more, they'll make more friends, and they'll feel part of something larger than themselves. And that's a rare thing to find these days.

Oh, Behave! Netiquette Rules Kids Should Follow

So, how should your kids behave online? The rules aren't particularly complicated. Start off with common sense. Tell them that the Internet is a lot like the real world, and they should follow the same rules for treating people online as they do in the real world.

There are a lot of sites that give advice on Netiquette. It's a good idea to send your kids to them. A good place to start is the Top Ten Netiquette Tips from Disney, at `http://disney.go.com/cybernetiquette/tips.html` (see Figure 18.1).

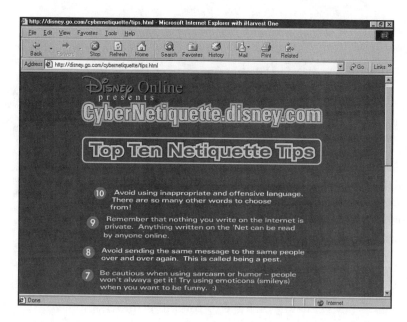

Figure 18.1

Kids love Disney, so send them to these Netiquette tips from Disney for some good advice.

There are a lot of specific things your kids should know about online behavior. Here's the rundown on what to tell them:

➤ **Don't use all capital letters in chats and email.**   WHEN YOU DO, IT LOOKS LIKE YOU'RE SHOUTING! And just as it's annoying when people shout at you rather than talk in the real world, it's also annoying on the Internet. If they keep doing it, people won't want to chat or email with them.

➤ **Avoid nasty language**.   Sometimes kids online think it's okay to use nasty language. It's not. Again, they shouldn't use nasty language in the real world, and for the same reasons shouldn't use it online.

➤ **Don't start or contribute to "flames."**   A flame is when someone behaves obnoxiously by attacking other people for no reason. A lot of kids act out online and flame. Make sure your kids don't.

➤ **Don't hurt others' feelings**.   As any parent knows, kids can be cruel to one another. Make sure your kids don't hurt other kids' feelings.

➤ **Don't ruin cyberspace for others.**   When kids are frustrated or angry, they sometimes act out. And for some kids, it's tempting to act out online. So a kid might be tempted to do something like going into a chat room and holding down the 9 key this many times: 999999999999999999999999.

➤ **Don't harass others or make threats.**   This one should be obvious, but sometimes kids get carried away. Your kids should know that there can be legal consequences to this kind of action.

Constantly Sending Sound Files on AOL Chats Is Obnoxious

On America Online, there is a way that kids can make everyone else's computer in a chat room make a sound or talk, such as having everyone else's computer say, "You've Got Mail." Doing that once a session might be funny. Doing it continually is obnoxious, and it should not be done. If your kids know how to do it, make sure they do it in moderation.

➤ **Keep calm if people attack you or annoy you.** The most common thing that makes kids behave improperly is losing their tempers. Tell them to walk away from the computer if they get angry, or come to you if they have a problem.

➤ **Don't crash a discussion area or chat.** Many discussion areas and chats are devoted to a particular topic, such as pets. When kids visit them, they should stick to that topic. They shouldn't talk about other things instead—it's like crashing a party when they're not invited.

➤ **Respect people's privacy.** If someone tells them a secret, they shouldn't tell it to others. On the Internet, it's easy to pass along secrets because kids can just forward an email or chat message. They should never do it.

➤ **Be careful when using humor or being sarcastic.** It's easy to be misunderstood when chatting or sending email. Humor or sarcasm can be misread and taken as nastiness. Tell your kids that a good way to make sure they're not misunderstood is to use what are called "smileys" or "emoticons" to express their emotions, such as <g> for grin and :) to show a joke is being told.

➤ **Don't impersonate others**. It's easy to pretend that you're someone else online. In small ways, kids do it all the time—they might add a year to their age or exaggerate their accomplishments. But impersonating someone else, such as an America Online employee, is another matter altogether. Make sure your kids never do it.

➤ **Don't post false information about someone.** One way that kids can be cruel to each other is lying about other people. They can do it online just as they can in the real world. So make sure they don't.

➤ **Don't send "spam."** Spam is email advertising something sent to someone who didn't ask for it. So if you're trying to sell something, don't send email about it to people you don't know.

Some Common Smileys

There are countless smileys your kids can use. Here are some common ones:

:-)	The original smiley shows humor or happiness	:-}	A smiley with an embarrassed smile—you're embarrassed
:-(	A frown shows sadness	;-)	A wink shows a joke
:=)	A smiley with a big nose	:'-(	A smiley crying shows sadness
:-D	A big smile—you're happy	=:-O	A frightened smiley
:-|	A bored smiley—you're bored	:-)8	A smiley with a bow tie
8-)	A smiley with glasses	:-()	A big-mouthed smiley
=:-)	A smiley with a punk haircut	:-b	A smiley sticking out his tongue
:-o	A surprised smiley—you're shocked or surprised	$-)	You just won the lottery

Hacking and Other Woes

Your kid, a hacker? No way! Not yours!

Well, you're probably right. Most kids aren't hackers. And your kid probably isn't.

But you can never be too sure. Have a talk with your kids and explain to them that breaking into another person's or company's computer is just like breaking into someone's house—and it's just as illegal. Let them know that harming other people's computers with viruses or other programs is dangerous and illegal as well.

The truth is, though, hacking often starts out as small pranks that even young kids can do. Talk to your kids about those. One common computer prank is posing as someone else, and trying to get that person's passwords. Kids often send false email or instant messages to other kids, saying they work for America Online and ask for passwords. It doesn't involve programming, but the truth is, that's pretty much the same thing as hacking.

Another prank on America Online is called "punting." That's the use of a program to kick someone else off of America Online. No special expertise is required. A kid can just download a program and run it. So make sure you kids don't do any punting, either. If you start early enough and make sure these pranks don't start, you'll go a long way toward making sure your kids never become hackers.

Yackers Away: What Your Kids Should Know About Chatting Etiquette

Kids love to chat and send instant messages. And when they do in places like America Online (see Figure 18.2), they should keep in mind all of the general rules for Netiquette outlined earlier in this chapter. They should also follow online safety rules. But there are some special chat rules they should follow as well.

Figure 18.2

Here's a typical chat room on America Online. Busy, busy, busy!

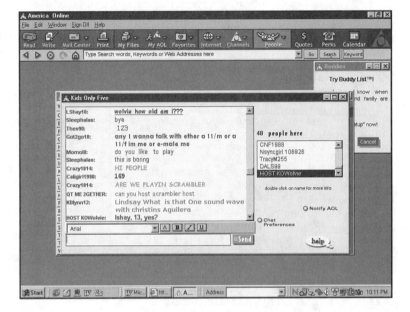

➤ **Before they enter a chat room, they should read the instructions for the room.**   Different rooms have different rules. They should know the rules of the room before entering.

➤ **Before they enter the conversation, they should listen for a few minutes, to see what the room is like.**   They should make sure that their tone and conversation fits in with the room.

➤ **They should find out who the host or SYSOP (System Operator) is who is in charge of the room.**   That way, if they have questions or concerns, they know who to go to.

➤ **They can use the "ignore" feature if someone bothers them.**   Most chat software has a feature that lets kids ignore someone who bothers them. They should use that, and can also report the person to the host.

Your Kids Should Never Send Large Attachments Without Asking

Kids love to send pictures and other things to each other as attachments to email messages, or directly to one another with instant message software. They should never send a large attachment to someone else without first asking if it's okay. It can take a very long time to receive a large attachment, tying up someone's computer for a long time. The person receiving it should be allowed to decide ahead of time whether he wants his modem tied up.

Get the Message? Netiquette for Kids on Message Boards

Kids love to hang out on message boards, especially when it's about a hobby. Figure 18.3 shows a kids' message board about dinosaurs on America Online.

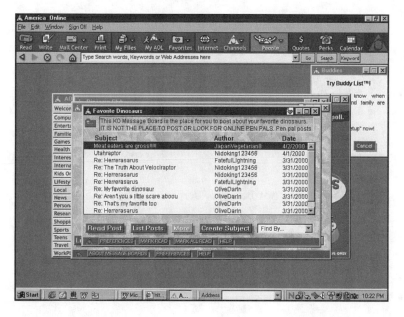

Figure 18.3

Here's an example of a message board on America Online; it's a popular place for kids to hang out.

Techno Talk

What's a FAQ?

At times, there will be what's called a FAQ posted about the rules of a particular chat room. FAQ stands for Frequently Asked Questions, and it contains basic information about the room. There are FAQs for many things on the Internet, not just chat rooms.

When spending time on these boards, kids should follow the same basic Netiquette rules and safety rules that you've taught them up until now. But there are a few specific things they need to know as well:

➤ **They shouldn't "spam" a message board with chain letters, jokes, advertising, or similar messages that have nothing to do with the purpose of the board.** This just annoys everyone and could get them banned from the message board.

➤ **They should read the rules of the board before posting.** The only way to follow the rules is to know what they are.

➤ **They shouldn't keep repeating the same idea or message over and over.** For some reason, kids sometime do this. It makes everyone angry at them and could lead to them being banned from the message board.

➤ **Before asking a question, they should see whether it's been answered already.** Few things are more annoying to people on message boards than people asking questions that have already been answered repeatedly.

The Least You Need To Know

Just as in the real world you teach your children to behave properly, you should also teach them the rules of online behavior, called Netiquette. If they follow these rules, their time online will be a lot more fun for them. Here's what you need to know:

➤ Kids need to follow basic Netiquette, or else they might find no one will want to communicate with them—and they could also get you kicked off America Online.

➤ Kids should avoid nasty language, not harass or demean anyone else, and treat everyone they meet online with respect.

➤ Kids should not use capital letters when communicating with others. It's interpreted as shouting, and annoys people.

➤ Before entering a chat room or message board, they should read the rules so they know how to act.

➤ Kids should be careful about using humor or being sarcastic. It can lead to misunderstandings. Use "smileys" and "emoticons, such as" <g> for grin and :) to show humor.

Chapter 19

Finding Law Enforcement When You Need It

In This Chapter

➤ A glimpse at what law enforcement is doing on the Internet

➤ Find out whom to contact if something bad happens to your child online

➤ Learn about valuable resources to help you protect kids online

Hopefully, most of you will never experience any of the online dangers described in this book, such as cyberstalking or unsolicited, obscene email. However, if you do, this chapter can assist you in finding the help you need. You'll find plenty of resources you can turn to in times of trouble and dozens of Web sites that offer advice and tips for protecting children on the Internet. Plus, you' also learn what law enforcement agencies are up to in their quest to combat online crime.

Law Enforcement on the Internet

Like most of the real world, law enforcement has been a bit slow in catching on to the Internet. This lag happens when any new technology hits the scene. Perhaps you feel this as well, especially if your kids know more about computers than you do. It takes a while for technological advances to trickle through the system, and there's no better example of a "system" than the government. Government agencies, including law enforcement, are typically burdened by bureaucracies that are mercilessly slow to take on new technologies. Depending on where you live, the changes can occur even more slowly than mercilessly slow (which is pretty darn slow, indeed).

Thankfully, this big, old ship we call "government" is starting to change course to address these issues. Today's law enforcement agencies are becoming increasingly cyber-savvy and are using the numerous tools at their disposal to fight online crime. They'd better get cyber-savvy fast—the criminals certainly are.

Laws Do Apply to the Internet

With all the stories about the Internet in the news these days, a person might get the idea that it is a lawless, criminal-infested place, much like the early days of the American West. Like the wild, wild West of yesteryear, the Internet is a sprawling wilderness teeming with new settlers, some of whom are out to stake a claim, and some of whom are just passing through. Just when you think things are going well, a gunslinger rides into town and causes trouble. That's when you need a sheriff, a noble lawman who can bring peace to the cyberstreets. Hold on a second while I cue up the theme music from "High Noon" (or another one of the classic western movies).

As explained in Chapter 2, "A Walk Down the Bad Side of Cybertown," the Internet is just a reflection of society. We've got bad guys and good guys offline as well as online. Remember, most Internet users are decent, upstanding citizens, but there is a percentage of the criminal element roaming about cyberspace.

You'll be happy to know that government laws that apply to crime offline apply to crime online too, so the Internet is not exactly lawless. For example, the U.S. government's laws concerning fraud apply to fraud that occurs on the Internet. The attractive anonymity of the Internet can make criminals feel very safe and hidden, but just because we can't see them physically doesn't mean their acts are anything less than criminal. They are not immune to the law if they use the Internet to commit a crime.

Take a look at Figure 19.1, from the U.S. Department of Justice Web site (www.usdoj. gov). It shows a list of recent reports the DOJ has published regarding computer crime. One of the reports lists various cases that were prosecuted in which criminals broke the laws.

Figure 19.1

Visit the U.S. Department of Justice Web site to find out more about laws and computer crime.

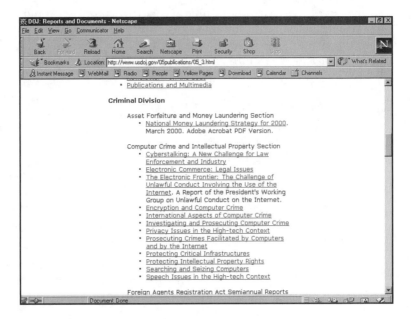

As far as children are concerned, any of the following incidents is considered unlawful in most countries around the world:

➤ **Manufacture, distribution, or possession of child pornography**   Any visual image of a minor engaged in, or seemingly engaged in, sexually explicit conduct (or simply posed in a lewd fashion) is considered child pornography. This even includes images that have been altered to resemble children.

➤ **Enticement of children to perform or engage in sexual acts and/or to meet a child offline**   Pedophiles have found a relatively anonymous way of befriending children through various chat rooms on the Internet. They spend numerous hours grooming potential victims with the goal of eventually exploiting them in some fashion or meeting them in person.

➤ **Promotion of child pornography in the form of advertisement or tourism**   Child-sex tourism is an underground problem in foreign countries. Some estimate that more than one million children in Asia are involved in prostitution. It's not uncommon to find brochures and advertisements online that solicit travelers seeking sex with children to visit areas in Asia, Latin America, and Eastern Europe.

➤ **Child molestation of any kind**
Enough said.

In your efforts to protect children online, you need to be aware of the laws. Most of the United States have established well-defined laws regarding child pornography; check to see whether your state has such measures in place. In addition to laws to protect children, there are also laws to protect everybody on the Internet—laws against fraud, harassment, stalking, impersonation, hate crimes, and so on. So, contrary to news reports, there is law on the Internet—it's just extremely hard to enforce, that's all.

Who's a Minor?

According to the Child Protection Act of 1984, the law defines a child as anyone younger than 18 years old. Laws in Europe differ, of course. Still, a picture of a nude 17-year-old that might be legal in Europe *is* illegal when it arrives on your stateside computer.

Crime Fighter Woes

In truth, most local police departments around the United States are ill-equipped to fight cybercrime, so enforcing the law on the Internet is problematic. If you were to hand a complaint to your nearest police officer, chances are he or she is unfamiliar with the Internet. Even if the officer did know what to do, catching a cybercriminal is no small feat. Cybercriminals know how to utilize Internet tools such as "scrubbers" and "anonymizers," special programs that help them hide their identities. Cybercriminals also use multiple anonymous email accounts. All this amounts to one profound point—criminals can be hard to track online. It's not easy to track someone electronically; there's no cyber-bloodhound for this sort of thing.

The Internet is practically without boundaries, which also makes it difficult to track criminals. The Internet crosses state and international boundaries, making it hard to determine what laws apply to criminals in which country. Jurisdiction problems come into play. Legislators are scrambling to pass new laws and amend old ones to cover this new technology.

The most difficult part of fighting online crime is in the prosecution of it. This is certainly true with any crime, but it's even more difficult with online crime. Investigators must really know their technology in order to gather evidence, and lawmakers must continue to test laws that uphold our online safety.

Don't despair. Law enforcement might be struggling to catch up in terms of Internet know-how, but catch up it will. More and more high-tech and computer crime divisions are cropping up among law enforcement agencies. Agencies such as the FBI and U.S. Customs are working extremely hard at catching crime on the Internet.

Look at an example of law enforcement at work—in the fall of 1999, a vice president at Infoseek heading up Walt Disney Company's Web sites was arrested for soliciting sex with a 13-year-old girl. The FBI began investigating the man earlier in the spring of 1999 when they found him soliciting minors in a chat room. Using an FBI agent who pretended to be a 13-year-old girl, the FBI communicated with the man throughout the summer. Eventually, the man sought to meet with the "girl." They met indeed. He approached the "girl," who was a female agent posing as the 13-year-old, at a roller coaster ride wearing the agreed upon article of clothing that would identify him to her. Agents rushed in and arrested him after he asked the "girl" to meet him on the beach. Seizing the man's computer, they found child pornography. He even directed them to his Web site where he had posted a picture of his...well, his naughty bits.

Watch Those Chat Rooms!

Nobody really knows how many pedophiles lurk in Internet chat rooms. Enter any chat room posing as a child and see how long it takes for someone to "approach" you. That's what one Seattle police detective does to demonstrate to parents the dangers of online chat. She poses as a young girl online and it's usually only a matter of minutes before someone makes a move. Parents are often quite shocked at the direction of the questions aimed at the seemingly "young girl."

Or take the example of a U.S. Customs agent who pretends to be a minor online to nab pedophiles. He arrests 30 or so pedophiles a year. Chat rooms are definitely an online danger for kids. For more information about chatting online, see Chapter 5, "Chat, Chat, and More Chat."

This is just one of the cases the FBI handled last year. Rest assured that agencies like the FBI, U.S. Customs, U.S. Postal Inspection Service, U.S. Drug Enforcement Association, U.S. Department of Justice, and many others are battling online crime even as you read this. So even if your local police officer doesn't know much about Internet crimes, she can hopefully put you in touch with law enforcement agencies that do.

On the Side

In addition to regular law enforcement agencies, there are independent agencies that can help you tackle Internet complaints and reports. Agencies such as InterGOV (www.intergov.org), WebPolice (www.webpolice.com), and ScamWatch (www.scamwatch.org) use a range of techniques to investigate complaints. They investigate cyberstalking, child pornography, drug dealing, child abductions, and online harassment.

Who You Gonna Call?

If you do suspect cybercrime activity or are a victim of it yourself (or your child is), what should you do about it? Report it, of course. You don't want the same crime to happen to anyone else, especially another child, right? You can take some practical steps to report a crime, and plenty of sources are available to help you find more information about protecting your family from online dangers.

Identify the Problem

When you or your child encounters an Internet problem, the first thing you need to do is evaluate its seriousness. Receiving unsolicited email, for example, is a nuisance, but it's not really a problem. Receiving *obscene* unsolicited email is a problem, particularly if it's addressed to your child. Start by evaluating the seriousness of the offense. Try not to overreact, as hard as that might be. Remember, the wheels of justice grind slowly, but surely.

Depending on the nature of the problem, there might be several sources you need to contact. With the obscene email example, you can contact your ISP or online service and forward them a copy of the message. Seek their advice for what to do about it. It's always a good idea to contact the organization that provides your Internet connection (your ISP or commercial online service); they handle similar situations everyday and should be able to help you.

Most of the commercial online services have guidelines for how users are to behave, telling you what's allowed and what's not. Familiarize yourself with the rules. If you or your child witness a violation, such as in a chat room, report it to the service. AOL's software has a **Notify AOL** button, shown in Figure 19.2, you can click from within the chat room to contact AOL representatives about a problem going on.

Figure 19.2

*Click the **Notify AOL** button to summon help. A form opens for you to fill out and paste the offending conversation into.*

Click here

If the offense is more serious in nature, you need to step up a level as far as who you contact. For example, if your child is approached in a chat room and lured to meet another user face-to-face, you should not only contact the online service, but also a law enforcement agency, such as the FBI or local police. The same is true for instances where you run across child pornography on the Internet—report it. It's your duty as a citizen of the online community to report serious crimes that happen to you or your child online.

Victim or Not a Victim?

If you need help determining whether your child is a victim of online crime, consult with any law enforcement agency, or check out the GetNetWise Web site (www.getnetwise.org) for some pointers.

Use common sense when evaluating the seriousness of an online problem. If the crime is an emergency, contact the local police. For example, if your child has been threatened with serious harm or is being stalked offline as well as online, call the police.

Regardless of the situation, *don't* punish your child for telling you about the problem. It's up to you to educate your child and make him or her aware of online dangers. Work with your kids and help them learn from the encounter. Online crime can happen to anyone.

The following section provides you with a list of various agencies you can get in touch with regarding cybercrimes.

Finding Law Enforcement

There are several national child advocacy groups who can help with online problems involving children. Most of these groups provide 24-hour hotlines parents can call for help. They can also assist you in contacting law enforcement officials. (See Table 19.1 for a complete listing.)

The National Center for Missing and Exploited Children (NCMEC) is a clearinghouse for information regarding child abductions, runaways, and child exploitation. The organization does not investigate cases, but it receives leads and forwards them exclusively to appropriate law enforcement agencies for investigation and review. This group partners with the U.S. Postal Inspection Service, U.S. Customs, and the FBI to sponsor the CyberTipline shown in Figure 19.3.

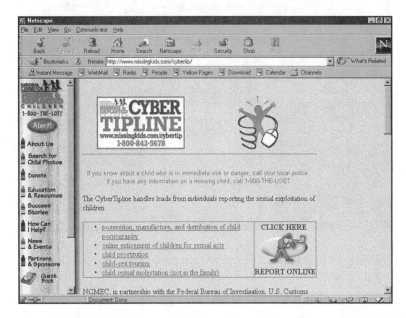

Figure 19.3

You can report a crime online using the CyberTipline.

The CyberTipline is open all day, every day, and it takes calls from around the nation, as well as from Canada, Mexico, and the United Kingdom. Use this line to report any sexual exploitation of children on the Internet, whether it's child pornography on the Web or child pornography received in an email message. You can also call this line if you have any information regarding abductions or missing children:

CyberTipline   1-800-843-5678
www.missingkids.com/cybertip

If you reside in Europe, you can contact the INHOPE Association (www.inhope.org)—Internet Hotline Providers in Europe. It's a site focused on protecting children online, and it provides access to other resources as well as letting you make reports on child exploitation.

If you suspect child exploitation or other Internet crimes, you can also contact the federal authorities. The U.S. Customs Service is a good place to start. You can check out their site in Figure 19.4.

> U.S. Customs Service
> Phone: 1-800-BE-ALERT
> Email: icpicc@customs.treas.gov
> Web site: www.customs.ustreas.gov

Figure 19.4

You can report child pornography found on the Internet at the U.S. Customs Web site.

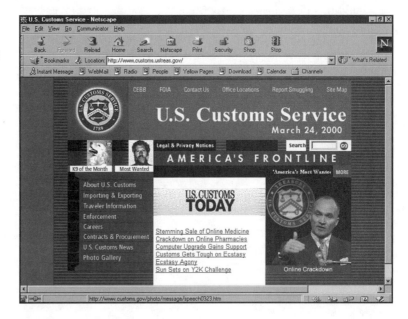

The Federal Bureau of Investigations (FBI) investigates reports of child exploitation as well as cyberstalking, fraud, and other online crimes (see Figure 19.5).

> Federal Bureau of Investigation
> Phone: 1-202-324-3000
> Web site: www.fbi.gov

Here are a few more federal agencies you can turn to for help:

> Bureau of Alcohol, Tobacco, and Firearms
> Web site: www.atf.treas.gov

> U.S. Drug Enforcement Association
> Web site: www.usdoj.gov/dea/

> U.S. Postal Inspection Service
> Web site: http://www.usps.gov/websites/depart/inspect/

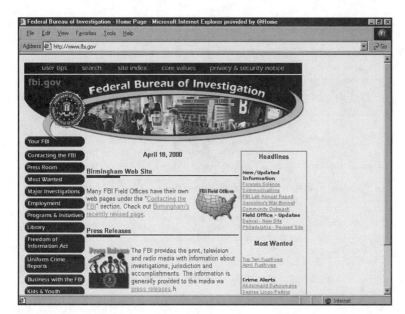

Figure 19.5
Not only can you report crime at this site, you can also check out the top 10 fugitives.

Don't Send It!

If you do run across anything you believe to be child pornography, *don't* download it or copy it even to provide evidence. It's a crime. Report it to the authorities and let them tell you how to handle it. If you're reporting a Web site, write down the URL to report it.

Where to Find Tips and Guidelines

Your best defense in protecting kids online is your own supervision. That's a no-brainer. Set some guidelines, get cyber-savvy yourself, and spend some time teaching your child about Internet safety.

To learn more about child exploitation and keeping kids safe online, check out the following Web sites:

Children's Partnership Organization www.childrenspartnership.org

Enough is Enough www.enough.org

Safe Surf   www.safesurf.com

Online Safety Project   www.safekids.com (see Figure 19.6)

Figure 19.6

SafeKids.Com is a great source for information about protecting kids online. It offers a directory of parental control software.

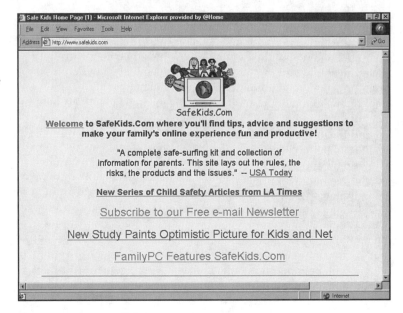

CyberAngels   www.cyberangels.org

FBI's Guide to Internet Safety
www.fbi.gov/kids/crimepre/internet/internet.htm

GetNetWise   www.getnetwise.org

Child Quest International   www.childquest.org

Family Education Network   familyeduction.com

Safeguarding Our Children-United Mothers   www.soc-um.org

Family PC   www.familypc.com

Kids Online   www.protectkids.com

Kidshield   www.kidsshield.com

Web Wise Kids   www.webwisekids.com (see Figure 19.7)

Figure 19.7
The Web Wise Kids site is another great spot for finding resources and links.

Table 19.1 presents a list of national child help hotlines.

Table 19.1   Important Phone Numbers

Organization	Phone Number
Alcohol and Drug Abuse Hotline	800-237-6237
Center to Prevent Handgun Violence	202-898-0792
Child Abuse Hotline	800-540-4000
Child Help USA	800-422-4453
Children Now	800-CHILD-44
Crisis Counseling Hotline	800-444-9999
Enough is Enough	888-2-ENOUGH
National Center for Missing and Exploited Children	800-843-5678
National Clearinghouse for Alcohol and Drug Information	800-729-6686
National Council for Child Abuse and Family Violence	800-222-2000
National Crime Prevention Council	202-466-6272
National Institute on Drug Abuse Referral Line	800-662-HELP
National Victim Center	800-FYI-CALL
Runaway Hotline	800-231-6946
Suicide Prevention Hotline	800-827-7571
Violence Prevention Coalition	213-240-7785

This is just the tip of the iceberg when it comes to finding assistance for dealing with and learning about online dangers. You can conduct your own online search to find other sites that might be able to answer your questions.

The bottom line—Nobody can protect your kids but you. If they do encounter an online danger, make sure they (and you) are prepared to deal with it. Thankfully, there are resources you can contact if the problem is serious. Keep things in perspective; the Internet is not all doom and gloom. There are plenty of great and wonderful things for your entire family online, and the next chapter, "Kid-Friendly Places on the Internet," points you to a few of them.

The Least You Need to Know

No doubt about it, it's a dangerous world these days—online and off. Chances are, you and your family will never experience any of these dangers—especially if you follow the guidelines recommended in this book. But if you do, there are sources of help you can turn to.

➤ Laws do apply to the Internet, but they're difficult to enforce at times.

➤ Various law enforcement agencies—local and national—are equipping themselves to fight online crime. Many are developing new departments and divisions to tackle the ongoing problem of cybercrime.

➤ Educate yourself and your children about online dangers; set guidelines on what to do if your child encounters something wrong on the Internet.

➤ The CyberTipline 1-800-843-5678 or www.missingkids.com/cybertip, sponsored by the National Center for Missing and Exploited Children, can help you report a problem or answer questions about your concerns.

➤ Contact your ISP or commercial service for help with problems like email solicitation, unsuitable behavior in chat rooms, and online harassment.

➤ Contact authorities to report incidents of child pornography, pedophilia in chat rooms, cyberstalking, and other serious crimes.

➤ Check Web sites such as GetNetWise (www.getnetwise.org) for help in determining whether a crime has been committed against your child.

Chapter 20

Kid-Friendly Places on the Internet

In This Chapter

➤ Find a collection of fun sites for kids and teens

➤ Check out learning sites to help with homework

➤ Learn how to find your kid's favorite hobby on the Internet

➤ Find sites that offer help with parenting

Although the focus of this book has been to educate you about many of the Internet's more dangerous aspects, don't let that be your only viewpoint of the Internet. The Internet has much to offer you and your children. To help prove this, we look at many kid-friendly offerings in this last chapter. If you and your family haven't already tapped into some of the wonderful things available on the Internet, let this chapter help show you the way.

Finding the Fun

With the constant bombardment of negative press in our culture, it's often easy to concentrate the bad instead of the good. But as the saying goes, don't let a few rotten apples spoil the whole online experience—or something like that. The Internet can be an exciting and fun place for kids as well as adults.

As you learned in Chapter 1, "What Do Kids Do on the Internet?" they can do a lot. Numerous Web sites offer fun stuff for kids of all ages. The tricky part is finding these sites. You can use a search engine, such as AskJeeves.com, to find kid stuff (try running a search on the words "fun kids"). You can also find sites recommended in magazines, such as *FamilyPC*. Another great resource to consult is other Internet-savvy parents. They usually enjoy rattling off a few fun sites to others as well.

To help you and your child get started, this section explores several sites, based on age-interest. Although your family can find great kid stuff among the many offerings of commercial online services (such as AOL), this chapter focuses on kid-friendly sites out on the Web.

Bookmark It!

When you find sites you think your kids will like (or when they find sites they like and you approve of), bookmark them with your browser's bookmark feature. You might want to set up a special folder that holds only your kids' favorite Web sites, and then show them how to return to their favorite places whenever they like.

To bookmark a Web page, first display the page. If you're using Internet Explorer, open the **Favorites** menu and choose **Add to Favorites**, give the page a name (or accept the default), and click **OK**. If you're using Navigator, press **Ctrl+D** on the keyboard to immediately add the site to the bookmark list.

Sites for Younger Kids

For sheer delight, especially with toddlers, check out the many dancing creature links found at NuttySites (www.nuttysites.com). This site offers links to numerous sweet little dancing things, such as the famous dancing hamsters. My current favorite is the dancing armadillos, shown in Figure 20.1.

NuttySites has links to dancing aliens, dancing cows, and other funny dancing drawings. Catchy music accompanies the dancing creatures, and kids can email their favorite site's link to friends. Be sure to check out the link to the dancing aliens; it's equally cute and includes a disco tune.

Fun for Kids by Jen (www.geocities.com/Athens/1850/) offers a variety of links to activities and crafts younger kids will enjoy. Children can access coloring pages, games, and educational information from this site. For example, one of the Coloring and Drawing links takes the user to Apple Corps Mr./Mrs. Vegetable Head game (apple-corps.westnet.com/apple_corps.2.html), a site that lets kids create their own vegetable/fruit faces, a la Mr. Potato Head (see Figure 20.2). Your kids (and perhaps you yourself) will have fun putting parts on the vegetable or fruit in any arrangement they so desire. The pictures can also be printed out for hands-on fun.

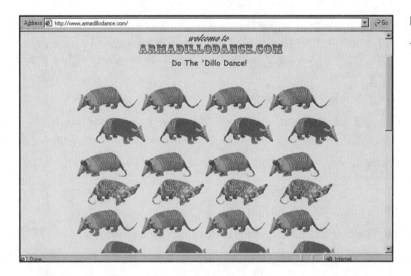

Figure 20.1

If only you could see these 'dillos dance in this figure!

Figure 20.2

Customize a vegetable or fruit character with attachable face parts.

There's nothing more amusing than vegetables that talk, as proved by the popular Veggie Tales characters. Join Larry Boy (the cucumber) and Bob (the tomato) at their Web site—www.bigidea.com. The site features plenty of games and activities to amuse younger children (and adults). Be sure to have a go at the Veggie Pile-Up game. It's like Tetris, but you have to line up dropping veggies. It's guaranteed to provide hours of online fun. Remember to try to let your kids play a few rounds, too.

Speaking of characters, stop by Dr. , Seuss's Seussville (`www.randomhouse.com/seussville`). This site includes Dr. Seuss-themed games, contests, and more. If your kids are hungry, print out a recipe for green eggs and ham, or sneetch snacks. Stop and read the Seuss-ism of the day or shop for SeussWear made by Esprit.

Coloring pages are very popular on the Web. You and your kids can find sites with pictures to print out and color, or sites that let kids color using an applet (a program that activates on the Web site with tools for filling in the picture onscreen). Here are a few coloring book sites your kids can try:

> **Kendra's Coloring Book**   `www.geocities.com/colorbook` (see Figure 20.3)
>
> **DW's Art Studio (from the PBS cartoon "Arthur")**   `www.pbs.org/wgbh/arthur/dw/paint/index.html`
>
> **Theodore Tugboat**   `www.cochran.com/theodore/activities/default.html`
>
> **The Color Site**   `www.thecolorsite.com`
>
> **Coloring 4 Kids**   `www.coloringpage.org/`
>
> **AnfyPaint**   `www.kiddonet.com/kiddonet/anfypaint/index.htm`
>
> **Klay Doodle**   `www.dreamworksgames.com/Games/Neverhood/klaydoodle.html`
>
> **Michael's Electric Canvas**   `www.michaels.com/e-canvas/e-canvas.html`
>
> **Warner Bros Coloring Book**   `wbanimation.warnerbros.com/cmp/ani_13cc.htm`
>
> **Billy Bear's Playground**   `www.billybear4kids.com/games/print/n-play.htm`

Figure 20.3

Color some frogs on Kendra's Coloring Book site, or print out the picture to color later.

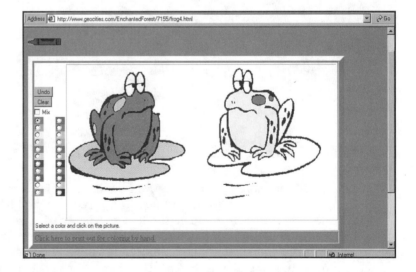

How about some interactive stories for kids? Check out Alex's Scribbles site (`www.scribbles.com.au/max`) for a point and click story that follows the adventures of Max the Koala bear. The stories are written by Alex and his dad, who live in Australia.

Are the Berenstain Bears a favorite at your house? If so, visit `www.berenstainbears.com`. It's not easy typing the name in, but the Web site has lots of fun stuff for youngsters. This site is interactive, and smaller children will enjoy moving the mouse around the screen to reveal various characters. Kids can also email their favorite bear and receive a message, or send Berenstain e-cards to their friends.

Commercial sites—such as Disney (`disney.go.com`), the Cartoon Network (`www.cartoonnetwork.com`), Nickelodeon (`www.nick.com`), and Fox Kids (`www.foxkids.com`)—have lots of kid appeal, and lots of advertising, too. There are gobs of graphics on these sites, so advise your kids to be patient if they're using a slower speed modem. All your kids' favorite TV shows have Web sites online these days. Try `www.pbs.org/kids`, for example, to find Teletubbies, Zoboomafoo, and good ol' Mister Rogers.

Most of your kids' favorite food makers have Web sites with kid stuff. For example, stop by and see what the Keebler elves are up to at `www.keebler.com/treehouse/treehouse.htm` (or just check out Figure 20.4). Or visit Tony the Tiger and the Kelloggs Game Zone at `www.kelloggs.com`.

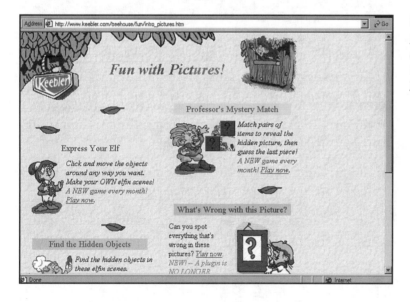

Figure 20.4

Have fun with the Keebler elves, but watch out—that theme song might haunt you the rest of the day.

Some of the more popular search sites have special areas for kids. For example, Yahoo! has Yahooligans! (`www.yahooligans.com`) and Lycos has Lycos Zone (`www.lycoszone.com`), as shown in Figures 20.5 and 20.6, respectively. The links at these sites change frequently, so be sure to check them out often.

Figure 20.5

Yahooligans! is Yahoo!'s Web site for kids.

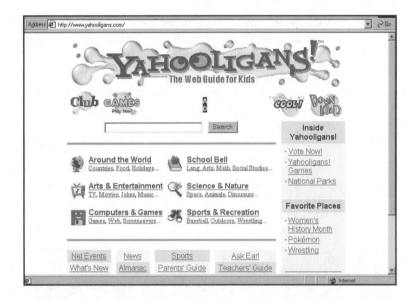

Figure 20.6

Search sites' kids' areas offer games, homework help, and more.

Sites for Older Kids

Older kids will most certainly enjoy several of the sites already mentioned, particularly the commercial ones, such as the Cartoon Network (www.cartoonnetwork.com), Nickelodeon (www.nick.com), or Fox Kids (www.foxkids.com). In fact, many of the sites on the Web for children appeal to all ages. As you know, the real appeal of any kid-related item depends more on the child's personality and maturity level and less on the child's actual age.

GusTown (www.gustown.com) is one of those sites that kids of all ages like. We're mentioning it in this section because it has a CyberBud area for chatting with other kids, a favorite older-kids pastime, as shown in Figure 20.7. GusTown is rated the number one Web site by *FamilyPC*, with good reason. There's lots to explore here, and a variety of activities to keep kids busy.

Figure 20.7

GusTown has something for everyone.

Squigly's Playhouse is another site that appeals to children young and old. The theme of Squigly's Playhouse (www.squiglysplayhouse.com) changes every month and includes games, crafts, puzzles, quizzes, jokes, and riddles. The writing corner features stories and poems from kids around the world, and your child can submit his or her own writing projects to be posted.

Headbone Zone (www.headbone.com) is a site that definitely targets older kids and offers chat, games, contests, and more (see Figure 20.8). There's even an online jukebox. Some of the features are silly (Pojo's Digital Destiny Machine), some are innovative (try the Dreamalyzer).

Is your kid looking for a pen pal? Numerous Web sites help kids meet other kids. World Kids Network (www.worldkids.net), for instance, offers international pen pal clubs for girls and boys. Kid City Post Office (www.child.net/kcpo.htm), Kids Space Connection (www.ks-connection.com), and 4PenPals.com (www.4penpals.com) are some more you might look into. Your kids can find more by doing a search of the words "pen pals."

A Word About Plug-Ins

Multimedia is all over the Internet, and with many of the online games, music, and videos, a plug-in is required for your browser to see and hear the multimedia. For example, many games require the Shockwave plug-in, a special *applet* (mini-program) for viewing animation and multimedia effects online. In many instances, when such a plug-in is needed, a link is provided to a download site where you can download the file and install it on your computer. Plug-ins work with the browser and open immediately to play multimedia files found on the Internet, so you don't have to worry about finding the program on your computer and starting it yourself, or worrying about teaching your child to do the same.

Figure 20.8

Headbone Zone is a Web site for older kids, ages 8 and up.

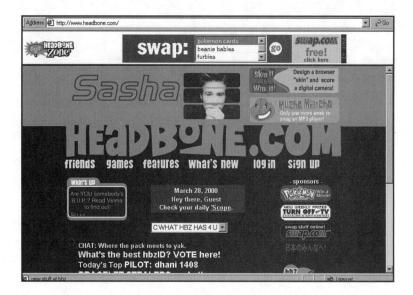

FreeZone (`www.freezone.com`), pictured in Figure 20.9, is another fun site that offers stuff for kids and teens, including clickable comics, jokes, advice from other kids, and bulletin boards. (The message boards are monitored, so rest assured there are no unseemly postings.) Parents, be warned—this site has a collection of practical jokes your kids are sure to try out around the house, like the tip about smearing Vaseline on all the doorknobs. You've got to admit, that's a pretty good one.

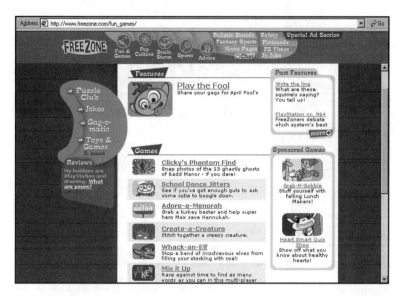

Figure 20.9

FreeZone has a lot of silly stuff any kid is sure to appreciate.

FunBrain.com (www.funbrain.com) has games that challenge the mind (see Figure 20.10), including word games, math games, even a virtual piano to play. This site's brainy games include Proton Don, a game to help kids learn the elements of the periodic table—how many other sites can boast that? We double-dare you to try this one yourself. When's the last time you could identify the symbol for Chromium?

Some of the best Web sites are home grown—not the slick commercially packaged pages, but sites created by kids and families. I'm especially fond of pages where someone has gone to a lot of trouble to list interesting links to other sites. For example, Not Just For Kids (www.night.net/kids) is for the whole family. The site includes an exhaustive list of links to other kid sites, poetry and stories, and a Java jukebox.

If your kids can't get enough mystery novels, they'll love the Kids Love A Mystery.com Web site (www.kidsloveamystery.com), as shown in Figure 20.11. This very cool site has online mini-mysteries to solve, quick-solve cases, magic tricks, and more. Something tells me it's not just kids who stop by this site for a little mystery solving.

Set Some Rules

Set some rules for your child regarding how much personal information to give out when corresponding online. Remember, in cyberspace not everyone is who they say they are.

Figure 20.10

Kids can hone their school skills at FunBrain.com.

Figure 20.11

Kids really do love a mystery, and this site offers mystery stuff for all ages.

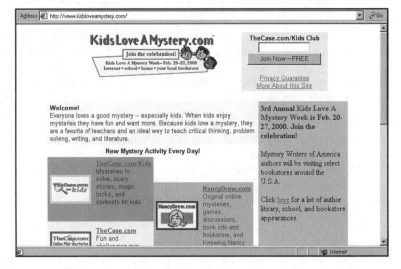

We've only just begun to scratch the tip of the iceberg regarding fun content online. There are many more kids' sites on the Internet for your entire family to explore, and new ones are added every day. The easiest way to find them is to use search engines to look up terms like "kids" or "fun for kids."

Sites for Teens

It's a bit harder finding sites for teens using search engines. If your teen enters words like "teens" or "teen fun," mixed results will appear, many of which will be unsuitable. For example, a search on the words "teen fun" on the Lycos search site resulted in a small number of actual teen-related links, but an equal or greater number of links to porn pictures and the like. Consider yourself warned. Despite this, we've put together several teen sites your family can check out.

Mark 'Em!

Don't forget to bookmark favorite sites so kids can easily return to them again.

Let's start with Teen-Net (www.teen-net.com), shown in Figure 20.12. Teens can find numerous teen-related "channels" (pages) on this site, including topics like music, movies, dating, sports, and games. The fashion channel offers links to popular fashion online magazines, such as *Glamour* and *Cosmopolitan* (not too teen-oriented, if you ask me), as well as makeup tips and links to popular teen shopping stops online (such as Abercrombie & Fitch and The Gap). The Speak Your Mind On The Net (SYMON) channel gives teens the opportunity to post original stories, poetry, and artwork.

Figure 20.12

Teen-Net claims to be the Web guide for teens.

TeenMag.com (www.teenmag.com) appeals mainly to teenage girls. The site covers fashion trends, show business news about the latest onscreen hunks, music news about the latest singing groups, and dating questions. Teens can find all the teen magazines online these days, including *Seventeen* (www.seventeen.com) and *Teen People* (www.teenpeople.com).

The Cyberteens Web site slogan is "where creative teens rule." That's catchy and seemingly on target. Follow the URL www.cyberteens.com to find the site, as shown in Figure 20.13. Once there, teens find links to an art gallery by teens, a young composer's site, and online novels, plus the usual game connections. The e-zine (magazine for the Web) called *Zeen* is not to be missed. It features original contributions from teens all over the world.

Figure 20.13

Visit Cyberteens to tap into the more creative efforts of teens online.

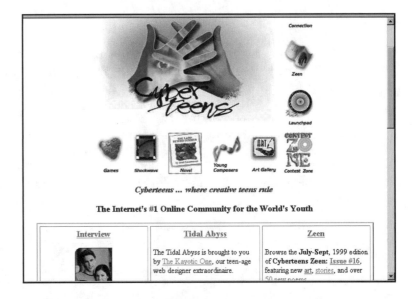

Hopefully, these sites will get you and your teen started.

Sites for Learning and Exploring

Web sites for kids aren't all about fun and games. They can also be extremely educational and helpful (think homework helpful). Although you and your child can use search engines to look up specific topics on the Internet, there are some sites worth visiting just because they exist. Take, for example, the National Geographic Web site (www.nationalgeographic.com). This site includes tons of wonderful links and features for exploring the world around us. In the summer, be sure to check out the Wild Bear Cam, a live camera feed from Alaska's McNeil River Sanctuary. When the salmon are running, the bears are at the river fishing and playing. How amazing is that—sitting in front of your computer anywhere around the globe and viewing bears fishing in Alaska at that same moment!

In addition to the site's regular features, the National Geographic Web site also has a special kids' area, shown in Figure 20.14, chock full of fun information your kids will enjoy. The site includes a link to the San Diego Zoo's Panda Cam (www.sandiegozoo.org), a camera set up to view the happenings in the panda pen. Find out what baby panda Hua Mei is up to, and learn all about pandas in general.

Figure 20.14

Kids can count on adventure, fun, and education at the National Geographic Web site.

Web cameras are quite amazing and they can be found set up in all sorts of interesting places. Zoos make great settings, such as the Penguin Cam at Sea World/Busch Gardens in Tampa, Florida (www.seaworld.org). Or try the Cheetah cam at Discovery.com. You can also search for the words "web cam," but again, be aware that this search might turn up live cams of an adult nature, as well as interactive kid stuff.

Check This Out

When to Tune In

Live Web cams take the viewer right to where the action is, but depending on the time of day of the visit, there might not be much going on. Try to visit such sites during their daylight hours or when the animals are active. Also try checking in periodically throughout the day to see what sort activities you and your kids can catch. Remember time zone issues, too. Tell your kids that if it's daylight where you live, it's dark on the other side of the globe. So if you live in the United States and decide to check out the kangaroo cam in Australia, don't be surprised to see a dark screen. It's nighttime there when it's daytime here.

For online action, you and your child can't beat Discovery.com's many live camera feeds (see Figure 20.15). They've got Ant Cam, Puppy Cam, Shark Cam, Eagle Cam, Bird Feeder Cam, and even a Bat Cam. You and your family might end up whiling away the hours trying to catch a glimpse of the Loch Ness monster via the Monster Cam. We, personally, spent forever waiting for the puppy to wake up at the Puppy Cam site, a live cam in the puppy pen at the Humane Society of Greater Miami. At one point, the puppy rolled in front of the Web cam and stayed there blocking the camera's view, so we never did get his picture for this book. (In fact, the puppy blocked the camera for so long we started to get worried. We hope the puppy didn't expire or anything.)

Figure 20.15

After much waiting, a woodpecker finally showed up at the Wild Birds Unlimited feeder. Can you see him?

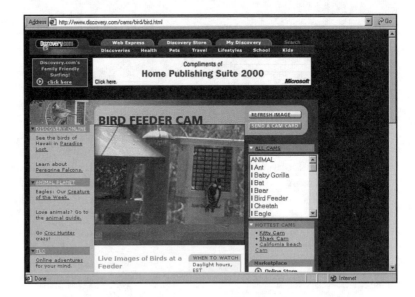

Something exciting was happening at the Oklahoma City Zoo's Baby Gorilla Cam (another link on the Discovery Web site) when we stopped by (see Figure 20.16). A zookeeper came in to play with the twin gorilla babies. 30,000 net surfers stop by to check on the gorillas' progress every day. These two babies will certainly remind you of your own kids, and the gorilla room probably looks like theirs, too.

There's more than just animals to watch online. The Discovery.com site also offers people cams (such as Taxi Cam), planet cams (like Volcano Cam), and travel cams. Your kids will never get bored at the Discovery.com site. There's always something going on, things to learn, and links to follow. The Kids section of the site includes games, message boards, and more (see Figure 20.17).

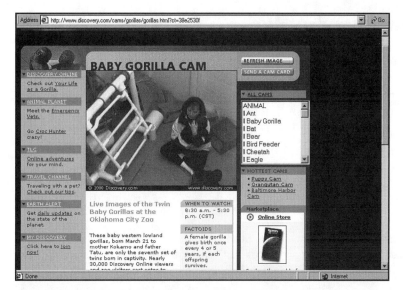

Figure 20.16

Check in on the baby gorillas at the Oklahoma City Zoo.

Figure 20.17

The Discovery.com site offers loads of educational fun.

If your kids like exploring the world of science, stop by Beakman's World (www.beakmansworld.com), a site based on the popular kids TV show. Your kids will encounter plenty of interactive science fun. For example, the site answers age-old questions like "What is ear wax" and "How does the moon power the tides."

Another good science site is Nye Labs Online, based on the *Bill Nye the Science Guy* TV show (www.nyelabs.kcts.org). The site features a Demo of the Day, as well as all the show's hit science songs (yes, science songs—don't miss the one about your Blood Stream), video clips from the show, and more than 40 home demo science experiment instructions. Time to buy little Johnny that junior lab coat and goggles.

Homework Help on the Web

The Internet is a wonderful resource for homework help. For example, the next time your child comes to you and asks about the Spanish revolution, don't wing it, send him or her online. If your child needs an encyclopedia, try the Encyclopedia Britannica site (remember, it's www.britannica.com). Also try www.encyclopedia.com, home to The Concise Columbia Electronic Encyclopedia, or Funk and Wagnall's (www.funkandwagnalls.lycos.com) online archives.

Many encyclopedias are taking their information online, such as Weather.com's weather encyclopedia (www.weather.com/breaking_weather/encyclopedia/), and the 3D Atlas Online (www.3datlas.com). Kids can even find the World Book Encyclopedia online (www.worldbook.com), but they want you and your family to buy their product, so they only offer a trial version.

If your child simply needs to look up a word, stop by Merriam-Webster's online dictionary (www.m-w.com). Kids can look up words in the dictionary or the thesaurus. The site also features word games, word of the day, jokes, and more.

Searchopolis (www.searchopolis.com) is another great place for kids to conduct a search of the Web or to find numerous resources that include architecture, history, social sciences, maps, and even online calculators (handy if your kids have lost yours).

Does your kid need some math help? Check out Aunty Math's Web site (shown in Figure 20.18) at www.dcmrats.org/AuntyMath.html. Try the math challenge of the day, or see how you do with past challenges. The site is sponsored by the DuPage Children's Musuem in Chicago.

Figure 20.18

Aunty Math helps young-sters practice their math skills.

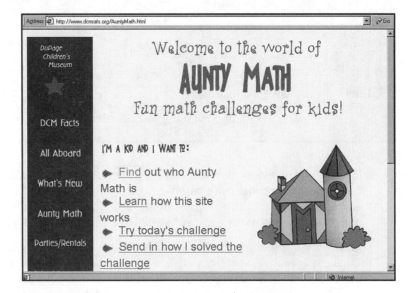

Many kids' sites on the Web offer homework help, such as Bonus.com (www.bonus.com). Take a look at Bonus.com's Homework Help area in Figure 20.19. Aside from the site's many games and other activities, the homework section has fun information about language arts, culture, science, and more. Your kids can find challenging games that help them build their math skills, learn about history, and test their memory skills. (This might be useful for parents, too.)

The Canadian Broadcasting Corporation has a spiffy educational site for kids (www.cbc4kids.ca). Your kids can learn about inventions, print out science experiments to try around the house, or send in their own stories for posting on the site.

No Plagiarizing Please

With such easy access to all kinds of information on the Internet, especially for homework purposes, parents need to teach their kids not to plagiarize the work they find online. Cutting and pasting text from a Web page into a homework project is plagiarizing, even if the project is due tomorrow.

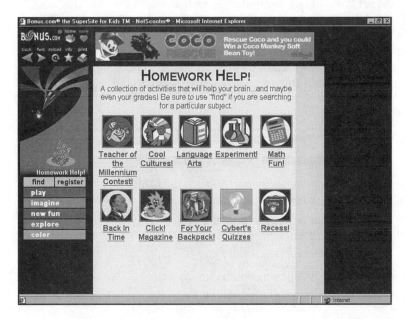

Figure 20.19

Be sure to visit the Bonus.com site for games and learning fun.

Younger kids can find learning games at Alfy, the Kids Portal Playground (www.alfy.com). Be sure to open the Brain-Train page for links to a variety of learning activities like letter flashcards and counting. The site features games that help youngsters learn to tell time, spell simple words, and more.

What's That Strange Suffix?

Some URLs have an odd extension attached to the end of the address that differs from what you're used to seeing (the typical .com or .org), such as www.cbc4kids.ca. In this example, the extension stands for Canada. Web site address extensions can indicate commercial sites, organizations, networks, educational sites, and more. Now you know.

Sites for Hobbies and Crafts

Looking for sites that direct kids off the computer, as well as on? There are numerous places on the Web that offer guidelines and instructions for performing tasks offline. Take cooking, for example. Kids can print out recipes they find at sites such as Jell-O Kids' Cooking Fun at www.kraftfoods.com/features/jello.html (see Figure 20.20), FamilyFoodZone (www.familyfoodzone.com), or AllRecipe.com's cookie site (www.cookierecipe.com) and try them out in their own kitchen—with your supervision, of course.

Figure 20.20

The Internet is a great source for food recipes; it even includes some that kids can follow.

Food and kids always go together, and you can find kids' recipes at just about every commercial food Web site. Try doing a Web search on the words "kids recipes" to find something edible for every kid in your house.

About.com (parentingteens.about.com/library/sp/blkidscook.htm) has a page of links to recipes for camping treats, holiday foods, even bath and spa recipes.

Maybe your child prefers crafts instead of food. It's easy to find craft ideas online. Try a Web search on the words "kids crafts." There are gazillions of sites that offer craft ideas, as well as recipes for kid stuff. For example, find recipes for play dough, modeling clay, finger paints, bubble-blowing solution, and even rock candy at the Skaarup Laboratories Kids site (homepages.skylink.net/~skaarup/kidscraft.html). Or try The Man in The Moon page (shown in Figure 20.21) where there's a recipe for homemade silly putty or a do-it-yourself kazoo (themaninthemoon.com/KidsCrafts.htm).

Figure 20.21

Craft recipes are just as fun as food recipes, perhaps even more so because kids can play with what they make.

The National Directory site offers links to all kinds of craft sites (www.nationaldirectory.com/Kids/Arts_and_Crafts). Check commercial Web sites from known hobby stores such as Michaels (www.michaels.com) or Hobby Lobby (www.hobbylobby.com), too.

That leads us to hobbies. There's no end to hobby sites online. The Internet is full of people sharing interests such as remote control cars, stamp and coin collecting, pet fish, Pokémon cards, Beanie Babies—you name it, it's out there. Use a search engine to help your kids find the way to their favorite hobby. Whether your kid is into sports, critters, movies, or music, information about that interest is somewhere on the Internet.

Sites for Parents

Well, we've covered all kinds of sites focused on kids, but what about parents? There are just as many sites for you, too. You can find parenting tips, message boards focused on parenting topics, and forums for swapping stories with other parents. There are numerous special interest groups on the Web, including support groups for parents who have children with learning disabilities or physical disabilities, single-parenting, grandparenting, and adoption.

To help you get started, here's a list of parenting sites that you may find useful:

FamilyPC Magazine www.familypc.com

Parenting Magazine www.parenttime.com

Women.com Family Page www.women.com/family/?lec

Home and Family www.homeandfamily.com

Parenthood Web www.parenthood.com

Parent Soup www.parentsoup.com

ParentsPlace www.parentsplace.com

The National Parenting Center www.tnpc.com

Family.com www.family.com

Parents.com www.parents.com

Family Education Network familyeducation.com

Parents Talk www.parents-talk.com

Spilt Milk www.spiltmilk.net

Interactive Parent www.interactiveparent.com

Parenting Q & A www.parenting-qa.com

Parent Zone www.parentzone.com

Adopt: Assistance Information Support www.adopting.org/parenting.html

Internet Resources for Special Children www.irsc.org

There's more where those came from, so get on the Internet and explore for yourself.

The Least You Need to Know

That about wraps up our book. We hope you feel more informed about protecting your child on the Internet, and are equipped with some good ideas for setting guidelines and making your family's computing safer. Don't let fears of online dangers keep your kids from all the fun and education found on the Internet. With a little help, your child can surf safely, have a great time, and learn a little, too.

➤ The easiest way to find Web sites for kids is to conduct a Web search on the words "kids fun," or a similar combination.

➤ Many kids' sites appeal to kids of all ages, so whether your kid likes the site or not depends on his or her personality.

➤ Teen sites are a bit harder to come by, unfortunately. If you perform a Web search on the word "teen," you'll end up with porn links, so be careful.

➤ Many of the educational sites online are both fun and enlightening, and adults will enjoy them, too.

➤ There's a Web site for every hobby or interest, even if your kid collects smelly socks as a hobby.

➤ The Internet offers plenty of helpful parenting sites, so be sure to visit them for moral support as well as ideas.

Glossary

ActiveX   A technology for Microsoft Internet Explorer that allows programs to be downloaded and run in your browser.

Anonymous email   A way of sending email so that no one can tell the true identity of the sender.

Anonymous posting   A way to send messages on Usenet newsgroups so that no one can tell the true identity of the sender.

Anonymous remailer   A program or Web site that lets you send anonymous email or post anonymously to a newsgroup.

Anonymous surfing   A way to browse the World Wide Web so that no information can be gathered about you from your Web browser.

Antivirus software   Software that can detect and kill computer viruses. See *Virus*.

AOL Instant Messenger (AIM)   A popular instant messenger program that enables anyone on the Internet to chat with America Online users, as well as with other users of AOL Instant Messenger.

Applet   A Java program. See *Java*.

Attachment   A file added to an email message. It can be a picture, a video, or any other kind of file.

BIOS (Basic Input/Output System)   The software that handles the most basic workings of your PC, such as ensuring that the keyboard, monitor, and other parts work together.

Blocking software   Software that blocks a computer from viewing certain Internet sites, such as pornographic or hate sites.

Bozo filter   A feature of some chat programs that enables you to block messages from individuals you find annoying.

Browser cache   A directory on your hard disk that temporarily keeps files, such as Web pages and graphics that have been downloaded to your computer, when you visit a Web site.

Buddy list   In instant messaging software, a list of friends you create so that you are alerted whenever one of your "buddies" comes online.

Cable modem   A device that hooks you up to the Internet through your cable television system.

Chat   A way in which people can communicate with each other in real time, by typing messages on their keyboards.

Chat channel   A place where you chat, particularly when using IRC. See *IRC*.

Chat room   A place where you chat, particularly on America Online.

Communications Decency Act   A law passed by Congress intended to control the kind of information available on the Internet, such as pornography. Many people believe that the act is unconstitutional.

Communications protocol   A kind of language that allows computers to talk to one another over a network such as the Internet.

Cookies   A bit of data, put on your computer by a Web server, that can be used to track what you do when you are on the Web.

CPU (Central Processing Unit)   The chip that is the brains of a PC, such as a Pentium III.

Cybercrime   A crime committed online, such as hacking or cyberstalking.

Cyberstalking   The act of stalking someone online, which includes sending unwanted email and instant messages, following someone into chat rooms, and sending unwanted messages.

DejaNews   A Web site at which you post and read newsgroup messages.

Download   To transfer information or files from the Internet to your computer.

Email filter   Automatically sorts incoming email so that some messages are automatically routed to certain folders or deleted, based on the sender and the content of the message. Email filters can be used to cut down on spam sent to you.

Email reader   A piece of software used to send and receive email.

Email spoofing   Forging the From address in an email message so that it appears that the message came from someone other than the real sender.

Encryption   A method of scrambling information as it's sent across the Internet so that no one can read it.

Eudora   A popular, free email program.

Ewallet   An electronic wallet that contains your credit card information or electronic money so that you can use it to easily shop at many online shopping sites.

File attachment   A file attached to an email message or a newsgroup posting. Any kind of file can be attached to email or newsgroup postings.

File extension   The three letters on the end of a filename that are used to identify it's file type. For example, files with .doc extensions are typically Microsoft Word files.

Filtering software   Software that can be used by parents to block children from viewing certain Web sites or using certain kinds of Internet services, such as chat.

Flame   To vociferously attack someone in a newsgroup or other discussion area, often for no clear reason.

FTP (File Transfer Protocol)   A way of downloading files on the Internet. See *Download*.

Hacking   The act of using a computer to access information over the Internet in an unauthorized way.

History list   A list, kept by your Web browser, of the recent Web sites you've visited.

Hyperlink   A link on a Web page that, when clicked, sends you to another Web page.

ICQ   Software that enables you to chat and communicate with others over the Internet.

IM   Slang for Instant Message.

Infomediary   A site or a piece of software that protects your privacy and gives you the opportunity to determine what information should be made public about you on the Internet.

Instant message   A message sent privately to an individual when both the sender and receiver are online at the same time.

Internet mailing list   See *Mail list servers*.

Internet Service Provider (ISP)   A company that provides dial-in or other kind of access to the Internet for a monthly fee.

IP address   The numerical address of something on the Internet—the address that computers can understand. It's a series of four numbers separated by periods like this: 147.23.0.124.

IRC (Internet Relay Chat)   A way of chatting on the Internet. To chat this way, you need special IRC software.

Java   A programming language that can be used to run programs in your browser.

JavaScript   A technology that enables Web designers to use a variety of interactive features on Web pages.

Macro   An automated set of commands in a file such as a word processing file or a spreadsheet. Macros can be infected with viruses.

Mail bomb   The automatic sending of dozens, or even hundreds or thousands, of email messages to a single email box so that the server or computer crashes.

Mail header   The part of an email message that contains the subject line, the sender, the receiver, and similar information.

Mail list servers   A public discussion, similar to a newsgroup, carried on via email.

Message board   A public area online where people can read and send messages.

Microsoft Outlook   A popular email program.

Moderated chat   A chat in which a monitor is present. The monitor has the power to kick participants out of the chat room if their behavior is inappropriate. See *Chat*.

Motherboard   The part of a computer to which all the components are attached.

MP3 file   A high-quality music file that can be downloaded from the Internet and played on a computer.

MP3 player   A piece of software that plays MP3 files.

Newsgroup   A discussion area on the Internet.

Newsgroup reader   A piece of software used to read newsgroups.

Online auction   Just like a real-life auction, except that it's done online.

Online profile   A profile put together by a Web site or marketing firm that contains information about what a person buys online.

Online service   A service, such as America Online or CompuServe, that provides access to the Internet and other features for a monthly fee.

Operating system   The basic piece of software that controls every aspect of how a computer works.

Opt out   A policy that gives you the option to reject junk mail or similar information.

Parental Controls   A feature of America Online that gives parents the power to decide where kids can go on America Online and the Internet, as well as how kids can use America Online and the Internet.

Password   A set of private letters and numbers or words you type in to give you access to a service or site.

Peripheral   A device attached to your PC, such as a printer.

PIN (Personal Information Number)   A set of private letters and numbers or words you type in to give you access to a service or site. Often used interchangeably with *password*.

POP3 server   A kind of Internet computer that lets you receive email. You usually have to put the name of your POP3 server into your email program to receive email.

Pretty Good Privacy (PGP)   A program used to encrypt and decrypt information. It's especially useful for sending out private email that only the sender and recipient can understand.

Private chat room   A chat room that isn't open to the public. Only people who are specifically invited in can join.

Public chat room   A chat room that is open for anyone to enter.

RAM (Random Access Memory)   The basic memory in your PC. This memory is temporary and stores information only until your computer is turned off.

RealPlayer   A popular piece of software that plays video and audio files.

Real-time chat   Another term for chat. See *chat*.

Registration form   A form on the Web you fill out to enter a special area of the Web site or to get special services.

Screen name   A person's name as it appears on America Online in chat areas and discussion areas. It's also that person's email address on America Online.

Secure site   A site that encrypts your credit card information as it's sent across the Internet so that the credit card number can't be stolen.

Server   A computer on the Internet that provides a basic service, such as delivering Web pages or sending email.

SET (Secure Electronic Transactions)   The electronic encryption and payment standard that a group of companies, including Microsoft, Netscape, VISA, and MasterCard, are pushing to become the standard for doing electronic commerce on the Internet.

Shareware   Software you can download from the Internet and try out free, paying for it only if you decide to keep it.

Site-blocking software   Software that can block children from accessing certain sites or resources on the Internet.

SMTP (Simple Mail Transfer Protocol)   A kind of communications protocol that lets you send email. You usually have to put the name of your SMTP server into your email program to send email.

Spam   Email sent to you that you've never asked for, trying to sell you a product or asking you to visit a Web site.

Spamoflauge   A method by which senders of spam hide their addresses by faking information such as who is sending the message.

SSL (Secure Sockets Layer)   A technology that scrambles information as it's sent across the Internet, making it impossible for hackers to read it.

SYSOP (System Operator)   Someone who moderates a chat room or is in charge of a message board.

TCP/IP (Transmission Control Protocol/Internet Protocol)   The two basic communications protocols that enable you to connect to and use the Internet.

Trojan horse   A malicious program that appears to be benign, but in fact damages your computer.

TRUSTe   A company that sets voluntary standards for privacy on the Internet and awards seals that companies can post on their Web sites if they adhere to those privacy rules.

Unmoderated chat   A chat in which there is no monitor or moderator present.

URL (Uniform Resource Locator)   The precise location of any spot on the Internet, such as www.mcp.com.

Usenet newsgroup   See *Newsgroup*.

Virus   A malicious program that can damage your computer.

Web browser   A piece of software, such as Netscape Navigator or Microsoft Internet Explorer, that enables you to visit Web sites.

Web database   A Web site that contains information that can be searched through, such as email addresses.

Web white pages   Web sites that contain information that can be searched through for identifying information, such as email addresses, phone numbers, and addresses.

WinAmp   An MP3 player. See *MP3 file* and *MP3 player*.

Windows Media Player   A popular piece of software from Microsoft that plays audio and video files.

Yahoo! Instant Messenger   A popular instant messenger program, available for users of the Yahoo! Internet site.

Index

Enough is Enough
Web site, 261
Enuff Web site, 191
expansion slots, 45

F

Family Education
Network Web site,
262, 284
FamilyConnect Web
sites, 191
FamilyPC Magazine
Web site, 284
FamilyPC Online Web
site, 262
FamilyPC Web site,
142
FBI Web site, 260
FBI's Guide to Internet
Safety Web site, 262
file sharing, turning
off, 174
files
downloading, 51
uploading, 51
zipping, 52

filtering email, 81-82
filtering programs. *See
also* parental con-
trols
controversies, 180
decisions about
using, 182
family filtering,
200-201
AltaVista, 203
Go Network, 203
Lycos, 203
hate groups, 155
installation issues,
190
keyword-based
filters, 183
Net Nanny, 187
functions of,
188-189
new features, 188
on/off feature,
188
screening options,
187
Web site, 187
PICS (Platform for
Content
Selection), 184

plug-ins, 192
server-based, 186,
193
utility programs,
193
filtering software,
95-97
Find command (Start
menu), 216
flaming, 125
floppy disk drives, 45
Fox Kids Web site, 269
fraud
credit cards, 20-21
debit cards, 20
freeware, 132
FreeZone Web site,
272
FTP'S (file transfer
protocol), 51
Fun for Kids by Jen
Web site, 266
FunBrain Web site,
273

301

N-O

safe shopping
tips, 112,
114-115
identifying crime,
257
law enforcement,
253-257
crime examples,
255
InterGov Web
site, 257
ScamWatch Web
site, 257
U.S. Department
of Justice
WebPolice Web
site, 257
reporting crime,
257-258
CyberTipline, 259
FBI, 260
Internet Hotline
Providers in
Europe
(INHOPE), 259
national child
help hotlines,
263
U.S. Customs
Service, 260

protection against
cable modem dan-
gers, 174
chatting, 70
Bozo filters, 72
monitored chat
rooms, 70
Neighborhood
Watch area, 72
Norton Interent
Security 2000,
71
parental controls,
71
self protection
rules, 73-74
file attachments, 79
harassment, 79,
229-230
hate groups, 155
mail bombs, 78
pornography, 94
browsers for kids,
98
filtering software,
95, 97
monitoring soft-
ware, 97

parental controls,
97-98
search engines for
kids, 98
spam, 81, 84
filtering, 81-82
software, 83
stalking, 79
viruses, 79
Web cookies, 166
disabling, 171
McAfee Internet
Guard Dog, 170
Norton Internet
Security 2000,
170
Web pages, blocking
access, 171-173

Quake III (online
games), 136

R

RAM (random access
memory), 44
regulations, Internet,
36
rejecting email, 79

System Requirements

Minimum Requirements

- Windows 95 or 98
- 486 Processor or higher
- Mouse or pointing device
- Minimum 4MB of RAM (8 MB or more recommended)

Installation

To avoid potential conflicts, exit all programs before installing Net Nanny.

Insert the Net Nanny Trial Version CD-ROM into your CD Drive. Use the "Start" button and choose "Run" and enter the source for the Net Nanny "Set Up" program (e.g. D:\SETUP) or use Windows Explorer, find SETUP.EXE on the CD-ROM, and double-click to run the program.

Follow the onscreen installation instructions.

If you would like the latest trial version
of Net Nanny, please come to our website at
www.netnanny.com/code25307